# TOURISM LOCAL SYSTEMS AND NETWORKING

## ADVANCES IN TOURISM RESEARCH

**Series Editor: Professor Stephen J. Page**
University of Stirling, U.K.
s.j.page@stir.ac.uk

Advances in Tourism Research series publishes monographs and edited volumes that comprise state-of-the-art research findings, written and edited by leading researchers working in the wider field of tourism studies. The series has been designed to provide a cutting edge focus for researchers interested in tourism, particularly the management issues now facing decision-makers, policy analysts and the public sector. The audience is much wider than just academics and each book seeks to make a significant contribution to the literature in the field of study by not only reviewing the state of knowledge relating to each topic but also questioning some of the prevailing assumptions and research paradigms which currently exist in tourism research. The series also aims to provide a platform for further studies in each area by highlighting key research agendas, which will stimulate further debate and interest in the expanding area of tourism research. The series is always willing to consider new ideas for innovative and scholarly books, inquiries should be made directly to the series editor.

Published:
*Destination Marketing Organisations*
Pike

*Small Firms in Tourism: International Perspectives*
Thomas

*Tourism and Transport*
Lumsdon & Page

*Tourism Public Policy and the Strategic Management of Failure*
Kerr

*Managing Tourist Health and Safety in the New Millennium*
Wilks & Page

*Indigenous Tourism*
Ryan & Aicken

*Taking Tourism to the Limits*
Ryan, Page & Aicken

*An International Handbook on Tourism Education*
Airey & Tribe

*Tourism in Turbulent Times*
Wilks, Pendergast & Leggat

Forthcoming titles include:

*Benchmarking National Tourism Organisations and Agencies*
Lennon, Smith, Cockerel & Trew

*Cold Water Tourism*
Baldacchino

*Tourism and Small Businesses in the New Europe*
Thomas & Augustyn

*Tourism Micro-clusters & Networks: The Growth of Tourism*
Michael, Mitchell, Lynch & Hall

**Related Elsevier Journals — sample copies available on request**
Annals of Tourism Research
*International Journal of Hospitality Management*
*Tourism Management*
*World Development*

# TOURISM LOCAL SYSTEMS AND NETWORKING

## LUCIANA LAZZERETTI

*University of Florence, Italy*

## CLARA S. PETRILLO

*Institute for Service Industry Research, National Research Council, Italy*

ELSEVIER   Amsterdam • Boston • Heidelberg • London • New York • Oxford
Paris • San Diego • San Francisco • Singapore • Sydney • Tokyo

Elsevier
The Boulevard, Langford Lane, Kidlington, Oxford OX5 1GB, UK
Radarweg 29, PO Box 211, 1000 AE Amsterdam, The Netherlands

First edition 2006

Notice
No responsibility is assumed by the publisher for any injury and/or damage to persons
or property as a matter of products liability, negligence or otherwise, or from any use
or operation of any methods, products, instructions or ideas contained in the material
herein, Because of rapid advances in the medical sciences, in particular, independent
verification of diagnoses and drug dosages should be made

**British Library Cataloguing in Publication Data**
A catalogue record for this book is available from the British Library

**Library of Congress Cataloging-in-Publication Data**
A catalog record for this book is available from the Library of Congress

ISBN-13: 978-0-08-044938-8
ISBN-10: 0-08-044938-7

For information on all Elsevier publications
visit our website at books.elsevier.com

Printed and bound in the Netherlands

06 07 08 09 10 10 9 8 7 6 5 4 3 2 1

# Contents

# List of Figures

# List of Tables

# Contributors

*Tom Baum*
The Scottish Hotel School, University of Strathclyde, Scotland

*Enrico Bonetti*
Department of Business Strategies and Quantitative Methodologies, Faculty of Economics, Second University of Naples, Italy

*Zélia Breda*
Department of Economics, Management and Industrial Engineering, University of Aveiro, Portugal

*Francesco Capone*
Department of Management Science, Faculty of Economics, University of Florence, Italy

*Jordi Comas*
Department of Business Management and Product Design, School of Tourism, University of Girona, Spain

*Carlos Costa*
Department of Economics, Management and Industrial Engineering, University of Aveiro, Portugal

*Rui Costa*
Department of Economics, Management and Industrial Engineering, University of Aveiro, Portugal

*Girolamo Cusimano*
Department of Cultural, Historical-Archaeological, Socio-Anthropological and Geographical Heritage, Faculty of Arts and Philosophy, University of Palermo, Italy

*Paolo Di Martino*
Department of Business Studies, Faculty of Economics, University of Naples "Parthenope", Italy

*Arvid Flagestad*
Norwegian School of Management and ETOUR (European Tourism Research Institute), Norway

*Maurizio Giannone*
Department of Tourism, Sport and Shows, Sicilian Regional Government, Italy

*Catherine Gorman*
School of Hospitality and Tourism Management, Dublin Institute of Technology, Dublin, Republic of Ireland

*Jaume Guia*
Department of Business Management and Product Design, School of Tourism, University of Girona, Spain

*Luciana Lazzeretti*
Department of Management Science, Faculty of Economics, University of Florence, Italy

*Kaija Lindroth*
Helsinki Business Polytechnic, Finland

*Géraldine Maulet*
IGEAT, Université Libre de Bruxelles, Belgium

*Antonio Minguzzi*
Department of Economics, Management and Social Science, University of Molise, Italy

*Alfonso Morvillo*
IRAT, Institute for Service Industry Research, CNR, National Research Council, Italy

*Sara Nordin*
Mid Sweden University and ETOUR (European Tourism Research Institute), Sweden

*Clara S. Petrillo*
IRAT, Institute for Service Industry Research, CNR, National Research Council, Italy

*Lluís Prats*
Department of Business Management and Product Design, School of Tourism, University of Girona, Spain

*Francisco Manuel Dionísio Serra*
University of Algarve, School of Business, Hospitality and Tourism, Faro, Portugal

*Maria Immacolata Simeon*
IRAT, Institute for Service Industry Research, CNR, National Research Council, Italy

*Michele Simoni*
Department of Business Studies, University of Naples "Parthenope", Italy

*Tuovi Soisalon-Soininen*
Helsinki Business Polytechnic, Finland

*Bo Svensson*
Mid Sweden University and ETOUR (European Tourism Research Institute), Sweden

*Immacolata Vellecco*
IRAT, Institute for Service Industry Research, CNR, National Research Council, Italy

*Kong-Yew Wong*
Department of Hospitality and Recreation, Faculty of Economics and Management, University of Putra, Malaysia

# Preface

The tourism industry is playing an increasing role in both new/old industrialized countries and emerging/developing countries. While the manufacturing sector is undergoing a deep crisis and transformation process at a world-wide level, the service and tourism industry is attracting new investments and capitals, often playing a crucial role in the international diversification processes; it is increasing its average size, involving multinationals as well.

Therefore the scenario has drastically changed and is constantly evolving. Tourism is no longer a prerogative of countries such as France, Italy, Spain, with their SME systems, but a wider and more complex phenomenon involving local and global networks, not only individual products/services, strictly linked to the area features. However, within such a context the European model still plays a crucial and specific role thanks to its wide range of different cultures (also allowing for the new entry of the eastern countries).

Developing countries are evolving as well and are directly involved in the competitive game. The new major Asian countries such as China and India, leaders of the world industrial development, are no longer playing a passive role as tourism destinations managed by the major international tour operators; they are rather becoming active subjects generating tourism demand and new entrepreneurship.

The competitive game is no longer controlled by individual organizations but involves the territories that, through the arrangement and multi-level co-ordination of their resources, become supply systems and, then, tourism destinations. Thus, the tourism destination becomes the unit of analysis and the focus shifts to "networking", co-operation, formal and informal networks and partnership management in order to gain a competitive edge and increase product quality.

Consequently, tourism firms are required to implement drastic management changes; first of all they are required to adopt a systemic approach to analyse the competitive context and manage relationships and resources. Achieving and retaining the firm's competitive advantage strictly depends on the firm's ability to include and define its product/service within the local area, to co-operate with other local stakeholders so as to provide an authentic, differentiated and unique tourism experience. In this scenario application and dissemination of ICT technologies can effectively support the new processes aimed at integrating firms and services.

With this work we want to participate in the debate on these issues, including a number of contributions presented at the session "Networking and Tourism Local Systems" of the ATLAS Annual Conference 2004 "Networking & Partnerships in Destination Development

& Management", held in Naples in April 2004 organized by CNR-IRAT[1] of Naples and by ATLAS, the Association for Tourism and Leisure Education, designated by the European Commission in 1996 as a "European Thematic Network for the Tourism and Leisure Subject Areas".[2]

Scholars, tourism operators and policy-makers have focused their attention on the issues related to networking and partnership involving firms and institutions; they have stimulated a lively debate and suggested analytical approaches and empirical applications.

From the theoretical point of view the papers included herein relate to two macro reference areas: economics and management sciences. The analyses range from national to local levels and focus on strategies, policies, and project experiences. The European matrix of the studies is clearly highlighted by the wide range of approaches followed and the empirical evidences presented.

This volume has been subdivided into two parts corresponding to the two theoretical approaches mentioned above which will be illustrated hereunder.

Prior to making a detailed analysis of the individual contributions, we would like to mention a number of common, cross-wise elements which can be found in all papers and viewed as a first starting point, common opinions on which a "European way" to approach the tourism issue could be developed.

These elements are:

- A widespread trend to "replicate" – within the tourism sector and often in a direct manner – models and experiences developed in industrial contexts.
- Adoption of a "systemic approach" enhancing inter-relationships instead of a sector-based approach (and then of the recognition of a sector's specificity).
- Importance of the "site" and its specificities in order to create networks and partnerships within the specific context.
- A greater attention paid to the public sector viewed as a support for the private sector (not only firms, but cluster of non-economic and institutional actors).
- A constant attention to the local/global relationship, often adopting the local approach.
- The TLS approach is often used to enhance the tourism value of peripheral, rural or under-developed areas.
- The constant research work and detailed analysis of excellent cases of territorial tourism management that, through benchmarking and process modelling, enable to identify crucial variables and replicate successful cases.
- Several cases from different areas (Finland, France, Ireland, Italy, Malaysia, Portugal, Spain, Sweden) are examined and provided features and issues that can be applied beyond the cultural and economic contexts.
- Academics, practitioners and tourism scholars should be interested in these important issues and in the actual case studies from all over the world.

*Luciana Lazzeretti and Clara S. Petrillo*

---

[1] National Research Council – Institute on Service Industry Research.
[2] www.atlas-euro.org.

# A Short Overview

The first part *Tourism Local Systems: Economics Approaches* includes the contributions based on approaches mainly related to Industrial and Regional Economics and a case on Malaysian tourism destinations connected to International Economics.

*Capone's* first work summarizes a first state of the art of studies on the travel and tourism industry with a specific view to systemic approaches. The author makes a distinction between management approaches (Destination Management, SLOT) and industrial economics approaches (Milieu, tourist clusters, tourist districts). He then suggests a first theoretical model developed from industrial districts and cultural districts. Within this context, the tourism system is considered as a territorial entity characterized by two elements: the cluster of economic, non-economic and institutional actors and the social local community. An interesting analysis highlights the differences between this framework and the one recently introduced by the Italian law on local tourism systems.

The same theoretical model is applied in the work of *Lazzeretti and Capone* aimed at identifying and analyzing the map of tourism districts and local systems in Italy, extending the Local Labour Market Areas (LLMAs) methodology, typical of the regional analysis and also used as a foundation to identify industrial districts, to the tourism context. While so far the traditional identification of tourism systems has been resorting to indirect variables, the authors classify the existing Italian TLS allowing for the actors of the system and the consequent structure of the supply. They also develop an ad hoc tourism filiére as a proxy for their territorial identification. By doing so, four different categories are identified, from the emergent TLS to traditional tourism destinations. Authors highlight the location of the Italian tourism local systems and how they can be identified.

Another theoretical model based on the industrial district approach is the one suggested by *Maulet*. The author categorizes the relevant features of the industrial district into four main descriptive dimensions: the systemic consciousness degree, the strategic means display, the degree of cumulativeness and the spatial concentration. Applied to tourism, these dimensions emphasize the elements required to build a long-term partnership among tourism actors. This paper focuses on the existing structure among tourism suppliers within a delimited area, on the advantages of building relationships and on the difficulties to function as a system. An interesting test of this theoretical framework is made through a case study of Rochefort, an entity situated in a rural area in the south of Belgium.

The innovation system and clusters are the concepts *Guia, Prats and Comas* refer to. In the tourism industry, local knowledge can play a major role in the configuration and evolution of the destination as a tourism product. In this way, a territory can become a local system of innovation (LSI) according to its innovation ability that, in its turn, depends on the variety and quantity of actors and the type of relations established among them. Although all these elements are important, two characteristics of the relational networks play a crucial role in determining the innovativeness and competitiveness of a specific destination: the clusters' centrality within the global system and its internal cohesion. These factors must coexist in order to improve the destination-innovation capability: actors cannot exploit knowledge without first acquiring it; similarly, they can acquire and assimilate knowledge but they should have the ability to turn it into innovation for profit generation.

The cluster approach guides the contribution of *Breda, Costa* and *Costa*. They maintain that developing networks and partnerships within the tourism sector is a tool to meet the challenges resulting from the constant changes taking place in the global market. Specifically, peripheral areas lack adequate infrastructures and growth dynamics; actually their isolation and the small size of most of their firms prevent the private sector from investing. In their work the authors present an interesting case study on Caramulo, a small backward region located in Portugal: the Regional Tourism Policy Program Anchored to Private Sector Investment (PITER) promotes strong relationships between public and private organizations and is a useful tool to develop remote regions. PITER is a successful example on how to promote socio-economic development in lagging areas behind by combining private and public sector investment in a concerted action aimed at encouraging tourism initiatives.

*Svensson*, *Nordin* and *Flagestad* participate in the debate adopting the governance-based approach to understand the dynamics of destinations and apply it to the different development models of partnerships, clusters and innovation systems. Few authors have adopted this approach and relatively low attention has been paid to clusters and innovation system models. It is argued that the governance-based approach is useful when dealing with these models within the tourism destination context. The models focus on the different governance features and even suggest different forms of governance and government involvement. The authors conclude that the partnership perspective is useful in basically all tourism destinations, while few of them are suitable for the cluster model, and even a smaller number of them for the innovation system model. Empirical observations are drawn from different studies on the Swedish ski resort of Åre.

The first part concludes with the paper of *Wong* and *Baum* on the relationships between multinational corporations and host governments of developing countries with a deep focus on the hotel industry of Malaysian tourism destinations. The entry and presence of new actors in a developing country's destination might have an impact on the existing equilibrium and force local firms or government to react and protect market shares and profits, or local human resources. Welcoming multinational corporations' presence in the local industry is a widely used strategy by host governments to close the technology gap and access new markets. However, the study addresses the prominent negativity of a long-lasting foreign involvement, i.e. over-dependence on foreign resources. The consequences of over-dependence are of core concern among academics and host destination country authorities. Authors capture evidence of the presence of productivity spillovers between local and foreign hotels, indicating the level of maturity of the industry and a state of dependency.

The second part *Tourism Local* Systems: *Management Approaches* includes the contributions basically referring to destination management and marketing areas, with a specific view to some regional cases in southern Italy.

The first contribution further analyses the state of art presented in the first part, focusing on the business economics literature; it presents a multi-level TLS interpretation model. *Bonetti, Petrillo* and *Simoni* suggest a breaking down into four levels, each of them characterized by its own specificity in terms of problems, interpretation keys, evolutionary dynamics, functioning and governance approaches. The first level is the territorial system, recognized as a new unit of analysis, to which concepts and tools already developed for firms and entrepreneurs can be applied to. The second level is the tourism system, meant as the network of local actors involved in tourism development, that generates offers capable of creating value for specific market segments. The analysis concludes with the tourism product level and with the evolution level including the process leading to the creation of a tourism system.

The adoption of a system approach is recommended by *Serra* to better understand and manage quality principles applied to tourism destinations: Integrated Quality Management which is very complex and strategically important for a destination-sustainable development. The concept of quality applied to a tourism destination as a whole is a soft (qualitative) concept resulting from its positioning and consolidated image in the minds of actual and potential tourists. It is then viewed as the aggregated average level of performance output provided by the many service activities included in the so-called tourism value chain within a specific destination. The author presents a framework showing the impact of some decisions on one specific dimension only, on the destination as a whole, and on the feedback cycles. In this way it is possible to understand the underlying behaviour of many system structures and prevent unintended consequences by acting in a more coordinated and informed manner, through networking, cooperation and dialogue.

*Gorman* analyses the use of relationship marketing in developing tourism destination and, in particular, Tourism Product Marketing Groups. Small and Medium Tourism Enterprises (SMTEs) are fragmented and lack organizational structures: co-operative marketing and evolving relationships can help to create a common group identity and a sense of belonging. TPMGs supply a common core product to visitors by bringing together a number of small and medium firms performing in a specific sector of the tourism industry; they also supply a wide range of tourism products and experiences which complement each other and are defined by a specific geographical parameter. Through the interesting case of the PMG "Great Houses and Garden of Ireland", the author explores co-operative marketing groups and their socio-cultural issues, product visions, perceived values as well as many of the constructs associated with the concepts of co-operative marketing, networking and relationship marketing.

The contribution of *Morvillo*, *Simeon* and *Vellecco* is focused on the dissemination of ICT in the tourism industry and on their strategic value as tools to support destination management. Through an economic-managerial approach, the authors analyse the determinants of the rapid dissemination of ICT in the tourism industry to understand how they (multimedia technologies specifically) can support destination strategic management and marketing.

Thanks to their effectiveness and flexibility, in the near future multimedia networks – universal and interactive link tools – will have high development potentials. The authors present a project illustrating the effective role played by ICT in enhancing a specific destination and promoting aggregation among actors, products and services with a positive impact on the way through which value can be created for end users.

The net-management approach is developed by the Finnish authors *Soisalon-Soininen Tuovi* and *Lindroth Kaija*. This article discusses regional tourism co-operation development processes using the network approach. The contribution focuses on the management of the network in its different phases and the roles of the actors in the existing network, identifying their future needs. Developing co-operation requires new management capabilities from the company. Understanding networks, their structure, processes, and evolution is essential.

At the net management level a company's behaviour can be analysed allowing for their positions and roles within these nets. The article concludes that the network-based view is a prerequisite both for a successful net management and an active net participation.

*Minguzzi's* paper deals with Destination Management Organizations (DMO), their role and activities. The development of an area is strictly related to the DMO's capability of developing meta-management functions to manage and promote tourism activities. In a new approach to local and regional policies DMO play a crucial role in organizing inter-actions among the actors of the territorial network. This paper analyses a specific Italian DMO in the Region of Abruzzo (Italy), evaluating how the actual functioning of a DMO influences destination competitiveness. The author highlights that DMO action is more promptly absorbed by company planning activities; however, to have local systems func-tioning effectively, a number of conditions are required: universally recognized and clear guidelines; effective and efficient planning and organizational systems; flexible and acces-sible institutional and organizational bodies; sufficient and stable financial resources, con-sistent with the initiatives to be implemented.

*Cusimano* and *Giannone* highlight how in the region of Sicily the development of new tourism supply organizational patterns is characterized by the cooperative nature of the rela-tions among public institutions, local communities and enterprises, like the ones that are just appearing in other Italian regions. This process is fostered by the latest legislation, issued to support enterprises and local development and integrate local stakeholders to make the best use of the territories from the tourism point of view. Local tourism systems are making the attempt to connect to international networks, and new opportunities for economic growth arise from the relations between local and global bodies. The different territories, although not yet ready, claim their right to build up their future development; new destinations will then enter the tourism market. New geographies are emerging, but the traditional represen-tation patterns are no longer suitable to the new organization of the tourism space.

The paper of *Di Martino* and *Petrillo* deals with a development framework for tourism destination based on partnerships. This framework has been developed allowing for a basic assumption: as local resources are the competitive advantage of the area, any development project must be built on their knowledge and enhancement. This must be achieved through an active and aware cooperation among all actors involved. This integrated management model was implemented and tested in a National project aimed at developing the Cilento and Vallo di Diano National Park from the tourism point of view, by creating networks and enhancing local resources. This paper illustrates the achievement of the project's objec-tives and the framework validity, i.e. when a destination development project has a clear and specific purpose and a limited duration, when it is based on the territory identity and on values and ideals shared by the actors involved, it is possible to create cooperation and destination networks.

# PART 1

# TOURISM LOCAL SYSTEMS: ECONOMICS APPROACHES

Chapter 1

# Systemic Approaches for the Analysis of Tourism Destination: Towards the Tourist Local Systems

Francesco Capone

## Introduction

The aim of this paper is to outline a review of systemic approaches to analyse tourism destination, with a specific view to the analytical models of a "site viewed as a system of actors". Multi-disciplinary approaches will be reviewed dividing them into management approaches and industrial economics approaches, outlining their various characteristics and specificities at Italian and international level. A general model to analyse a tourism destination, i.e. the *tourism local system* (*TLS*) will then be suggested.

This paper is divided into five sections. The first section includes a review of contributions to management approaches (Destination Management (DM), SLOT). The second section illustrates the approaches generated by industrial economics and applied to the tourism industry (cluster, *milieu* and district). The third section illustrates a model drawn from the "industrial district theory", the TLS, as a clue to interpret the system of actors specialized in tourist activities. The fourth section deals with a recently issued Italian law on local tourism systems (LTS) and highlights the differences between the framework proposed and the one introduced by an Italian law. Lastly, some conclusions are drawn.

## Systemic Approaches to Tourism Destinations Developed by Management Science: Destination Management and Local System Tourism Offer

### Destination Management

The systemic approach to a tourism destination is not unique. Within this context, a number of authors (Franch, 2002) differentiate the managerial approach to a destination from the supply side (SLOT) and the demand side (DM). From the demand side, a destination is defined as a whole set of products and services acting as attractions for tourists, while from the supply side it is identified as a correlated system of offers related to a specific site, differentiating it from the tourism product (Franch, 2002, p. 3).

What is a tourism destination? The European Commission (2000) defines a Tourism Destination as:

> an area which is separately identified and promoted to tourists as a place to visit, and within which the tourism product is coordinated by one or more identifiable authorities or organizations (p. 149).

The European Commission (EC) stresses the importance of the tourist's perception of the locality and the need for a systemic approach to management and quality:

> As far as tourists are concerned, however, the satisfaction derived from staying at a destination does not just depend on their experience of tourism services, but also on more general factors such as hospitality, safety and security, sanitation and salubrity, traffic and visitor management (ibidem, p. 13).

Based upon this definition, in the past 10 years, the international specialized literature coined the concept of "Destination Management". Following this view, the attention focuses on the strategies and marketing actions implemented in a specific site considered as a system of players co-operating to supply an integrated tourism product.

The concept of DM and Marketing, which analyses a tourism site as a unique system of players located in a specific area, was originally developed by Ritchie, Laws and Buhalis and by International Association of Scientific Experts in Tourism (AIEST)[1] members, Bieger, Keller, Pechlaner, Weiermair among others. Specifically, Pechlaner and Weiermair (2000) make a detailed analysis of a destination with a specific view to destination management, financing tools, organization development and need for competencies and development of marketing strategies. Bieger (1998, p. 7) defines a destination as "as an area consisting of all services and offers provided to a tourism consumers during his/her stay". As already mentioned, this approach mainly focuses on the demand side; the destination is then viewed as a mix of products capable of attracting a given number of visitors.

From this perspective, the tourism destination is viewed as a bundle of products (the final experience) supplied by a wide number of co-operating players (tour operators, travel agents, passenger carriers, hotels and other service providers), and the competitive advantage of the *filière* is increasingly depending on the system of local actors. A destination is described as a place characterized by two key elements: its internal reality — i.e. a territorially coherent geographical space where players co-operate — and the external perception

---

[1] International Association of Scientific Experts in Tourism, www.aiest.org, last three congresses were devoted to DM and Marketing 1996, 1997, 1998 (Pechlaner & Weiermair, 2000, p. 4).

of it, which is founded on its image, i.e. its significance for tourists. Although tourism is defined as a heterogeneous mix of services (Crouch & Ritchie, 1999) from the consumers' point of view, it is no longer a service or a product, but an experience (Otto & Ritchie, 1996).

Systemic literature on tourism also refers to the whole set of relations among local actors resorting to the concept of "coo-petition" (Edgell & Haenisch, 1995), namely co-operation *and* com-petition. Therefore, emphasis is placed on the role of these two forces, which are crucial for a tourism destination, like for any other territorial model (district or cluster). Such a theoretical similarity to territorial models is also underlined by Crouch and Ritchie (1999), who introduce the well-known Porterian "five forces model" to analyse competitiveness in a tourism site,[2] and represent it as a prototype of the tourism cluster.

A similar study was carried out by Buhalis (2000), who examined a destination as a combination of tourism products providing the consumer with an integrated experience. The author also emphasized the local actors interdependence and showed how the offer system depends on every single player involved. Buhalis and Cooper (1998) highlighted instead the small and medium size of the enterprises performing their business in the tourism industry.

Attention was paid to the relationships between the DM approach and the ones typical of Italian scholars, particularly the SLOT model (illustrated in the next section) (Tamma, 1999; Franch, 2002). Specifically, a number of Italian authors (Franch, 2002, p. 2) deal with three main issues. The first issue relates to the definition of destination as a target area for government strategic choices and tourism policies. The second issue deals with multiple *destination management* forms and mainly relates to the co-ordination of the decision-making process, regardless whether it refers to the analysis of the segments to be attracted or to the composition of the local offer. The last issue relates to the policies alternative to *destination management*; it focuses on how to develop a decision-making process shared by local actors, social community.

From this perspective, Franch (2002, p. 7) maintains that these problems can be addressed as follows: identifying a body capable of analysing and orienting the behaviour of the destination area; having a public organization capable of co-operating with the local stakeholders; and, lastly, self-regulating the actors involved in order to pursue shared objective for the area development.

## Slot

In the past 10 years, the Italian literature on travel and tourism industry has widely accepted the systemic approach, mainly referring to the studies by Rispoli and Tamma and to the SLOT concept . The systemic approach applied to a tourism destination analyses the attraction factors and the whole set of local activities. A strong emphasis is put on the relations

---

[2] The authors suggest an interesting model, aimed at increasing a place's competitiveness by means of a micro- and a macro-economic pattern of actors. This model relates resources with the achievable competitive and comparative advantages, and it might be interpreted as an elementary form of Porter's cluster. Although the unit of analysis is the local system, the focus is rather on managerial aspects, such as strategy, marketing and management.

between what is supplied by the firms and the total offer provided by a specific site, which overtly relates to the definition of SLOT, that is:

> a bundle of activities and factors of attractiveness situated in a specific place (site, locality, destination) [which] can provide a well-constructed and integrated tourism offer, that represents a distinctive system of tourism hospitality enhancing local resources and culture (Rispoli & Tamma, 1995, p. 41).

SLOT is characterized by the four following fundamentals (Ibidem, 1995, p. 41):

(a) The *system*: a bundle of integrated activities rooted in the territory and requiring coordination and involvement of all stakeholders;
(b) The *local*: the reference being made to a specific area that determines the fundamental and peculiar characteristics representing a local attraction;
(c) The *tourist offer*: the aim of the system is to provide a wide range of tourism products.
(d) The *local system of offer*: it defines the area as a system open to relations with the external world.

These factors are the pillars, which enable us to evaluate the capability of a specific area of producing wealth and employment opportunities, and setting up a virtuous circle of local development. They also are a common foundation to analyse the industrial economic models extended to the tourism industry.

Both the models illustrated herein (DM and SLOT), while including different factors, emphasize the role of local players, their relations with local resources and the interaction of the local system with the external environment.[3]

A branch of specialized literature focused on systemic approaches to tourism industry starting from the SLOT definition (Casarin, 1996; Tamma, 1999). For example, Casarin (1996) emphasizes some crucial aspects of the TLS, such as direct management of the territory by local stakeholders, through their participation in the decision-making process aimed at promoting local development.

Tamma (1999) generally refers to DM allowing for two correlated aspects; firstly, the management of the tourism products supplied to the market place; secondly, the resources, activities and players making up the local supply system. The author highlights that DM is the attempt of promoting and organizing the integration of the resources of a specific area to provide a distinctive, sustainable and competitive tourism offer. As the literature includes many system approaches (Laws, 1995; Leiper, 1995), the aim is to give

---

[3] The main difference between this approach and the territorial models is that, in the former case a single leading subject, a meta-manager, is delegated and charged not only with the management of the place but also with the strategic planning of the whole system. This feature is quite different in the various environments, such as in the agglomerations of small and medium enterprises (SMEs), where sometimes there is not even an established managing consortium, and the managing role is played by different subjects and disseminated within the local system. In other words, there is a sort of widespread entrepreneurship at the local level. Additionally, the strategic-managerial foundation of this model is meant to develop targeted strategic paths and is mainly based on a "project" perspective where a specific subject represents the interests of the site.

a "collective dimension to the strategies and actions implemented by the individual actors performing their activity in tourism, so as to identify potential decision-making centers, tools, processes" (Tamma, 2002, p. 21). The systemic approach to tourism sites has been widely accepted, and its influence was also recognized by the new Italian Law (L. 135/2001) on LTS (see next section). To analyse the systemic approaches from the industrial organization perspective focusing on the supply side, it is now necessary to refer to other disciplines and analyse the territorial models applied to tourism industry, such as tourism cluster, district and *milieu*.

## Territorial Models Developed by Industrial Economics

### Tourism Milieu

Illustrating the approaches developed by industrial economics, we analyse for the first time the social reality of the destination and the role played by the local community. This approach is mainly focused on these points and on the *milieu innovateur*.[4] The concept of *milieu* comes from the French and Swiss literature; original contributions were developed by Aydalot in the 1980s (Aydalot, 1986), and recently by the GREMI[5] group: Maillat, Crevoisier and Camagni among others. Some scholars of the GREMI group tried to apply the territorial model to other sectors, for instance to the cultural (Costa, 2004) and tourism (Peyrache-Gadeau, 2003) sectors.

The latter contribution analyses the development of mountain sites using a model characterized as a social-economic *milieu* with a tourism vocation. In this research, two typologies of skiing resorts are described: the "territory-resort of tourism economy" and the "place-resort of tourism production". The first typology is characterized by a spontaneous local *milieu*, where innovations spread smoothly and organizations develop in continuity with the past. In the second typology there is no *milieu innovateur*, but the actor's origin is exogenous and development is merely based on tourism, which is often in conflict with the place's history. This paper also explains the important role played by the local community and the relationships among local players. Making reference to this taxonomy, the authors distinguish resort sites by their different development paths followed in the past few years.

The theory of *milieu innovateur* mainly focuses on the role of an innovative social-economic environment and on the ability to create a virtuous circle of development, with a strong emphasis on the relations between productive organizations and social communities. Some studies with a similar background were also developed in the Italian literature, but they generally extend the idea of *milieu* without identifying a definition of the concept specifically related to the tourism sector.[6]

---

[4] The literal translation of *milieu innovateur* is "innovating environment".

[5] Group européenne de recherche sur le milieu innovateur (European Network on Innovative Environment).

[6] Other authors view territorial local systems specialized in tourism activities as a social *milieu*, see for instance Dematteis (2003).

### Tourism Cluster

The renewed interest in industrial clusters was initiated by Michael Porter's studies.[7] Porter maintains that in a globalized economy increasingly competitive advantages are rooted in local systems and in specific places. In *The Competitive Advantage of Nations* (Porter, 1990) he defines a geographic cluster as "a geographic concentration of interconnected companies and institutions in a particular field".[8] Porter's analysis is mainly focused on traditional industries, but it also makes references to the tourism industry:

> a host of linkages among cluster members result in a whole greater than the sum of its part. In a typical tourism cluster, for example, the quality of a visitor's experience depends not only on the appeal of the primary attraction but also on the quality and efficiency of complementary businesses such as hotels, restaurants, shopping outlets and transportation facilities. Because members of the cluster are mutually dependent, good performance by one can boost the success of the others (ibidem, p. 77).

Researches about tourism clusters are still limited in number. One of the most interesting works on this subject is that by Nordin (2003), who applies Porter's diamond to tourism industry and focuses on the role of a cluster of tourism enterprises and innovators.

Nordin stresses the need for developing collaboration strategies and synergies among local players, in order to catch up a sustainable competitive advantage as "the purpose of the report is to emphasize clustering as a means of developing tourism industry" (Nordin, 2003, p. 8). A number of examples of "clustering" are given: the tourism cluster of Napa Valley, South Africa, North Queensland and some Swedish cases.

Conversely, criticism of Porterian cluster approach can be severe. For example, Martin and Sunley (2003, work cited in Nordin, 2003, p. 25) maintain that Porter's approach is far from being universally accepted in the areas of business economics, industrial organization and management studies, and that it often lacks specificity and measurability.

Nonetheless, Porter's cluster approach was applied to tourism as well, and it assumed a specific definition, "clustering strategy", i.e. a strategy aimed at developing initiatives that can involve a network of local actors in the attempt to catch up the typical advantages of the industrial cluster (collaboration, synergies and competition).

In this context, some studies refer to a cluster initiative (NEDLAC, 1999) carried out in South Africa and related to the project of re-launching tourism in the region. The analysis of the South African cluster is mainly aimed at promoting support activities for national tourism. Specifically, the points of strength and points of weakness of travel and tourism industries at the national level are investigated, applying the Porterian approach.[9] The

---

[7] Although we use Porter's concept of industrial cluster, there are many approaches to the concept. For a review of the definition of cluster, see European Network for SME Research (ENSR) (2003).

[8] This concept is similar to the concept of agglomeration of enterprises. The main difference vis-à-vis the industrial district is represented by the close social relations between the local community and most of the SMEs.

[9] The analysis highlights how the distributive system and accommodation facilities should be better developed and integrated. The main future goal is to develop agreements and synergies within the national cluster.

consortium, including private and public stakeholders, aims at improving the vertical and horizontal components of the value chain. However, the criticisms moved on the outcomes resulting from a top-down strategy are still valid.

The cluster theory directly refers to the role played by Marshall's external economies as source of competitiveness in an enterprise system (Porter, 1998). In particular, the crucial role not of concentration, but of the industry's structure and level of inter-firm rivalry is recognized. Contributions in this line of research underline that industrial rivalry drives enterprises to compete in an increasingly intense and efficient manner so as to develop innovations.

### *Tourism District*

In Italy, the importance of Porter's cluster has been recognized only recently; the national literature mainly refers to Marshall's industrial district, also because the Italian manufacturing industries mainly includes small- and medium-sized firms, which are similar to the English firm agglomerations of the early 1900s.

There are only few contributions on tourism districts; one of them is a research carried out by ACI-CENSIS (2001) analysing Italian territory:

> a new model for an offer that draws its origin from natural vocations (sea, art, mountains, etc), and that goes beyond the traditional reading by "points" (tourism municipalities), "lines" (the Romagna coasts, or the Amalfi Coast) or "systems" (Val Gardena, Val Pusteria, etc).

The document identifies Italian tourism sites in relation to their multiple activities (if any). A choice that does not correspond to the traditional concept of district; from this point of view, the analysis is rather based on Porter's cluster, where there are no mutual connections between enterprises and social community.[10]

On the other hand, other studies use the term "district" just to refer to an area from the territorial point of view, but focusing on different aspects. Santarelli' survey (1995) on the tourism district of the Adriatic coast — including the provinces of Forlì, Ferrara, Ancona, Ascoli Piceno and Macerata — makes reference to Mashall's district theory. The local system investigated is characterized by low entry-barriers and negligible levels of sunk-costs that determine a thriving process of natality and mortality, typical of district enterprises. There is a strong division and specialization of labour among enterprises; hotels are separated from enterprises providing recreational activities or transport facilities, etc. (*ibidem*, p. 350).[11]

---

[10] Using some indexes, the report records 299 Italian "tourism districts" (96 sea-side districts, 37 artistic-cultural districts, 137 skiing districts and 29 integrated districts), for a total number of 2841 municipalities, 22.4 million people, 16,600 restaurants and 24,300 hotels. As a whole the district group records over 200 million tourists.

[11] The author defines a tourism district as follows: "the Emilian coast, in fact, turns up to be a local system specialized in the supply of tourism products and, from this point of view, it is similar to the widely diffused industrial districts with a manufacturing vocation of the central and northern-eastern regions of the country". The district is characterized by the following factors: (1) intensive process of creation of new enterprises, incubators of entrepreneurship; (2) cumulative process of learning built on a professional labour supply; and (3) external economies that scale down entry barriers and abate the problems associated with the small size of the enterprises.

An interesting study on tourism district by Antonioli-Corigliano (1999) analyses a tourism-gastronomic district, and investigates into the role of a wine-route, assuming that it functions like a service centre in the area. The description given by the author resumes Becattini's definition of a district as: a stable and reasonable thickening of relations among enterprises along time (Antonioli-Corigliano, 1999, p. 145).

Enterprises are viewed as being strongly rooted in the territory, and their identification is not necessarily based on geographic parameters,[12] but also on social-economic parameters. Moreover, every enterprise is considered as a ring in the chain representing the local system. Relationships among agents in a specific small area favour the building up of a Marshallian "industrial atmosphere", defined as an "eno-tourism atmosphere", namely:

a particular state in which information, culture, innovations and abilities are transmitted and learned in an unconscious way, and exchanged thanks to the indirect action of social institutions (family, school, enterprises, associations, and so on) and due to proximity (*ibidem*, p. 150).[13]

The industrial district theory directly refers to Marshall's external economies as sources of competitiveness for the local area.[14] In this context Antonioli-Corigliano (1999) subdivides scale economies into two groups: promotion and commercialization economies at enterprise and local system level,[15] agglomeration economies that are internal to the enterprise, but external to the tourism district.

The models of tourism district illustrated in this paper analyse a site as a whole district, while other contributions on tourism deal with a limited part of a city (or a neighbourhood) viewed as an urban district.[16] For instance, Pearce (1998) investigates the various structural characteristics of Paris tourism quarters. The contribution is mainly focused on various urban *nuclei* as heterogeneous tourism districts of the French capital: Ile de la Cité, Montmartre and the Opera quarter. Stansfield and Richert (1970) analyse the recreational business district of Niagara Falls, while Getz (1993) examines the tourism business districts. All these studies are focused on a specific and restricted geographic area. Other authors, such as Judd, analyse instead the role played by agglomeration economies in an urban tourism district.

> Agglomeration economies apply to tourism districts not principally because concentration lower costs or increase the efficiency of business transaction, but because to full panoply of services and business is necessary to make the space maximally attractive to consumers of the tourism space (Judd, 1993, p. 179).

---

[12] See, in opposition, the identification methodology used in the report by ACI-CENSIS (2001).

[13] In this tourism district, the *impannatore pratese*, or pure entrepreneur, might be featured as the tour operator who runs the information concerning the national and international markets, and the supply of tourism services.

[14] For the analysis of the sources of competitiveness in Italian TLS, see Capone and Boix (2004).

[15] In other words, economies of specialization and scale (or target) economies due to the supply of specialized services in the local system.

[16] Initially, studies on urban tourism developed in the 1990s were mainly carried out by geographers (for instance, Jansen-Verbeke and Pearce). In the last decade, this field of research was very much enlarged in Europe, particularly by Cazes and Poitier (1996), Van der Berg, Van der Borg, Van der Meer (2001) and Ashworth (1991).

The author finds out that agglomeration economies develop when the localization of an economic unit depends on that of all other actors, not only because of the economic advantages or efficiencies, but also because a total offer of services can maximize the overall attractivity of a specific area. Judd also analyses recreational activities for leisure time, conference centres, etc.

Jansen-Verbeke and Ashworth (1990) maintain that tourism development in a specific site depends more on concentration rather than dispersion, on the functional combination of activities rather than on their segregation, more on multifunctional environments rather than on mono-functionality. Ashworth (1991) analyses these district relations in the historical cities of Groningen and London, considering the entire city as a district.

In our opinion, systemic approaches, that gained an increasing importance in the past few years, are useful and crucial for the analysis of a tourism locality. In this context, and using the industrial district approach as a starting point, in the next section we suggest an analytical model for the tourism production system, the *TLS*.

## Towards the Tourism Local System

### *The Theoretical Context of Reference: The Industrial District Theory*

The aim of this section is to illustrate a general model to study tourism destinations so as to analyse the supply structure of a specific area. An analytical model will be suggested to investigate a site as a system of actors and probe into the composition of the local supply. This model will focus on a multi-sector firm system, allowing for the interconnection with the local community and institutions. The theoretical context of reference of our analysis is the district theory as a model to analyse a local industry, mainly consisting of SMEs, characterized by its interconnection with its social community.

In Marshall's seminal work, industrial districts were described as agglomerations of small and medium enterprises specialized in a given productive activity. The concept of Mashallian industrial district was reviewed by Becattini in the 1980s: since then, the Florence school has played a major role in the study and dissemination of this concept (Becattini, 1990; 2004).[17]

Some scholars have recently paid a particular attention to local development models of non-industrial origin (Bellandi & Sforzi, 2003), thus clarifying the interconnection between industrial districts and the complex paths to local development.

The industrial district theory can be helpful and provide a suitable interpretation key to break down a complex entity, such as a tourism destination. Our attempt is to suggest a model for local development: the TLS, where small- and medium enterprises co-exist. In the first phase of our work, we define an agglomeration of enterprises specialized in tourism activities and analyse its ability to reproduce itself, generate employment opportunities and

---

[17] Becattini (1990, p. 58) defined an industrial district as a "social-territorial entity characterised by the active presence of both a community of people and a population of firms in a naturally and historically bounded area. Unlike other environments, in the district, such as the manufacturing towns, community and firms tend to merge".

produce wealth, allowing for its territorial dimension and social-cultural characteristics. Our investigation focuses on enterprises that enhance artistic and cultural resources through shared work and social experiences.

Firstly, tourism industry is typically based on medium and small enterprises; secondly, these *places* are characterized by close ties enterprises and local communities. Therefore, there is the opportunity for a territorial approach: the *TLS* might assume these characteristics as an interpretation model.

### *The Starting Points: The Cultural District (and Cultural Districtualization Processes)*

In the past few years, there has been a lively debate on the extension of industrial territorial models to other fields of analysis, such as cultural district in Italy (Preite, 1998; Valentino, 2001; Santagata, 2002; Lazzeretti, 2003, 2004) and abroad (Garreau, 1992; Scott, 1996; Frost Kumpf, 1998).

In this context, we applied the approach of Lazzeretti (2003, 2004) as an extension of the Industrial district theory to the cultural district. In particularly, there are two elements at the base of the configuration of a cultural district that can be extended to the tourist local systems. The two elements to verify are: the presence of local resources to be enhanced as the artistic, cultural and environmental heritage and the existence of economic, non economic and institutional stakeholders willing to develop the local resources to achieve a competitive, durable and sustainable development for the whole community. These two elements are the foundations of the TLS, we will refer to in this paper. In other words, the cultural, artistic and environmental heritage (CAEH) and the cluster of actors.

### *Cultural, Artistic and Environmental Heritage and the Cluster of Actors*

The existence of resources to be enhanced and promoted constitutes the pre-requirement for a TLS. The growth of industrial districts has often resulted from the enhancement of local resources by the leader enterprises of a local community. From this point of view, we must verify the existence of the CAEH, a notion introduced by Lazzeretti (2004, p. 9). The CAEH factor does not refer to the tangible resources of a specific place only — monuments and works of art —, but it includes the whole set of tangible and intangible resources included in the following three categories:

- *artistic resources*: monuments, architectural works, works of art, etc.;
- *cultural resources*: typical arts and crafts, sense of belonging, atmosphere of the city as a whole and of its single neighbourhoods, exhibitions and events, cultural activities, etc.; and
- *environmental resources*: urban and hillside landscape, gardens, parks, squares, flora and fauna, etc.

Cities, coastlines, valleys and tourism destinations are highly characterized by the CAEH factor; and on this basis, it is possible to map a place, a nation or a region.[18] The resulting heritage can be viewed as a driver for local development. In fact, once it is

---

[18] For a geo-referencing of artistic and cultural heritage of Tuscany, see Bacci (2002).

viewed as a resource not only to be preserved but to be enhanced as well, it can play an economic role.[19]

Following Lazzeretti (2003), we can view a tourist local system as a system characterized by the presence in its area of a large endowment of the CAEH factor, and by a network of economic, non-economic and institutional actors specialized in tourism activities. Firstly, CAEH is a platform for a competitive tourism attraction and, if enhanced and preserved, it is able to create a competitive, sustainable advantage, and act as a driver for the development of the local community.

Secondly, it relates to the networks of actors, which — according to the literature —, result from the two main pillars of an industrial district: the productive organization — i.e. a system of localized and specialized enterprises working with a flexible division of labour —, and the local social-institutional environment. Therefore, as a first approximation, the TLS is a group of SMEs — a strong concentration of small- and medium-sized firms — creating wealth and employment, thanks to the combination with CAEH: the cluster of actors. The cluster of enterprises will include hotels, travel agencies, catering firms and other firms related to the tourism business widely meant.

Two specific elements, the population of enterprises (the cluster) and the social community, enable TLS to be a self-reproductive model of local development. TLS is a group of localized and interconnected enterprises, mainly SMEs, generating wealth and employment by enhancing local resources. Therefore, a cluster of economic, non-economic and institutional actors is a necessary, but non-sufficient, condition to create the model of TLS as proposed.

The second necessary condition for reproducing a local development model over time, is represented by the social relations among the local community members. As underlined, a cluster of interconnected and localized actors develops relationships within the local community. If a thickening of this kind of relations exist, reproductive effects will be generated, along with the *humus*, which is crucial for the economic development of a specific area.[20]

The relationships between CAEH, enterprises, local community, institutions, together with the specific social-economic aspects, can be the starting point for verifying the existence of different degrees of tourism districtualization as a test of TLS similarity/diversity with a typical Marshallian tourist district.[21] From this point of view, a tourism district can

---

[19] In addition to preservation, we think that the assets belonging to CAEH cannot be considered as resources only, but they must be regarded as well as limitations. In fact, they cannot be exploited without constraints: just think of over-exploited protected areas or art cities, where the excess of tourist flows can conflict with local communities. Although, it is not possible here to probe into the sustainability issue, we would like to point out how CAEH, if properly maintained and increased, can act as an autonomous driver for sustainable development.

[20] An example of these vertical relationships among economic, non-economic and institutional players aimed at developing inter-firm co-operation can be found in Lazzeretti (1995) and in the case of the city of Florence.

[21] The study of districtualization processes is a dynamic district analysis focused not on the district as such, but on the forms of districtualization, by means of a process analysis. Starting from suggestions made for the agrarian district (Becattini, 2004, p. 197), Lazzeretti (2003, p. 641) proceed with an analysis of the cultural district with the support of an ex-post study carried out in a mature, complete and, strictly speaking, Marshallian district. The author (2001) tries to find various degrees of cultural districtualization in different cultural local systems that are more or less well developed compared to the mature, achieved form of the 'Marshallian cultural district'.

be viewed as a specific typology of TLS with close economic and social links, including all elements typical of a social community (trust and social capital).

### The Tourism Local System

Based on what has been mentioned above, and following the industrial district approach, a TLS can be described as having the following attributes:

- First of all, a TLS is a place where the social community and the economic community co-exist (for example a local labour market area).[22]
- There is a stable and durable core industry developing wealth, and thus generating local activities, i.e. tourism activities; other complementary activities are also performed.
- The main tourism productive process is localized within the district and developed by resident people; a crucial part of the production is made within the district's boundaries. CAEH has an impact on the consumption process in the area.
- The area can be represented as a tourism *filière* as SMEs are specialized in one or more phases of the "productive process" offering tourists a special experience.
- Most enterprises are SMEs. There is not a prevailing enterprise, but an autonomous population of SMEs.

As to the local community, the distinctive factor of a TLS is a shared homogenous system of values (ethics of work, family, etc.). The territorial boundaries and staying of people in the area over the years favour the creation of an authentic local community with shared social values (for example, the mountain communities).

Enterprises are specialized in one or more phases of the process aimed at supplying tourism services; every enterprise is a ring of the chain that constitutes the whole local system, within a multi-industrial entrepreneurship context.

TLS enterprises are interconnected and can benefit from scale and scope economies. Competition and co-operation interact within the local system: on the one hand, there is an intense competition (every firm strives to supply the best product or service); on the other, firm-interconnection and local social relations support an inter-firm co-operation.

From the supply side, a TLS is mainly characterized by three elements: (a) a substantial number of enterprises enhancing the tourism destination CAEH (tourism-related activity); (b) a cluster of SMEs based on tourism destination; (c) economic and social relationships between the local social community (citizens) and the productive community (enterprises).

## Local Tourism System: A Comparison to the Italian law 135/2001

In this paragraph, we want to highlight the differences between the framework proposed and the one recently introduced by an Italian law on local tourist systems. The legislator's

---

[22] Think, for example, of the role played by labour local systems in the identification of industrial districts as social-economic unit of analysis local labour market areas (LLMAs). See, for instance, Lazzeretti and Capone (2004) for the identification of TLS through Italian LLMAs.

approach to tourism systems and specifically Law 135 provides for a national reform of tourism activities, as it covers many issues related to the activity and, specifically, introduces the concept of LTS (art. 5).[23] The legislator defines LTS as:

> homogenous or integrated tourism contexts, comprising territorial areas that can belong to different regions, characterized by an integrated offer of cultural and environmental assets and tourism attractions, including typical products of agriculture and local handicrafts, or by the widespread presence of individual or associated tourism enterprises (L. 135/2001, art. 5).

Synthetically, the subject of the law is a public–private system, which — through an integrated offer — promotes tourism resources, such as cultural and environmental assets, ethnic and artistic events, and typical food products. The territorial reference context can include one or more municipalities, with the involvement of territorial agencies, such as provinces, Chambers of Commerce or Regions.

The main objective of this law is to up-grade the Italian tourism offer, which can no longer be based on traditional tourism destinations only. The law 135/2001 aims at meeting the local stakeholders' need for co-operation and networking so as to create an integrated tourism organization and improve the quality level of the tourism destination.

Unfortunately, after three years from its issue, there are still conflicting interpretations as to what kind of LTS the law refers to. While a number of regions decided to enforce the law and implement the relevant actions, other regions have not made the necessary amendments to the regional tourism legislation (and it seems that they are not looking forward doing it).

At the end of 2003, a research work carried out by "Il Sole 24 ore" highlighted that the national law was enforced in Marche[24] and Umbria only. A number of regions (Liguria, Lombardia, Lazio, Molise, Campania, Calabria, Sicily and Abruzzi) are still debating whether to enforce it or not and, to the date, only few of them have accepted it.

Moreover, most of the projects submitted were planned through a top-down approach; only few of them are characterized by a bottom-up approach. Multiple forms of territorial promotion and partnership still exit, for instance APT (*Provincial Tourism Boards*), and IAT (*Tourist Information and Support Offices*) or the Plans for Territorial Integration (PIT).[25] For example Tuscany did not accept the law 135/2001 and maintained its APT, while in Sicily, a PIT was called "From traditional tourism to an integrated local tourism system".

---

[23] The law refers to LTS, not to TLS. We distinguish the two concepts as we considered a TLS firstly as a local system then specialized in tourism activities and not a general tourism system. When identifying a system, the territory is viewed as the main element, not as a sort of a variable depending on the system of actors performing in the tourism industry.

[24] Marche Region, whose territory includes 10 LSTs, was the first Italian region to enforce the 135/2002 (d.r.g. 578/2002). The application diagram develops in a top-down way, by means of reference parameters, such as: the import of the territorial area involved, its territorial dimension, product typology, homogeneity, integration, presence of diverse offer typologies (1500 beds), existence of a public–private network and dimension of tourist flows.

[25] It is worth mentioning again that the PIT are projects, which may have a tourism qualification and the municipalities falling within Objective 2 of European Structural Funds that can create local consortia for promotion and management.

To date, the law is not sufficiently accepted and is strongly criticized by operators and experts (Becheri, 2003). Additionally, while the new legislation encourages local stake-holders to create a consortium aimed at promoting a specific area (leaving to operators the opportunity to act, or the freedom not to act), its aim of promoting a product-place on the market might hinder super-local marketing plans.

The important role played by systemic approaches and networking of tourism destinations is therefore recognized at the national level. In our opinion the widespread acceptance of these approaches (above all in the past years) drove the Italian legislator to develop political initiatives in this field, although they are mainly focused on promotion and characterized by a top-down approach.

In comparison to the proposed TLS model, the law 135/2001 approach dedicates an increasing attention to the territory and the effective reference area of tourist destinations. Nonetheless, a right emphasis still lacks on the social aspects on those sites where a thickening of relations between productive and social community exists, as the main elements render TLS model auto-reproductive along time. In this context, this model risks to develop strategies and policies for "weak"-tourist destinations, not considering the degree of presence of a tourist filiére and the local endowment of CAEH. On the other hand, the emphasis put on financing projects and partnerships helps to create co-operation among local actors and share a common mission, but the voluntary participation may exclude opinions of leaders and important economic and non-economic players, as already recognized in literature (Pechlaner & Weiermair, 2000).

## Conclusions

In this paper a review of systemic approaches on tourism destinations was presented. After a first analysis of management models, the state of art for industrial economics models extended to the tourism industry was illustrated. A model for a TLS was then defined, using the industrial district theory as a theoretical context of reference. The specific characteristics and analytical advantages of each approach were described.

The aim of this paper was to outline the systemic approaches adopted to study and analyse a tourism destination, focusing the analysis on the main features of the various models and the specificities of each individual approach.

A tourism destination can be viewed from two perspectives: as a whole set of products and services acting as attractions for tourists (demand-side); a correlated supply system related to a specific area (supply-side). From this perspective both DM and SLOT are approaches mainly focused on the management of the tourism products supplied on the market place and, then, on the resources, activities and actors constituting the local supply system.

Within this context other economic-industrial models can be adopted, mainly focused on the supply side. Reference was made to tourism cluster and district. The tourism cluster is mainly focused on advantages resulting from the location and on the local market structure/rivalry; the main unit of analysis is the network of enterprises and associated institutions. The tourism *milieu* basically analyses the socio-cultural environment of a specific place and the network of actors who wanted to develop innovations and new knowledge.

The tourism district is a place and a set of "close inter-relations", where the role played by the social community is strictly linked to the industrial world.

The TLS is a territorial entity characterized by two elements: the cluster of economic, non-economic and institutional actors and the social community.

The models illustrated in this paper have different reference territorial units. The cluster does not assume a geographic limitation and can include a city or a region. The district is instead a restricted area and a social-economic unit where the community of citizens coincides with working people.

The value of each model lies in its focusing on a specific element of the tourism enterprise system, according to the distinctive field of study. As a whole, these approaches highlight the multifarious competitive advantages resulting from firm agglomeration, and suggest a multidisciplinary model to analyse TLS. The important role played by systemic approaches and networking of tourism destinations is therefore recognized at the Italian level as in the proposed law 135/2001. The widespread acceptance of these approaches (above all in the past years) drove the Italian legislator to develop political initiatives in this field, although it mainly focuses on promotion, characterized by a top-down approach, lacks of the main feature of theoretical models proposed.

## Acknowledgments

The author expresses his gratefulness to Prof. Lazzeretti for guidance and aid.

## References

ACI-CENSIS. (2001). *I distretti turistici italiani: l'opportunità di innovare l'offerta.* Roma: Censis servizi S.p.A.

Antonioli Corigliano, M. (1999). *Strade del vino ed enoturismo. Distretti turistici e vie di comunicazione.* Milano: Franco Angeli.

Ashworth, G. (1991). The historic cities of Groningen: Which is sold to whom? In: G. Ashworth, & B. Goodall (Eds), *Marketing tourism and places.* London: Routledge.

Aydalot, Ph. (1986). *Milieux Innovateurs en Europe.* Paris: GREMI.

Bacci, L. (2002). *Sistemi locali in Toscana. Modelli e percorsi territoriali dello sviluppo regionale.* Milano, IRPET: Franco Angeli.

Becattini, G. (1990). The Marshallian industrial district as a socioeconomic notion. In: F. Pyke, G. Becattini, & W. Sengenberger (Eds), *Industrial districts and inter-firm co-operation in Italy.* Geneva: ILO.

Becattini, G. (2004). *Industrial districts: A new approach to industrial change.* Cheltenham, UK: Edward Elgar.

Becheri, E. (2003). I sistemi turistici locali: uno strumento superfluo. *Rivista del Turismo 1* (pp. 12–14). Touring Editore, Milano.

Bellandi, M., & Sforzi, F. (2003). The multiple paths of local development. In: G. Becattini, M. Bellandi, G. Dei Ottati, & F. Sforzi (Eds), *From industrial districts to local development. An itinerary of research.* Cheltenham, UK: Edward Elgar.

Bieger, Th. (1998). Reengineering destination marketing organizations — The case of Switzerland. *The Tourist Review, 3,* 4–17.

Bramanti, A. (1997). Il milieu turistico del Garda Bresciano. *Commercio 60* (pp. 171–193). Franco Angeli, Milano.

Buhalis, D. (2000). Marketing the competitive destination of the future. *Tourism Management, 21,* 97–116.

Buhalis, D., & Cooper, C. (1998). Competition or co-operation: Small and medium sized tourism enterprises at the destination. In: E. Laws, B. Faulkner, & G. Moscardo (Eds), *Embracing and managing change in tourism* (pp. 324–346). London: Routledge.

Capone, F., & Boix, R. (2004). *Sources of competitiveness in tourist local systems.* Working Paper 04.08. Departament d'Economia Aplicada, Facultat de Ciències Econòmiques i Empresarial, Universidad Autonoma de Barcelona, Barcelona.

Casarin, F. (1996). *Il marketing dei prodotti turistici. Specificità e varietà.* Torino: Giappichelli Editore.

Cazes, G., & Potier, F. (1996). *Le Tourisme urbain.* Paris: Presses Universitaires de France.

Costa, P. (2004). Milieux effects and sustainable developments in a cultural quarter: The 'Barrio alto-Chiado' area in Lisbon. In: R. Camagni, D. Maillat, & A. Matteaccioli (Eds), *Ressources naturelles et culturelles, milieux et développement local, Neuchâtel,* IRER, Institut de Recherches Economiques et Régionales. Neuchâtel: Editions EDES.

Crouch, G.I., & Ritchie, B.J.R. (1999). Tourism, competitiveness, and social prosperity. *Journal of Business Research, 44,* 137–152.

Dematteis, G. (2003). Il modello Slot come strumento di analisi dello sviluppo locale. In: C. Rosignoli, & C.S. Imarisio (Eds), *Slot Quaderno 3* (pp. 13–27). Bologna: Baskerville.

Edgell, D., & Haenisch, T. (1995). *Coopetition: Global tourism beyond the millennium.* Kansans City, MO: International Policy Publishing.

European Commission. (2000). *Toward urban tourism-integrated quality management (iqm) of tourist destination.* Luxemburg: EU.

European Network for SME Research (ENSR). (2003). *Regional cluster in Europe.* Luxembourg Office for Official Publications of the EC, Luxembourg.

Franch, M. (2002). *Destination management: governare il turismo tra locale e globale.* Torino: Giappichelli.

Frost Kumpf, H.A. (1998). *Cultural district: The arts as a strategy for revitalizing our cities.* Washington, DC: Institute for Community Development and the Arts, Americans for the Arts.

Garreau, J. (1992). *Edge city.* New York: Anchor Books.

Getz, D. (1993). Planning for tourism business districts. *Annals of Tourism Research, 20,* 583–600.

Il Sole 24 ore. (2003). *Rapporto sul Turismo.* Il Sole 24 ore Editore, Milano.

Jansen-Verbeke, M.C., & Ashworth G. (1990). Environmental integration of recreation and tourism. *Annals of Tourism Research, 1714,* 618–622.

Judd, D.R. (1993). Promoting tourism in US cities. *Tourism Management, 16,* 175–187.

Laws, E. (1995). *Tourist destination management.* Edinburgh: Napier University.

Lazzeretti, L. (1995). Per una teorizzazione del Modello Firenze. In: E. Becheri (Ed.), *Il Turismo a Firenze. Un modello per le città d'arte* (pp. 399–411). Mercury: Firenze.

Lazzeretti, L. (2003). City of art as a HCLocal system and cultural districtualisation processes. The Cluster of art-restoration in Florence. *International Journal of Urban and Regional Research, 27*(3 September), 635–648.

Lazzeretti, L. (2004). *Art cities, cultural districts and museums.* Florence: Florence University Press.

Lazzeretti, L., & Capone, F. (2004). Networking in the tourist local system. In: J. Swarbrooke, & C.S. Petrillo (Eds), *Proceedings of the 12th Atlas international conference, Networking & Partnerships in Destination Development & Management,* Irat-Cnr, Albano, Napoli.

Leiper, N. (1995). *Tourism management.* Australia, PB: RMIT Press.

Martin, R.L., & Sunley, P. (2003). Deconstructing clusters: Chaotic concept or policy panacea? *Journal of Economic Geography, 3*(1), 5–35.

Nedlac. (1999). *South Africa's tourism cluster.* Harvard, ITC: Harvard Business School.

Nordin, S. (2003). *Tourism clustering and innovations.* Ostersund, Sweden:, ETOUR, 14.

Otto, J.E., & Ritchie, B.J.R. (1996). The service experience in tourism. *Tourism Management, 17*(3), 165–174.

Pearce, D.G. (1998). Tourist districts in Paris: Structure and functions. *Tourism Management, 19*(1), 49–65.

Pechlaner, H., & Weiermair, K. (2000). *Destination management: fondamenti di marketing e gestione delle destinazioni turistiche.* Milano: TCI.

Peyrache-Gadeau, V. (2003). Le développement durable des territoires de montagne: un objet de concertation sur le devenir des stations touristiques? Paper presented at the meeting concentration et ségrégation dynamiques et inscriptions territoriales, Lyon, 1–3 septembre.

Porter, M.E. (1990). *The Competitive advantage of nations.* London: MacMillan.

Porter, M.E. (1998). *On competition.* Harvard: Harvard Business School Press.

Preite, M. (1998). *La valorizzazione del patrimonio culturale in Toscana: una valutazione di alcune esperienze.* Fondazione Michelucci, mimeo.

Rispoli, M., & Tamma, M. (1995). *Risposte strategiche alla complessità: le forme di offerta dei prodotti alberghieri.* Padova: Cedam.

Santagata, W. (2002). Cultural districts, property rights and sustainable economic growth. *International Journal of Urban and Regional Research, 26*(1), 9–23.

Santarelli, E. (1995). Sopravvivenza e crescita delle nuove imprese nei distretti industriali. Il settore turistico del medio adriatico. *L'industria, 16*(2), 349–362.

Scott, A.J. (1996). The craft, fashion, and cultural-product industries of Los Angeles: Competitive dynamic and policy dilemma in a multisectoral image-producing complex. *Annals of the Association of American Geographers, 86*, 306–323.

Stansfield, C., & Richert, J. (1970). The recreational business district. *Journal of Leisure Research, 2*, 238–251.

Tamma, M. (1999). Destination management e logica di sistema. *La Rivista del Turismo, 1*(2), 46–48.

Tamma, M. (2002). Destination management: Gestire prodotti e sistemi locali di offerta. In: M. Franch (Ed.), *Destination management: Governare il turismo tra locale e globale.* Torino: Giappichelli.

Valentino, P.A. (2001). *I distretti culturali. Nuove opportunità di sviluppo del territorio.* Roma: Associazione Civita.

Van Den Berg, L., Braum, E., & Van Winden, W. (2001). *Growth cluster in European metropolitan cities.* Aldershot, Burlinghton: AshGate.

Chapter 2

# Identification and Analysis of Tourist Local Systems: An Application to Italy (1996–2001)

Luciana Lazzeretti and Francesco Capone

## Introduction

The intent of this paper is to identify and analyse the Italian tourist destinations seen as "a system of actors specialized in tourist activities". First of all, a tourist local system (TLS) model is reminded as a model to analyse tourist destinations and second, an empirical proxy is proposed for their territorial identification.

The identification of Italian tourist systems has so far been of the indirect type, that is, deriving from other territorial classifications of economic character (local industrial systems, etc.), starting by determining local industrial and/or commercial systems and then by pointing out tourist localities specialized exclusively in tourist activities.

In this paper, instead, we mainly try to answer two questions: where the TLS in Italy are and how they can be singled out. In this process, we concentrate our attention on the actors of a TLS and upon the consequent structure of the offer. An identification proxy will be proposed reflecting upon its applicability to the tourist industry, placing particular attention on the variability of outcome resulting from adopting different definitions of tourism.

The paper is divided into six sections. In the first one, we remind a definition of TLS as a place with a "system of actors specialized in tourist activities". In the second section, we review those contributing to the identification of TLS in Italy. In the third part, a reminder of the analysis of local labour market areas (LLMA) in Italy is addressed. In the following section, we propose different definitions of tourist activities and we apply these definitions to the identification of TLS through geographic information systems (GIS) tools. In the fifth section, a taxonomy of the Italian TLS is presented. Finally, conclusions and policy implications are expounded.

# Tourist Local Systems

## *A Tourist Local System: A Reminder*

In the last 10 years, the international specialized literature has coined the concept of *"Tourist Destination"*.[1] In this concept, attention is focused on the strategies and marketing actions in a place characterized by a system of actors that co-operate in order to supply an integrated tourism product. The opportunity of using a territorial systemic approach emerges by focusing on *places* in order to develop a process of local economic development. In fact, territorial models of industrial origins have been recently extended to the tourist industry.

The theoretical bases for the study of (manufacturing) local systems started at the end of the 19th century, when Marshall described the existence of some concentrations of small and medium enterprises (SMEs) specialized in a specific production activity in certain districts of some English industrial cities (Marshall, 1920). Starting from his contribution, Italian scholars have paid particular attention to this local system of production coined by Marshall under the term "industrial district" (Becattini, 1990, 2004). In other countries, different but related territorial models have played a central role, such as the "milieu" (Aydalot, 1986) or the "geographical industrial clusters" (Porter, 1990, 1998). Recently, these models have been extended to nonindustrial fields like culture (Lazzeretti, 2003; Santagata, 2004; Costa, 2002), rural activities and tourism (Nordin, 2003; Peyrache-Gadeau, 2003).

In this contribution, we utilize the concept of the TLS as proposed in another contribution of this same volume.[2] TLS can be seen as a *"thickening of socio-economic relations among the various members of the local society, to favour the formation, the spread and the maintenance of a system of values, productive acquaintances, typical behaviours and institutions through which the local society interacts with the productive organization"* (Becattini & Sforzi, 2002, p. 21), using as point of departure the industrial district theory (Becattini, 1990, 2004; Bellandi & Sforzi, 2003).

Following the approach of Lazzeretti in cultural districtualization processes (Lazzeretti, 2003, 2004) used for identification of different degrees of cultural districts,[3]

---

[1] European Commission (2000, p. 149) defines a tourist destination as: *"an area which is separately identified and promoted to tourists as a place to visit, and within which the tourist product is co-ordinated by one or more identifiable authorities or organisations"*. The concept of destination management has been developed by the original contribution of Laws (1995), Pechlaner and Weiermair (2000), Franch (2002) and contribution of AIEST (International Association of Scientific Experts in Tourism, www.aiest.org), among others, that analyse tourist systems as a unique group of actors localized in a common place. See the contribution of Capone in this same volume for any deepening.

[2] See the contribution of Capone in this same volume.

[3] The study of cultural districtualization processes is a dynamic district analysis focused not on the cultural district as such, but on the forms of cultural districtualization, by means of a process analysis. Starting from suggestions made for the agrarian district (Becattini, 2004, p. 197), Lazzeretti (2003, p. 641) proceeds with an analysis of the cultural district with the support of an expost study carried out in a mature, complete and, strictly speaking, Marshallian district. She tried to find various degrees of cultural districtualization in different cultural local systems that are more or less well developed compared to the mature, achieved form of the 'Marshallian cultural district'.

the TLS represents a system characterized by the presence, in its territory, of a large endowment of artistic, natural and cultural resources (cultural, artistic and environmental heritage [CAEH]), and a network of economic, noneconomic and institutional actors who are specialized in tourist activities. Therefore, as proposed, a first approximation of a TLS is a group of SMEs having a strong concentration of enterprises that creates wealth and employment through its connection with CAEH. Extending the approach of cultural districtualization process of Lazzeretti (2003, 2004) three conditions will be tested: (a) verification of the presence of a consistent number of enterprises enhancing the cultural, artistic and natural heritage in a tourist destination (tourism-related activity); (b) verification of the set of enterprises composing a cluster of SMEs localized in the tourist destination; (c) verification of the presence of a set of economic and social relationships between the social local community (citizens) and the productive community (enterprises). In this paper, we will verify the first two conditions by applying specialization indexes to specific territorial units. In this context, we extend for the theoretical model, the cultural districtualization process as already discussed in the cultural districts approach and we apply the methodology of territorial identification of industrial district to TLS.

### The state of the art of Tourist Local Systems identification in Italy

In this section, we propose a review of the territorial identification of the Italian TLS. We particularly attempt to recall those contributions that have a quantity and/or geographic approach and have proposed analyses considering the wider regional or national territory.

An analysis essential for the study applied to the (industrial) districts is that relating to the identification of local labour systems. This study, proposed by Sforzi (1997a) and discussed in the well-known "*Local labour systems 1991*", brings forth the territorial classification of a nonadministrative type, relating to a group of communities singled out by a relevant regionalization algorithm based upon workers residing in the area. These groupings of communities constituted local labour systems (LLMA).

Subsequent analyses have made it possible to construct a map of Italy based upon local systems of tourist services in the strict sense of the words (restaurants, travel agencies, etc.) (Sforzi, 1997b). This contribution particularly analyses the development of the Italian urban systems by sectors. The author, in fact, analyses the evolution from 1981 to 1991, based on the data furnished by the Central Statistics Institute (ISTAT), of the local labour systems divided according to the following categories: industrial, commercial, services to firms and to persons and services exclusively to persons (hotels, restaurants, bars, etc.). This study reveals interesting points for reaching our purpose, however, tourist services are not measured, only systems specialized in people services. Therefore, we think it necessary to widen the definition to — services to persons *in the tourist sense.*

The ISTAT only recently proposed several analyses of the LLMA, but with few variables, very aggregated and produced as estimates of the National Accountancy (gross domestic product, occupation and population). Furthermore, such classification is often subdivided according to the part characterizing the system: industrial, services, tourism or mixed. The ISTAT analysis is developed through cluster analysis of the activities predominant in the local area at a three-digit level. Such an analysis is of a certain importance for industrial systems and for their temporal development, but not (in our opinion) when applied to local tourist systems, because it registers only pure systems, excluding systems that contribute to other industries. It also registers only local tourist systems that have a specialization which is dominant and exclusively in the tourist sector, excluding from the analysis, the various relationships with other sectors.

Another important contribution to the concept of tourist economic systems is supplied by the Regional Institute for Economic Planning of Tuscany (IRPET) with Bacci's analysis, *"Tuscan Local Systems"* (2002). It is based on local economic systems (SEL)[4] constituted by the 1999 Regional Decree #219. The study goes into the ties between territory and local production systems and reaches the construction of a taxonomy of local systems, through the use of the input–output tables for SEL.[5] This contribution is interesting for our analysis; however, the author's object is the classification of SELs in Tuscany and not the identification of the TLS. This perspective measured only the substantive presence of tourism, not its impact upon the systems or the eventual firm concentration. Another study is that of the ACI-CENSIS (2001) that identifies *tourism districts* in the Italian territory through the use of seven indicators.[6] The report registers 299 tourist districts identified by supply and demand characteristics, however, the concept of district utilized does not coincide with the traditional economic–industrial concept and the study is mostly based upon the identification of certain typologies of enterprise agglomerations (high quality hotels and restaurants, etc.).

## Tourist Local Systems as Specialized Local Labour Market Areas

This section is a reminder of what local labour market areas (LLMA) are and is addressed mainly to the Italian experience, explaining why this kind of territorial unit has been chosen.

In fact, the first step related to the concrete identification of a theoretical concept is to define measures and weights. Also, the history of the industrial district theory has always faced the difficulties of quantitative analysis. The industrial district surpasses administrative borders and in reality is composed of a group of municipalities. In this background, the efforts of the first scholars were to give a territorial acknowledgement to a concept that was strictly related with the territory and could not be considered separately.

We use LLMA for three reasons (Menghinello, 2002). First, LLMA allows us to go beyond the administrative definitions and refer more to the effective industrial organization

---

[4] The Tuscany regions configured regional local systems in 1999 as defined by the law 219/1999. These local systems were then defined as "SEL" (local economic systems).

[5] An analysis was carried out by calculating the prevalence of the import–export balance per business. See the text of Bacci (2002) for further information.

[6] These are the indicators used: degree of expansion of the tertiary industry (indicator upon which the rating was constructed); outline of the evolution service offer (in relation to the primary vocations and the opportunities for entertainment, shopping, sports, etc.); catering quality (concentration of high quality catering activities); hospitality quality (concentration of hotels recommended in most of the important guide books); segmentation of catering (degree of diversification of the gastronomic offer); segmentation of hospitality (degree of diversification of the hotel system: number of stars); and homogeneity *vs.* integration antinomy (interlacing of the vocations of the different communities that constitute the single district), "plus oenological and gastronomic".

of the territory. Second, LLMA are territorial units more suitable to the socio-economic analysis referring to the intensity of relations between residents and the labour force of a certain area. Third, they respect a rigorous identification methodology as described in the 1997 volume of the ISTAT (Sforzi, 1997a). This geographical methodology is also suitable for local systems characterized by the presence of a cluster of SMEs working on tourist activities. In fact, the final object of our analysis, the TLS, is a place where persons share life and job experiences with a sure stability in time: a local system.

In order to identify industrial districts in the territory, the methodology was the following: the national territory, examined in first approximation in Tuscany (IRPET), was subdivided into territorial units: LLMAs (Smart, 1974; Coombes & Openshaw, 1982), which interpret the daily commuting flows due to work reasons defined in Italy by the ISTAT in the 1991 Census on industries and services.

Therefore, the analysis identified a "thickening of socio-economic relations among the various members of the local society, to favour the formation, the spread and the maintenance of a system of values, productive acquaintances, typical behaviours and institutions through which the local society interacts with the productive organization" (Becattini & Sforzi, 2002, p. 21). The LLMA emerged as a big city, as a rural system or as TLS in relation to the specialized production.

The question of daily movement for study or job reasons was introduced by the ISTAT in 1971, but it only gathered a consistent analytical value in 1991, thanks to the geographical information system and to the possibility of using a greater number of geographical data.

With such methodology, the national territory was subdivided through criteria inspired by the district theory. Later on, through the application of location quotients (Lq) to the LLMA, a map of industrial districts was proposed (Sforzi, 1997a).

The driving concept was to identify a concentration of productive activities and services in such amounts so as to offer job opportunities to a wider portion of the residential population. The concept was then called autocontainment.

This indicated a territory's "ability to comprise a larger amount of human relations which take place between areas where production activity is carried out and areas where social reproduction is based" (Sforzi, 1997a, 19 ss.).

A territory of this type was called local labour market area, "a socio-economic entity that includes occupation, purchases, recreation and social opportunity ... given a residential base and the necessity of coming back at the end of the day" (*idem*).

This methodology identified 784 LLMA in the Italian territory. These 784 territorial units were the result of the aggregation of daily commuting flows of 8100 Italian municipalities in the 1991 Census.

After this brief review, in our opinion this geographical methodology is suitable also for local systems characterized by the presence of a cluster of SMEs working on tourist activities. In fact, the final object of our analysis, the tourist district is a place where persons share life and job experiences with a sure stability in time: a local system.

In the next paragraphs, we will try to apply an Lq to the LLMA constituted by the 1991 Census. Although they were defined 10 years ago, we think that the undeniable evolution of a local system is pretty durable and we can use the LLMA of 1991 in order to underline a concentration of tourist enterprises. Moreover, we think social life and socio-economic relations are pretty steady in time. This empirical suggestion may be a first approximation of empirical recognition of local systems characterized by the tourist business. Moreover, the possibility of using LLMA is valid at the moment only for the constructed local systems in the 1991 Census, because LLMA of the 2002 Census will be available only in 2005.

The methodology of location of the industrial districts (Sforzi, 1997a) assumes as its territorial unit of analysis the LLMA and contemplates the following stages:

1. Identification of manufacturing local systems.
2. Identification of manufacturing local systems that are mainly constituted by SMEs.
3. Identification of the main industry of every local system of SMEs.
4. Identification (as industrial districts) of the manufacturing local systems that are mainly composed of SMEs whose main industry is constituted of SMEs.

The aim of the paper is to identify those local systems that have a higher concentration of enterprises specialized in the tourism and travel industry (TTI) in comparison to the national average, and then to ascertain if it is a local system of SMEs as defined.

## Identification of Tourist Local Systems in Italy

### A First Analysis: The HoReCa Sector and 1996 Census

Following the described approach and starting from the LLMA of 1991, we can verify the social and productive characterization of tourist destinations. The aim is to identify those local systems through the characteristics of their SMEs.

The first issue is to define what belongs to the field of tourist activities and what cannot be considered tourism. We can use a broader or a narrower definition of tourism. For instance, we can either include in our analysis only hotels, camping and accommodation facilities and travel agencies, or also include those indirectly connected with it, like transportation, recreational activities and car rentals, or include those that are connected to the normal life of all places like bars, restaurants and coffee shops.

As a methodological simplification, in this operation we will adopt the ISTAT definition of activities connected with tourism, through ATECO codes of the H voice: hotels, restaurants and cafes (HoReCa). The voice H, hotel and restaurants, described in the table below (Table 2.1) is recognized as the HoReCa sector.

Also the OECD (1999) recognizes that the workforce in the TTI pertain to three main pillars. Referring to the two digits ISIC international classification, OECD classifies the activities connected with tourism as:

• 55 hotels, restaurants and cafes;
• 60–63 transportation and travel;
• 92 recreational, cultural and sports activities (market and nonmarket services).

Naturally, all the workplaces created in these industries cannot be attributed to tourism. However, OECD mostly refers to the HoReCa sector in its analysis of territorial employment in the European community, as it is directly connected with tourism instead of with the other two categories.

Table 2.1: HoReCa sector.

| | |
|---|---|
| 55.11.0 | Hotels and motels, with restaurant |
| 55.12.0 | Hotels and motels, without restaurant |
| 55.21.1 | Hostels |
| 55.21.2 | Mountain shelters |
| 55.22.0 | Camping areas and areas equipped for trailers and caravans |
| 55.23.1 | Tourist villages |
| 55.23.2 | Youth camps, rest homes (without medical care) |
| 55.23.3 | Sleeping cars |
| 55.23.4 | Short-stay rentals, vacation homes |
| 55.23.5 | Farm holidays |
| 55.23.6 | Other accommodation businesses (including apartment hotels) |
| 55.30.1 | Restaurants, diners, taverns and pubs with kitchen |
| 55.30.2 | Take away, pizza houses |
| 55.30.3 | Dining car management |
| 55.30.4 | Self-service restaurants |
| 55.30.5 | Restaurants with entertainment and shows |
| 55.40.1 | Bars and cafes |
| 55.40.2 | Bars selling milk products |
| 55.40.3 | Wineries and wine cellars |
| 55.40.4 | Bars and cafes with entertainment and shows |
| 55.51.0 | Cafeterias |
| 55.52.0 | Caterers |

*Source*: ATECO 1991 (ISTAT, 1991).

We think that this simplification can be suitable and this analysis can identify specialized TLS within a broader definition of tourism activities. In other words, we expect a stronger specialization in these activities in TLS.

The ISTAT collects this data in the 1996 *"Intermediate census of industry and trade"* for each municipality: the smallest unit of analysis available. This data can therefore be clustered for the LLMA on the census of 1991, as described in the previous pages. The successive step has been to apply the indexes of territorial concentration to the approximately 8100 municipalities in Italy as a whole, grouped into LLMA. These are the Lq used for tourism concentration:

1. Tourist local systems: this first Lq evidences those LLMA that have a strong specialization in tourist activities:

$$\text{Lq of HoReCa specialization} = \text{Lq}_{is} = \frac{E_{is}/E_s}{E_i/E}$$

where $E_{is}$ is the number of employees in local units in the local system s specialized in the sector i; $E_s$ the number of employees in local units in the local system s; $E_i$ the number of employees in Italy specialized in the industry i; and $E$ the total employment in Italy.

This Lq indicates the concentration in the LLMA of tourist activities (voice H, ATECO, 1991) in comparison with the national average.

2. Local systems composed of SMEs: this Lq indicates those local systems that are characterized mainly by SMEs with under 250 employees, where these variables are the same of the previous Lq but calculated in local units with less than 250 employees.

$$\text{Lq of SMEs} = \text{Lq}_{is} = \frac{E_{is}/E_s}{E_i/E}$$

The second Lq is not presented in the results because it goes from the national average up to 1.05. It means that there are no LLMA that have a percentage of SMEs below 95% in tourist activities. More information is presented in the next section. The first Lq indicates those local systems that are more characterized by SMEs in comparison with the national average. In particular, if the value of the Lq is more than 1 for a local system, it shows a concentration level over the national average. Moreover, regarding the representation of the Lq, we adopted a fixed scheme with defined classes, in order to more easily interpret the results. In particular, these are the defined classes: [0–1), [1–1.5), [1.5–3) and above 3. These classes define particular concentration levels, for instance [1–1.5) identifies concentration levels between the national average and 50% more than the national average.

The results of the first analysis are presented in Map 2.1.

The proposed map, constructed with the first Lq, identifies roughly 300 TLS with an index of more than a unit. The values go from below the national average up to 12 (12 times more than the national average identified in the darkest spots). The Lq values go from the national average up to 12. The 300 TLS have in average eight employees, therefore they are mainly characterized by small enterprises. The LLMA are heterogeneous and present in tourist destinations such as "sea, sand and sun", "snow and ski" and "lakes". The whole of Italy is recorded, but in the north there is a higher Lq value. The coast has a high rate, but the highest Lq values are recorded in mountain localities. At an administrative level, Trentino, Veneto, Tuscany, Liguria and Emilia Romagna are the regions that register the highest quotients.

Art cities have Lq values below most of the other specialized local systems. For instance, Florence, Rome and Venice have an Lq equal to two. This is because the Lq recognizes a strong specialization only in one activity and on the supply side. In the big cities, there is often a diversification of industries so that the TTI weight is less in an "only tourist place". Moreover, the top 25 LLMA have a percentage of employees of more than 41% under voice H, with a peak of 60% in the "snow and ski" LLMA (for instance in Canazei and Bardonecchia).

The TLS analysed belongs to the heterogeneous tourist segments. Some like Canazei, Badia and Cortina are typically of the snow tourism and of wintertime, others like Amalfi, Diano Marina, Porto Azzurro and Elba belong to the sea tourism of summertime. Other TLS are mixed, like Limone sul Garda or Fiuggi. Moreover, there is a prevalence of skiing stations, in approximately 45% of the local systems analysed.

The fact that the TLS follow the characteristics of the industrial districts is confirmed by the fact that they are mainly composed of small-and medium-sized enterprises.

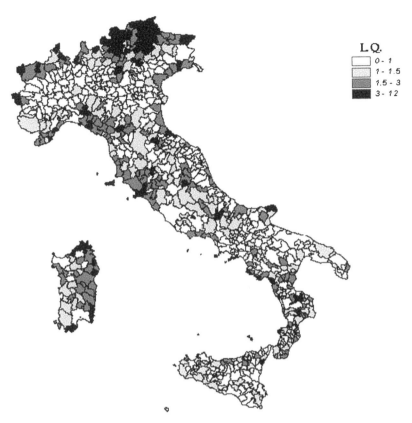

LQ.
☐ 0 - 1
☐ 1 - 1.5
▨ 1.5 - 3
■ 3 - 12

Map 2.1: Tourist local systems in Italy.
*Source*: Our elaboration from Census ISTAT (2001).

Approximately 90% of the labour force in the local systems works in SMEs with less than 20 employees. This estimate is strengthened when the percentage of enterprises with less than five employees is analysed, whose average is around 75%, with peaks close to 90% in Porto Azzurro and Limone sul Garda. This underlines the fact that most of the activities analysed are based on small enterprises.

In this context, a TLS is characterized by agglomerations of SMEs. Finally, the average of employees in the enterprises reaches five units with minimum peaks of three units in Malcesine and Porto Azzurro and maximum peaks of seven in Cortina of Ampezzo, Limone sul Garda and Pinzolo.

Therefore, these results confirm how the analysis through LLMA is applicable to the tourist industry so as to identify the TLS as described in the first part of this work. The TLS are strongly specialized in the tourist industry, their "core industry", and local units are localized inside the borders of the LLMA.

We think it useful to point out two problems. The first is the definition of tourism adopted. Although it can be a proxy to tourist activities, it could lose local systems specialized in other activities in parts of the *filière* other than in the HoReCa sectors. The other issue is the year of reference: 1996. We will try to face and solve these problems in the next section. First of all, a tourist *filière ad hoc* will be proposed on which to calculate the localization quotients and the database will be updated with the 2001 ISTAT Census.

### A Second Analysis: The Tourist filière and the 2001 Census

In the previous study, we have applied tourist specialization indexes (Lq) to the HoReCa sector represented by voice H of the 1996 ISTAT *"Intermediate census of industry and services"*. Such analysis has allowed us to describe a first landscape of the Italian TLS. Unfortunately, we have to face two types of problems. The first regards the definition used for tourism. Although it can be approximated to tourist activities, it does not count a real estimation of the incidence of these activities in the tourist industry. Therefore some local systems could be omitted for being specialized in other areas of the tourist *filière* (transportation and recreational activities, for instance). The second problem regards the temporal reference of the data. The Census refers to approximately 10 years ago: 1996. In this section, we will update the source of the data by using the 2001 ISTAT Census in order to present a temporal evolution of the Italian TLS. Finally, we will try to construct a *tourist filière* referring to institutional contributions like ISTAT, European Commission (2003) and OECD (1999).

Moreover, it is necessary to open a parenthesis regarding the territorial unit used. The territorial borders taken into consideration have the administrative reference of 1991 regarding the municipalities updated only to that date. In the period 1991–2001, eight new provinces have been instituted, while another eight have given municipalities to new ones.[7] Therefore, the data of 2001 have been recounted to the borders of 1991 in order to carry out a comparison of the homogenous data and territorial units. Finally, other territorial modifications[8] have been carried out and have been brought back to the municipalities of 1991.

Finally, regarding the census codes (ATECO, 1991–2002), several voices are changed, but the ISTAT internet site allows analyses based on the 1991 codes and makes directly available homogenous data from the 2001 ATECO Census.

After deciding the territorial unit of analysis, we must define what belongs to the tourist field of activity and what does not. In the previous study, a narrow definition through the HoReCa sector was adopted. In this section, we propose a new analysis through a *filière* as shown in Table 2.2 of the three digits ATECO 2002-NACE 1.1 definitions.[9]

It is expected that this simplification will be suitable for the identification of specialized TLS in a broader definition of tourist activities. In other words, we expect a stronger

---

[7] New provinces of Biella, Verbano-Cusio-Ossola, Lecco, Lodi, Prato, Rimini, Vibo Valentia and Crotone, instituted in 1992 with municipalities detached from the provinces of Vercelli, Novara, Como, Milan, Bergamo, Forlì-Cesena, Florence and Catanzaro.

[8] In the same period, 11 new municipalities have been instituted, nine have been abolished, and the borderlines of 28 municipalities have changed (not including the municipalities that have englobed or detached uninhabited areas between 1991 and 2001). For further information, see the ISTAT website regarding the 2001 Census.

[9] The 2003 European Commission presented a model of competitiveness for the tourist sector of European tourist enterprises. We recall this contribution and insert the activities in the model into the proposed *filière* (Table 2.1) adding two voices, artistic artisans and agriculture, so as to evaluate any relationship with these two activities. The *filière* presented is then similar to the tourist sector model of the 2003 European Commission.

Table 2.2: Broad tourist *filière*.

| | |
|---|---|
| Agriculture<br>  01.13 Apiculture, growing of fruits,<br>  nuts and beverages | Recreational, cultural and sports activities<br>  92.3 Other entertainment activities<br>  92.5 Libraries, archives, museums and<br>  other cultural activities |
| Artistic artisans<br>  26.1 Manufacture of glass and glass<br>  products (artisans)<br>  26.2 Manufacture of ceramic household<br>  and ornamental articles (artisans) | 92.6 Sports activities<br>  92.7 Other recreational activities<br><br>Transportation<br>  60.1 Railway transportation<br>  60.2 Other land transportation |
| Hotels and restaurants (HoReCa)<br>  55.1 Hotels<br>  55.2 Camping sites and other provision<br>  of short-stay accommodation<br>  55.3 Restaurants<br>  55.4 Bars | 61.1 Sea and coastal water transportation<br>  61.2 Inland water transportation<br>  62.1 Scheduled air transportation<br><br>Travel agencies<br>  63.3 Activities of travel agencies and tour<br>  operators, tourist assistance activities |
| Real estate and rental<br>  70.2 Letting of own property<br>  71.1 Renting of automobiles | |

*Source*: Our elaboration from ATECO (2002, Nace 1.1).

specialization in these activities in TLS. Thus, in order to identify TLS, we apply to the LLMA a concentration index for the ATECO, 2002 definition:

$$\text{Lq of concentration activities of the filière: } Lq_{is} = \frac{E_{is}/E_s}{E_i/E}$$

where $E_{is}$ is the number of employees in local units in the local system s specialized in the sector i; $E_s$ the number of employees in local units in the local system s; $E_i$ the number of employees in Italy specialized in the industry i; and $E$ the total employment in Italy. An Lq above 1 indicates that an LLMA has a specialization (concentration) in the industry i above the national average. Regarding the representation of the Lq we adopt a fixed scheme with defined classes, so as to interpret easier the results: [0–1], [1–1.25], [1.25–2] and [>2].

Following the approach of Sforzi (1997a), we analysed the 784 LLMA selecting first those local systems specialized in: (1) industry and (2) services, then those specialized in (3) services to enterprises, (4) services to consumers and finally in (5) the tourist *filière* as defined. Data have been collected from the Italian *Industry and Trade* Census 2001 for each municipality.

Map 2.2 shows those LLMA with an Lq for the tourist *filière* above the national average, subdivided by specialization in other activities for the year 2001.[10] Map 2.3 presents

---

[10] (1) No specialization in tourist activities, (2) specialized in tourism and industry, (3) specialized in tourism, service and commerce and (4) diversified as in Sforzi (1997b).

No specialized in tourist activities
Tourist and Industry
Tourism and Services + Commerce
Diversified

Map 2.2: Tourist local systems in Italy. HoReCa sector (1996).
*Source*: Our elaboration from Census ISTAT (1996).

TLS with an Lq for the tourist *filière* above 1. It indicates around 300 TLS with an Lq up to 8. The highest values are concentrated in the North (Trentino and Alto Adige) and centre of Italy (Liguria, Toscana e Lazio). The map also shows art cities like Florence, Rome and Venice,[11] localities specialized in the three Ss (Sun, Sand and Sea), skiing destinations (Alps, in particular Trentino Alto Adige) and lake localities (such as around Garda Lake).

The results between 1996 and 2001 are very similar and present in the same territorial patterns. The HoReCa proxy registers more TLS than when the *filière* is used, although the latter has been constructed with a wide range of activities. From our point of view, one of the problems of using the HoReCa sector is that the medium–large centres weigh more than the small ones, since their specialization in these activities is greater than for the tourist sector.

---

[11] The Lq recognizes a strong specialization only in one activity. In the big cities, there is a diversification of industries, so that the TTI weighs less in a "tourist place".

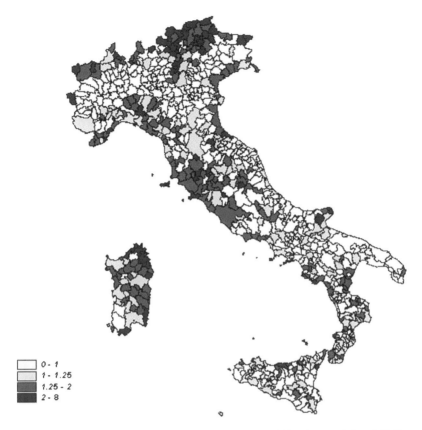

Map 2.3: Tourist local systems in Italy and specialization activity (2001).
*Source*: Our elaboration from Census ISTAT (2001).

The aim of this epigraph was to identify TLS in Italy. Regarding the first topic, the main hypothesis was to focus on clusters of localized SMEs specialized in tourist activities in a broader sense. [12]

We developed a methodology in two stages: firstly, we tested the methodology on the HoReCa sector that was generally considered a part of the tourist activities, then we constructed a tourist *filière* and applied an Lq to this *filière* for the identification of local systems through GIS tools. The results of this analysis indicate that this methodology is applicable to the travel and tourist industry. The TLS recorded are heterogeneous and strongly specialized in the tourist industry, their core industry. They represent tourist destinations such as "sea, sand and sun", "snow and ski" and "lakes" and Italian tourist destinations are suitably represented.

---

[12] See the contribution of Capone and Boix (2004) for any deepenings regarding the sources of competitiveness of Italian tourist local systems.

# A Typology of Classification to Analyse Tourist Local Systems

Extending the approach of Suzigan et al. (2004), we introduce a classification of the local systems in order to propose some policy indications regarding the different characteristics of the TLS calculated on the 2001 ISTAT Census. The authors propose a classification of the local system based on: (a) degree of specialization and (b) contribution to the national economy. The localization coefficient, although it is weighted to a minimum threshold, does not capture the level of contribution to the national industry. In other words, mono-specialized places in average weigh more than the diversified places that contribute in a substantial way to the Italian tourist industry. The classification in two dimensions gives the solution to this problem.

While there exists a wide acknowledgement of the importance of the local systems, there lacks an agreement on how these systems should be promoted and managed and on which policies should be implemented. This grid allows us to focus and differentiate the approach for four types of TLS.[13]

The first category (TLS of local development) has a very high localization coefficient, but its contribution to the Italian tourist industry is limited. This group is composed of small mono-functional destinations that base their economy mainly on tourist activities.

The second category (Tourist centres) is composed of TLS that register a high Lq, but contribute to the national industry in an important way. The importance of these destinations configures them as highly specialized regional and national tourist centres.

The TLS that are in the third category (Embryonic TLS) have a low concentration co-efficient and low contribution to national tourism, where tourism is in a development phase.

The last category (Tourist destinations) is composed of diversified TLS that register low localization coefficients, but give the largest contribution to the national tourism. This group is composed of destinations of medium–large dimensions, mostly art cities, like Rome, Venice and Florence. In Table 2.3, we introduce some of the classified TLS in the proposed grid.

*Tourist destinations* are those local systems that have the greatest problems of tourist sustainability, such as urban congestion and over-affluence of tourists. In these cases, it could help to place greater attention to the diversification of the supply side in order to avoid dead seasons and to reach a better development with other centres close by. This could help to increase the permanence of visitors and develop tourist routes.

*Tourist centres* are those TLS recognized as being strongly based on the tourist industry. These local systems follow optimal ways of development and supply an important contribution to the national industry. They are the TLS that deserve the greatest attention from policy makers. The enhancement of such centres should focus mainly on developing other links of the value chain, like the activities of marketing and quality certification. Finally,

---

[13] Based upon their specialization and contribution to the Italian national tourism sector, the TLS are classified into four categories: (1) high degree of concentration and low degree of contribution to the national economy; (2) medium high degree of concentration, but high degree of contribution to the tourism economy; (3) low degree of contribution and low degree of concentration; (4) low degree of concentration, but high degree of contribution to the national tourist sector. The authors instead present four categories named: vectors of local development, centres of industrial and regional development, embryonic local production systems and advanced vectors.

Table 2.3: Typologies of tourist local systems in Italy.

| Lq | Contribution to the national tourism | |
|---|---|---|
| | Low (0.5% > x > 0.1%) | High (x > 0.1%) |
| High (>1.5) | TLS of local development | Tourist centres |
| | Limone Sul Garda, Positano, Malcesine, Amalfi, Canazei, Porto Azzurro, Nova Ponente, Vieste, Capri | Forio, Badia, Taormina, Saint-Vincent, Ischia, Ortisei, Sorrento, Alassio, Bormio, Montepulciano |
| Low (1 > x > 1.5) | Embryonic TLS | Tourist destinations |
| | Nuoro, Domodossola Lamezia Terme, Follonica, Porretta Terme, Spoleto, Orvieto, Rosignano Marittimo | Roma, Napoli, Firenze, Bologna, Venezia, Genova, Padova, Verona, Palermo, Cagliari, Bolzano, Trieste |

*Source*: Our elaboration on ISTAT Census (2001).

the development of training courses and other forms of education could increase technical abilities and the functionality of these destinations.

*Embryonic TLS* are the most difficult to promote. These local systems have still not taken a defined path and although tourism is an important sector of the local industry, their contribution to the national economy is still limited. The most common error could be to use the same strategies as for the *tourist centres*. In fact, the latter can have their own unique characteristics that are not easily replicable in the short term. From our point of view, in this group, policy makers should develop a specific political approach for each case regarding the presence of the *filière* at a local level and synergies with nearby tourist destinations.

*TLS of local development* register the highest localization coefficient. They are small and medium centres that contribute little to the national industry. The enhancement of such centres should focus on developing all links of the value chain and creating collaboration with nearby tourist destinations, in order to increase the weight of the local industry.

## Conclusions

The object of this paper is to present a model for TLS and to propose an identification of TLS as defined. We have identified TLS in Italy and tested the coherence of the results with the outline of the situation of the Italian tourist destinations.

First of all, the choice of using the district theory and the local labour system theory was proven satisfactory. Both the first study and the second analysis show that the TLS register a substantial percentage of small-and medium-sized firms. This confirms the adequacy of the district model for the study of the tourist industry, because it is based on a network of small and medium-sized localized firms.

The inspection of the state of the art has highlighted the fact that quantitative identification of the TLS is still underdeveloped. From a certain point of view, the ISTAT supplies some data on tourist districts, but they are identified by their specialization exclusively on tourism. Other studies, such as the IRPET, instead reveal the relationship of the tourist systems with the other sectors, but are not extended to cover a national level (only Tuscany). A part of the contribution of Sforzi (1997b) analyses consumer services such as hotels, restaurants, cafes and travel agencies, but does not focalize on those activities exclusively dedicated to tourists.

That is why we have proposed and constructed a tourist *filière ad hoc* so as to identify the TLS by activities chosen for the purpose, taking inspiration from the institutional contributions of the European Commission and the OECD. The *filière* has given satisfactory results and seems to be an original contribution. It has then been shown that interrelations exist between the tourist industry of the TLS and other sectors, such as agriculture, industry, commerce and particularly manufacturing activities.

This work brings forth a solid base of quantitative information for the identification of Italian TLS updated to the 2001 Census. Furthermore, it proposes specific research on their evolution in the last 5 years (1996–2001).

The TLS identified represent the Italian tourist destinations and through the application of GIS systems, we have been able to construct several representational maps about their evolution in time, which also shows the variability of results based upon the definition of tourism that is used. Further studies are surely necessary, but the utilization of the LLMA and the applicability of the district theory have brought us to a more rigorous identification of the Italian TLS. This serves as a basis for future analysis of a more specific type for tourism operators and scholars studying tourism.

## Acknowledgements

The authors express their gratefulness to Dr Stefano Menghinello, researcher of ISTAT (Department of Statistics on the international activities of enterprises) for his empirical analysis and collection of data aid, and Prof. Sforzi for his theoretical advises.

## References

ACI-CENSIS. (2001). *Rapporto Turismo: I distretti turistici italiani: l'opportunità di innovare l'offerta*. Roma: Censis servizi s.p.a.

Aydalot, Ph. (1986). *Milieux Innovateurs en Europe*. Paris: GREMI.

Bacci, L. (2002). *Sistemi Locali in Toscana. Modelli e percorsi Territoriali dello sviluppo regionale*, IRPET, Franco Angeli, Milano.

Becattini, G. (1990). The Marshallian industrial district as a socioeconomic notion. In: F. Pyke, G. Becattini, & W. Sengenberger (Eds), *Industrial districts and inter-firm co-operation in Italy*. Geneva: ILO.

Becattini, G. (2004). *Industrial districts: A new approach to industrial change*. Cheltenham, UK: Edward Elgar.

Becattini, G., & Sforzi, F. (2002). *Lezioni sullo sviluppo locale*. Torino: Rosemberg & Sellier.

Bellandi, M., & Sforzi, F. (2003). The multiple paths of local development. In: G. Becattini, M. Bellandi, G. Dei Ottati, & F. Sforzi (Eds), *From industrial districts to local development. An itinerary of research.* Cheltenham, UK: Edward Elgar.

Capone, F., & Boix, R. (2004). *Sources of competitiveness in tourist local systems*, Working Paper 04.08. Departament d'Economia Aplicada, Facultat de Ciències Econòmiques i Empresarial, Universidad Autonoma de Barcelona, Barcelona.

Coombes, M.G., & Openshaw, S. (1982). The use and definition of travel-to-work areas in Great Britain: Some comments. *Regional Studies, 16*, 141–149.

Costa, P. (2004). Milieux effects and sustainable developments in a cultural quarter: The 'Barrio alto-Chiado' area in Lisbon. In: R. Camagni, D. Maillat, & A. Matteaccioli (Eds), *Ressources naturelles et culturelles, milieux et développement local, Neuchâtel*, IRER, Institut de Recherches Economiques et Régionales. Neuchâtel: Editions EDES.

European Commission. (2000). *Towards quality tourism: Integrated quality management (IQM) of tourist destinations.* Tourism Unit, Luxembourg: Office for Official Publications of the EC.

European Commission. (2003). *Structure, performance and competitiveness of European tourism and its enterprises.* Luxembourg: EU.

Franch, M. (2002). *Destination management: Governare il turismo tra locale e globale.* Torino: Giappichelli.

ISTAT. (1991). *ATECO 1991 — Classificazione delle attività economiche.* Roma: ISTAT.

ISTAT. (2002). *ATECO 2002 — Classificazione delle attività economiche.* Roma: ISTAT.

Laws, E. (1995). *Tourist destination management.* Edimburgh: Napier University.

Lazzeretti, L. (2003). City of art as a HC local system and cultural districtualisation processes. The cluster of art restoration in Florence. *International Journal of Urban and Regional Research, 27.3*(September), 635–648.

Lazzeretti, L. (2004). *Art cities, cultural districts and museums.* Florence: Florence University Press.

Marshall, A. (1920). *Principles of economics.* London: Macmillan.

Menghinello, S. (2002). *Le esportazioni dai sistemi locali del lavoro. Dimensione locale e competitività dell'Italia sui mercati internazionali.* Roma: ISTAT.

Nordin, S. (2003). *Tourism clustering and innovations* (No. 2003:14). ETOUR, Ostersund, Sweden.

OECD. (1999). *Territorial indicators of employment.* Geneva: OECD.

Peyrache-Gadeau, V. (2003). Le developpement durable des territoires de montagne: Un objet de concertation sur le devenir des stations touristiques? Paper presented at meeting concentration et segregation dynamiques et inscriptions territoriales, Lyon, 1–3 September, 2003.

Pechlaner, H., & Weiermair, K. (2000). *Destination management: Fondamenti di marketing e gestione delle destinazioni turistiche.* Milano: TCI.

Porter, M.E. (1990). *The competitive advantage of nations.* London: Macmillan.

Porter, M.E. (1998). *On competition.* Boston: Harvard Business School Press.

Santagata, W. (2002). Cultural districts, property rights and sustainable economic growth. *International Journal of Urban and Regional Research, 26*(1), 9–23.

Sforzi, F. (1997a). *I sistemi locali in Italia.* ISTAT, Rome.

Sforzi, F. (1997b). Il cambiamento economico nel sistema urbano italiano. In: G. Dematteis, & P. Bonavero (Eds), *Il sistema urbano Italiano nello spazio unificato Europeo.* Bologna: Il Mulino.

Smart, M.W. (1974). Labour market areas: Uses and definition. *Progress in Planning, 2*, 238–353.

Suzigan, W., Furtado, J., Garcia, R., & Sampaio, S. (2004). Local production systems: Mapping, typology and policy suggestions. Paper presented at European Regional Science Association (ERSA) 2004 Congress, University of Porto, Porto, Portugal, 25–29 August, 2004.

Chapter 3

# A Framework to Identify a Localised Tourism System

Géraldine Maulet

## Introduction

Nowadays, destinations do not focus exclusively on their intrinsic resources to develop tourism. To analyze how tourism actors organize their implementation, this paper focuses on factors that could influence tourism implementation and in particular on the operating mode among tourism actors within a delimited geographical area. The objective is to identify one operating mode among actors within a destination that we shall call 'the localized tourism system' (LTS). The aim is to develop a tool of analysis that focuses on the features of the LTS. This tool allows to analyze a destination, highlighting the elements that bring it close to the LTS.

An LTS is considered here as a destination including all tourism actors within a local predetermined area that work together in order to provide a coherent supply. The term 'tourism actors' is used here in a broad sense. An actor is an association or a firm, financed by the public or private sector, which has direct contact with tourists at the destination by offering a service to them during their stay. This conception includes an association that organizes events as well as cafés and restaurants or a bicycle rental services. The diversity of tourism actors has an important influence on the tourism system. Their territorial implantation influences the tourism flux, and consequently tourism development. As tourism analysis does not often consider the destination as a whole, including all types of tourism actors, the aim of this paper will be to build a new analysis model. This model, the LTS, has two main features: the diversity of actors working in the same industry and their concentration within a specific area.

To build a framework that groups the features of an LTS, the applied method consists in finding another system that shares features with an LTS. Looking through economic literature, the industrial district (ID) concept proved to be an interesting basis to develop the analysis framework of the LTS. Indeed, the ID's main features are firms' co-location and a network of relations that serves to participate in a specific trade activity, which corresponds to the LTS's features.

Building the analysis framework on the basis of ID's operating mode will allow to analyze the relationships between tourism actors, while focusing on the geographical area. This paper starts from the assumption that tourism actors have many possibilities to organize their implementation. The LTS is only one of many organizational profiles. The organizational mode among tourism actors can be considered as a continuum between two extreme situations: the LTS and the absence of structural links among tourism actors within a destination. This paper aims to develop a diagnostic tool in order to determine whether a destination matches the profile of an LTS. Furthermore, it analyses, from a territorial perspective, the co-operative culture in tourism. The ability to identify the variables that distinguish one profile from another could help solving synergy problems between different categories of actors in the tourism sector.

The chapter is organized as follows: Section 2 discusses the main features of an ID and identifies the structural parameters that could be transferred to a local tourism system. It presents a brief review of the literature on the main features of an ID. After this contextualization, an analysis framework is proposed, grouping the main features of the ID that are useful to analyze a destination. Section 3 provides an overview of the existing literature related to local systemic tourism. Then, after discussing the specificity of tourism, the LTS is analyzed with the aid of the proposed ID's framework, focusing on indicators that could categorize the LTS. Those indicators are then tested on the entity of Rochefort (Belgium) in order to examine their effectiveness.

## Industrial District

The objective of this section is to understand the main features of an ID in order to develop an analysis tool that can be adapted to a tourism system. The first part offers various definitions of an ID and briefly presents the evolution of the concept over time. This part classifies the IDs without any intention of exhaustiveness. Afterwards, these features are structured in a framework that is meaningful in the context of the paper's objectives.

### Definitions and Evolutions

In the literature, the notion of ID groups a very vast array of views. An ID may differ from another one in several ways, e.g. through the involvement of a variety of product specializations, a degree of organization or network complexity and cultural and social backgrounds (Humphrey, 1995 cited by Guerrieri & Pietrobelli, 2003). A historical perspective has been included in this section to help categorize the ID concept.

The phenomenon of geographical concentration of firms was analyzed at the end of the 19th century by the economist Alfred Marshall. He discovered that the co-location of small firms had consequences on external economies. Several concepts emerge from Marshall's notations, e.g. "industrial atmosphere", long-term socio-economic relationships among local firms and the role of local institutions. Based on the concept of Marshallian externalities, many authors have described firm agglomerations, commonly referred to as IDs.

A key characteristic of IDs is that they contain a large number of mostly small-sized specialized firms that produce a product at various stages or in various ways, which is homogeneous in a certain way (Brusco, 1982; Becattini, et al., 1992). These firms are also characterized by a high degree of geographical propinquity that encourages the exchange of information through personal and informal communication (Becattini, 1990).

Marshall's definition of ID is considered to be restrictive in the present day context. A broader definition refers to the ID as "a sizeable and spatially delimited area of trade-oriented economic activity, which has a distinctive economic specialization, be it resource-related, manufacturing or services" (Park & Markusen, 1995). This conceptualization focuses on firm size, inter-firm relations and internal versus external orientations (Guerrieri & Pietrobelli, 2003, p. 3). Markusen suggests categorizing districts in four distinctive levels. These different levels take different parameters into account: the firm size, the influence variability that they exercise on each other and the bottom-up or top-down implementation.

Nearly at the same period, Censis[1] suggests analyzing IDs with a life-cycle model. "Based on empirical research on several Italian districts, this model recognizes three different evolution stages of IDs. Each of them corresponds to a specific pattern of the ID evolutionary process: Formation, Development and Maturity" (Carbonara et al., 2002).

The first stage refers to the agglomeration of a craftsman-like entrepreneurial system within a local area or, in the case of a large firm surrounded by smaller ones, to the decentralization of production in the local area. This stage is characterized by a low transfer of operative knowledge that supports the production co-ordination mechanisms between firms. In the second stage, the ID involves small- to medium-sized firms that are specialized in a few phases of the production process and one or several hub firms that have a focal position in the network. The hub firms generally have direct access to the external market and co-ordination between firms is achieved by the exchange of both codified and tacit knowledge. In the third stage, IDs can pursue several goals, "depending on whether the hub firms pursue industrialization, decentralization or vertical integration" (Carbonara et al., 2002). So, Censis focuses on knowledge transfer, cooperation, firm size, firm position in the network, access to external market and ID future evolution.

More than 5 years after Markusen's categorization and Cencis' life-cycle model, Guerrieri simplifies Markusen's ID categories even further, emphasizing one key characteristic in addition to the geographical agglomeration that he considers as a permanent element. The first category, *geographical clustering of firms*, focuses on occasional inter-firm relations, no (or few) experiences of cooperation and non-existent (or little) developed local institutions. The second type, the *Marshallian ID*, is characterized by "smoother inter-firm transactions, much better developed practices of cooperation, more developed and effective local institutions, economies of scale at the district level made possible by substantial enterprise specialization, deep integration between economic activities and the local socio-cultural fabric" (Guerrieri & Pietrobelli, 2003). The last category, *enterprise network with some form of leadership*, draws attention to the existence of a leader, who provides "the strategic services and impetus for diversification into different products and sectors, with reorganization of production and new relationships with firms, local institutions, and factor

---

[1] Classified in the references under the name Unioncamere (1995).

and product markets" (Ibidem). Additionally to the focal Markusen features, Guerrieri focuses on cooperation practices, specialization and differentiation processes and integration in the local socio-cultural environment. He considers spatial agglomeration as a permanent feature of IDs.

Before concluding over these approaches of the ID concept through some literature currents, it has to be said that other aspects of ID, which are not going to be developed here, have been analyzed in the literature. Indeed, the objective of exploring ID features is to find common features between the ID and the LTS in order to transfer an analysis method that integrates the territorial perspective while exploring the operating mode of the system as a whole. This contextualization allows grouping ID features in order to study a LTS.

### Theoretical Framework

The framework that is proposed below is thought of as a comprehensive tool of analysis, which aims to give concrete examples of IDs that shows the chosen features. As a consequence, the paper does not claim to be exhaustive in its choice of ID features. The aim is to identify the features that are most relevant from the perspective of tourism in order to produce a specific investigation model. The selected features are spatial agglomeration, social and economic relationships and the firm's size and bottom up implementation. These identified features are divided into four main descriptive dimensions: the degree of systemic consciousness, the strategic means display, the degree of cumulativeness and the degree of spatial concentration. The first two dimensions result from thought processes of the firms themselves and can consequently be modulated. The last two dimensions are facts and as a consequence, they can neither be adapted by firms, nor by authorities.

First of all, the degree of systemic consciousness refers to the awareness of the firms that they are part of a transversal chain, which creates one product. Furthermore, in IDs, relationships between firms are based on both competition among firms that are dedicated to the same production phase and cooperation between firms that occupy different and interdependent phases of the production process. This mix allows the ID to innovate and thus to compete on bigger markets. For instance, an ID such as Murano (glass product, Italy) gathers small direct competitor firms with just a few reciprocal relationships. If a local leader (medium-size firm) emerges within the ID, as in the case of Sassuolo (ceramics, Italy), the systemic view and its benefits appears more clearly and increase the relationships building probabilities. If the ID is based on subcontracting of small firms, such as in Prato (wool textiles, Italy), the systemic consciousness also increases. IDs constituted by firms that possess only part of the resources that are necessary to build the end product, i.e. interdependent firms, are more likely to develop a global view of the product. The degree of consciousness mainly depends on firms themselves, their integration, their view of the district and their objectives. This dimension can evolve through diverse actions and is in this way similar to the strategic means display.

The second dimension is the strategic means display, which groups the means that are displayed by firms in order to create a coherent and competitive system. These strategic means focus on one hand on the system's creation by the bottom up implementation.

On the other, the strategic means display concerns the building of a strategy at the system level. The bottom-up process includes the role of local authorities, the distribution of financing sources, the existence of internal technical assistance or the decision-taking level (inside or outside of the system or the district). These factors indicate a bottom-up or top-down implementation. Judging from literature on IDs, the implementation was originally perceived as a bottom-up process. However, the notion of ID today acknowledges a larger conception that allows the intervention of authorities. In the north of Belgium, the government has been encouraging firms since 1994 to agglomerate in one single area (Flanders Language Valley in Ypres, Biotechnology in Gent, Telecoms in Antwerp) in order to create knowledge centers. Authorities intervene at the level of the promotion campaign and provide financial support for projects, after evaluation and within certain limits.

The development of a strategy at the system level is analyzed through the social and economic relationships that connect firms. The establishment of relationships between firms is influenced by their predisposition to collaborate their mutual trust and adhesion, their potential mutual profits and the transfer of knowledge. This cooperation level depends highly on the notion of social capital. Indeed, social capital is considered to be a soft infrastructure and is defined as the relational infrastructure in connection with the collective action, which presupposes trust, adhesion, reciprocity and a pre-disposition to collaborate, thus facilitating mutual benefits (Henderson & Morgan, 2001). Social capital highlights the fact that the district results from a collective learning process and from a social construction based on a shared socio-cultural identity. The first Italian districts have been created thanks to familial links based on informal personal contacts within a social culture founded on local historic traditions. The existence of common cultural bases on which firms can communicate reinforce the cooperation capacity (Capron, 2002, pp. 73–74). The notion of social capital and consequently the possibility to display strategic means at the district level arises with a higher degree of cumulativeness.

Thirdly, the degree of cumulativeness is the amount of facts resulting from previous periods that increases the probability of implementing a district in the present. The degree of cumulativeness concentrates on the firms of the district themselves: how long they have been in business and the workers' competencies. The size of the firms and the influence they exercise on each other determine the type of district that is developed. For instance, the first Italian districts are based on informal relationships among small and medium enterprises (SMEs). When firms have been established since a long period of time in an area, the implementation of a district comes easier. Besides, this approach moves towards the concept of the local share of identity. Firms originating from the local environment share a cultural identity that facilitates the implementation of a network system. Moreover, the socio-economic environment has an influence on both firm and product. In this respect, this dimension is firmly connected with the resources management of the studied area.

Finally, the degree of spatial concentration indicates the extent to which the firms are linked to their local environment. This point focuses on the borders of the district as well as the connections with external firms. The borders of the ID correspond to the sum of the conjunct areas where firms that work in the same trade sector and having relationships with each other, are established.

The concentration rate can be evaluated by the quantity and frequency of contacts among firms of the analyzed geographical area. If actors communicate with others within the district, it reveals that their connection with this area is significant for them. Consequently, links among internal district firms and external ones have to be determined.

Communication, which indicates the degree of openness of the system, influences the district's future projects.

The classificatory features mentioned above provide a starting point for the following specific tourism territory analysis.

## Application to the Tourism System

This section examines how the systemic tourism product is structured from the suppliers' perspective, including all suppliers that are directly and indirectly linked with tourism. These suppliers correspond to the tourism actors in a broad sense of the term, as defined before. This approach tends to analyze a specific tourism area through four dimensions in order to understand the specificities of tourism implementation.

First, we shall discuss some relevant literature about clustering in tourism, followed by an analysis of the LTS resulting from the application of the ID theoretical framework to tourism. Finally, we shall test the accuracy of this theoretical framework with a case study of Rochefort, an entity situated in the south of Belgium.

### Literature

In current literature, the notion of tourism district is mainly used in reference to urban tourism. Some authors made accounts of districts, observing and describing the clustering of tourism facilities (Obiol Menero, 1997; Priestley, 1996).

In their analysis of the Belgian city of Leuven, Jansen-Verbeke et al. evaluate its urban tourism potential through a morphologic and functional analysis of build heritage. This analysis focuses on historic buildings and introduces the notion of 'network' and 'cluster' in the town planning for an urban tourism implementation. From this point of view, interactions among actors depend on local authorities. To determine a cluster in this case, an external person of the area that will be considered as a cluster, identifies the tourism district based on both a location and an occupation index (Jansen-Verbeke et al., 2000). This study also shows that tourism actors located in some specific parts of the city, called tourism clusters or tourism corridors, benefit from agglomeration advantages and greater attractiveness, only due to their location. However, the objective here is not to improve tourism integration in a city but to analyze how tourism actors are integrated within a determined area. In the present chapter, the analysis framework shows the potential of tourism actors to create a local tourism system through relationship building that aims to improve the product as a whole.

However, the case study of Leuven is not the only one that refers to tourism clusters or districts. Pearce classifies tourist districts into six categories. The *Historic District* is defined as an area that agglomerates interesting buildings.[2] In the United States, the notion

---

[2] See on this subject Ashworth G. (1990), The historic Cities of Groningen: which is sold to whom? In: Ashworth G. and Goodall B., Editors, Marketing Tourism Places, Routledge, London, pp. 138–155. And also Ashworth G. and Tunbridge J.E. (1990), The Tourist-Historic City, Belhaven, London.

of district is used as an attractive strategy that catches the attention of tourists and shoppers.[3] The second category is the *Ethnic District* that promotes places where ethnic groups live, as an attraction.[4] Thirdly, *Sacred Spaces* are considered as a constellation of spaces, specific to pilgrims and tourists.[5] *Redevelopment Zones* are defined as specialized areas, which are spatially protected from usual life.[6] The fifth category covers *Entertainment Destinations*, i.e. high-tech entertainment centers, cinema complexes, theme restaurants, etc. Finally, the *Functional Tourism District* examines particular parts of cities under a spatial and functional perspective. Interesting case studies have been developed over different tourism districts in Paris (Pearce, 1998) and over theme districts of Singapore (Teo & Huang, 1995). This district categorization identifies tourism areas where co-location of tourism resources benefits to the tourism development. These areas are specialized in one element that attract tourists such as historic heritage, exotic culture, sacred places, a (perfect) place out of usual life problems, high-tech entertainment centers or specific tourism sector agglomerations.

The specificity of the ID framework analysis, compared with what has already been done, allows to analyze urban tourism as well as rural tourism. It defines the features of the LTS, focusing on all tourism actors within a determined space. This framework considers tourism actors in the broad sense of the word and analyses their organization method to work as being part of a system. The specificity of the ID framework for tourism is to identify the profile of a local tourism system, considering the destination as a whole and from a four-dimensional approach.

### Application of the Framework to Tourism

The fact that local actors move together in a chosen direction is the chief factor in creating a systemic tourism (systemic consciousness). The quantity and quality of connections (strategic means display) among actors determine the will to communicate. This communication is intensified when there is a common cultural capital (degree of cumulativeness) and also by geographical proximity (degree of spatial concentration).

- Systemic consciousness degree

Owing to the diversity of tourism actors, it appears to be difficult for them to include others of their local environment in the end product that is perceived as a whole by tourists. Considering tourism actors within a territory as being part of a LTS is equivalent to

---

[3] See on this subject Ehrlich B. and Dreier P. (1999), The new Boston Discovers the Old: Tourism and the Struggle for a Livable City. In: Judd D.R. and Fainstein S.S., Editors, Tourist City, Yale University Press, New Haven, CT, pp. 155–178. And also Lew A.A., Authenticity and sense of Place in the Tourism Development Experience of Older Retail Districts, Journal of Travel Research 27 4, pp. 15–22.

[4] See on this subject Conforti J., Ghettos as Tourism attraction, Annals of Tourism Research 23, 1996, pp. 830–842.

[5] See on this subject Sachachar A. and Shoval N. (1999), Tourism in Jerusalem: A place to pray. In: Judd D.R. and Fainstein S.S., Editors, The Tourist City, Yale University Press, New Haven, CT, pp. 198–211.

[6] See on this subject Judd D.R. (1999), Constructing the Tourist Bubble. In: Judd D.R. and Fainstein S.S., Editors, The Tourist City, Yale University Press, New Haven, CT, pp. 35–53.

considering local actors as one part of a transversal chain forming the end product, the destination. To sell this product, suppliers are grouped on a geographical base by distributors such as tourism offices (locally-based) or tourism houses (gathering together several border tourism offices). Consequently, suppliers are presented as being part of a whole but this does not always reflect the field reality. The dimension of systemic consciousness degree is highly significant to analyze a LTS because it allows to explore the basis of the system, its foundations.

If one adopts the tourist's perspective, the supply of a destination appears as a systemic product. Tourists consider all suppliers within the destination, from the basic services to the main resources, as being part of one product. Thus, through tourists themselves, tourism actors could become aware of the LTS. On top of this, the existence of structured transversal relationships among all actors that participate to the supply is required to enhance the work experience schemes of the destination actors. Consequently, structured tourism production and reception implies a minimum of cooperation among all actors and their integration in the system. Producing a coherent tourism destination concerning demand perceptions and expectations requires developing a systemic product (Ruffino, 2006).

On the other, when adopting the tourism actor's perspective, the systemic product does not always seem to be so obvious. Other suppliers can be considered both in a competitive or restrictive way. The trend for tourism actors to consider others as competitors only impedes to develop a systemic view of tourism within a destination. To consider tourism supply in a restrictive way is the main trend observed. Indeed, tourism gathers together a number of sectors such as accommodation, the cultural sector, entertainment, recreation, catering, transportation or other tourism-related services. These sectors collaborate mostly in an intersectorial way (implying only actors from one sector) while a trans-sectorial collaboration (implying actors from several sectors) is significant for the coherence of the localized system. As a result, the difficulty in tourism is that actors are not always aware of their participation in a broader than sectorial system. Therefore, two extreme types of tourism actors have to be distinguished: actors who have a systemic view and increase their potentials by implementing the system and actors who only develop strategies to increase their own profits.

The systemic consciousness of a destination is firstly submitted to the existence of a grouped implication of tourism actors, resulting in concrete actions at the destination level (for instance, promotion of the destination as a whole). From this statement, it is possible to determine how actors relate to each other. If tourism actors consider others only as competitors, they have no systemic consciousness. If partnership exists among actors of one sector, there is a low degree of systemic consciousness. If partnership exists in various or all sectors, there is a high degree of systemic consciousness. The degree of systemic consciousness increases with the integration of actors in the system, which can be seen more concretely through the strategic means display.

- Strategic means display

In order to be competitive and enhance the system performance, tourism can be analyzed through the major means developed by ID. Analyzing the role of local authorities, the origin and distribution of financing sources, the existence of technical assistance and the decision taking level, allows to determine a bottom-up or more top-down-oriented implementation, which highlights the system creation process. Furthermore, in order to determine the potentialities to build a coordinate strategy among all actors, a significant element is to identify the bases of the systemic strategy. The willingness of actors to collaborate is the first necessary condition to display strategic means. The second condition occurs when actors trust each other and agree about the way to implant tourism in their area. The following stage occurs when actors share mutual profits and are part of a network of information exchange. Finally, actors can combine all aforementioned forms of cooperation.

A structured network of formal or informal relationships can facilitate partnerships among actors who are not automatically aware of their contribution to the systemic tourism product as demonstrated in the first dimension. The ability to develop strong and dense connections among a large range of actors within the limits of a destination depends mostly on actors themselves but also on a general sector trend. Indeed, tourism encourages actors to communicate with each other in multiple ways, e.g. by making itineraries effective for tourists, hotels, restaurants, museums, attractions, etc. need to communicate. Another common collaboration process of the tourism sector is to propose packages at a lower price than all services taken separately.

Furthermore, small actors realize that they have to develop a system and mobilize knowledge in order to keep a competitive position in the global or even national tourism market. The tourism industry includes a large array of actors that are mostly small-sized firms. Small- and Medium-sized enterprises play a vital role in tourism. These firms are pushed by the economic context to be part of a larger supply in order to be competitive.

The strategic means displayed by tourism actors can be analyzed through several variables. If the public sector interferes in the development of a common promotion plan or a common strategy that groups all tourism actors of a specific area, the system is going to be more integrated than if the strategy only concerns some big actors of one sector. Other indicators are the existence of technical assistance at the destination level, the intervention of external actors in taking decisions about the destination and cooperation among actors (e.g. packages, itineraries or other forms of collaboration).

- Cumulativeness degree

While researching the diversity of tourism actors and their respective knowledge field, their location appears to be the main aspect they have in common. Sharing a territory, *a fortiori* during a long period of time, seems to favor transversal relationships. If tourism actors share a common cultural identity, they are more apt to communicate and to participate in a tourism system. Ruffino (2006) uses the concept of systemic product, with the purpose of studying the tourism supply from the perspective of learning processes. He explains the need for all actors to have a common relationship protocol, which includes local memory, professionalism and actor values. In this way, he gives some indicators to approach the concept of local identity shared by tourism actors.

The degree of cumulativeness focus both on tourism actors and the social, cultural and economic context. The size of the actor, the personality of the manager, the reason of the implementation in a specific area and the period of time since the establishment of the actor determine the influence they exercise on each other. The experience of actors within a geographical area to act as a receptive sphere for tourists also seems to be significant to the implementation of the system.

The trend for tourism actors to work as a LTS increases with the sharing of identity throughout time. The degree of cumulativeness gathers together elements highly linked with actors established area.

- Degree of spatial concentration

The spatial concentration in tourism is often linked with temporal concentration and perceived in terms of impact on natural and cultural resources at a tourist destination. The concentration of tourism actors within an area is considered here as an opportunity to collaborate and to build a coordinate strategy but also to attract other actors within the area. This notion raises the questions of the LTS borders.

Limits of the area identified as localized system can be defined by following the administrative division and taking the territory of the competent tourism authority into consideration. Different scales of tourism space can then be analyzed within this approach, from national to provincial or local scale. This paper focuses on a local approach for its case study. The aim is to analyze a relatively simple situation in order to understand LTS mechanisms and specificities.

The borders of the tourism system can also be seen by means of actors themselves, i.e. localizing the area where partner actors are established. In this case, the limits of the LTS are the result of strategies that are developed from existing networks between actors. This approach raises the question of the attractiveness of the LTS for external actors.

A combination of these two approaches, administrative and fictive borders, is chosen in this case. Analyzing systemic tourism from a local perspective would mean taking the territory of competent local authority as a maximum space scale. On the contrary, the minimum space scale is determined by the area where tourism actors entertain relationships. To compare the two approaches should underscore the importance of administrative limits for building a tourism system. The objective is also to be able to identify cores of tourism actors within the administrative limits.

The degree of spatial concentration for a destination that claims to have a coherent supply is quite variable. It can be regarded as a high degree of concentration if tourism actors have mutual dependency relations. By contrast, many actors having a lot of connections with external firms could point to a low degree of spatial concentration. This situation shows the foundations of another type of system, the reticular tourism system, which has no territorial bases.

### Application of the Framework to the Rochefort Entity

The framework does not aim to analyze an area in an exhaustive way, but intends to focus solely on key elements that are determinant to qualify an area as LTS.

Rochefort is an entity gathering together 13 villages (12,000 inhabitants), situated in a rural area of 165 km², between Namur and Bouillon (South Belgium). The tourism actors established in Rochefort are attractions (Domain of the Caves of Han, Centre for Country Life and Forgotten Crafts, the Gallo-Roman Archaeopark of Malagne, Cave of Lorette-Rochefort, Tourist Train of Rochefort), museums (Lavaux-Sainte-Anne Castel, Feudal Castle of Vêves, Domain of the Caves of Han "Museum of the Subterranean World",

Permanent Animation Centre of Railway and Stone, Remains of the Castle of the Counts, Ecomuseum "La Besace"), three tourism offices ("syndicat d'initiative") acting only in the entity, a "tourism house" ("Maison du tourisme") focusing on Rochefort and two other entities and the local public authorities (tourism represents approximately 1.5% of the whole entity's budget). The accommodation and gathering is composed of 19 hotels, 8 B&B's, 14 self-catering cottages, 5 campings and 40 restaurants. Other tourism actors in Rochefort comprise various associations involved in sports or the organization of events. The methodology used to study Rochefort is mainly based on field experience and interviews with tourism actors.

Partnerships exist through various sectors in Rochefort. First of all, there exists a high participation of actors during talks organized by the Tourism House once every year. Second, the main objectives are shared by tourism actors wanting to sell an integrate and coherent product in order to attract more tourists to the area, but whose priority is the visibility of their own product. A joint promotion of the area is organized by the Tourism House. Furthermore, there is a convention of partnership in order to develop a joint and more egalitarian form of promotion. Every actor donates an amount of money, corresponding to their profits. These indicators show a high degree of systemic consciousness in Rochefort.

The local authorities intervene in the promotion and strategy by financing the tourism office. The convention of partnership among actors favors the distribution of financial resources. No technical assistance exists at the destination level but one actor (Cave of Han) organizes language classes every year in order to professionalize their staff. Finally, decisions are taken locally without major intervention of external actors. These indicators show a high display of strategic means at the system level.

The oldest actor in the area was established in 1895, while the two most recent firms are strategically set up in the vicinity of existing big attractions. The management education level is similar in most cases (majority of master degree). This education level combined with the manager establishment in the entity, are indicators that point in the direction of a cultural identity. The actors' size indicates that there is a leading firm within the area. This leader helps structuring the partnerships among all smaller actors of the same sector (attractions and museums), even if they are involved in the same phase of the production process and normally tend to compete rather than to co-operate. The presence of this leader creates a balance between competition and cooperation, increasing the profits of every actor of the "cultural-leisure" sector. Other sectors are involved as well and brought into this process through the creation of packages (cooperation with the transportation sector and with the accommodation sector). The fact that the leader is both the oldest firm in the area and the greatest in terms of profits or visitor number, reinforces the indicators of the framework. The degree of cumulativeness in Rochefort appears to be very high according to these indicators.

Finally, the administrative border of the entity combined with the fictive border, determined by the actors' relationships, show the presence of two cores of spatial concentration, grouping a majority of tourism actors.

To conclude, Rochefort's entity can be classified as a destination close to the LTS. The indicators chosen for the ID framework reflect the presence of a LTS in this case.

## Conclusion

The existence of a local tourism system as well as its development results from a judicious combination of multiple factors. Indeed, competencies of local tourism actors, even if they are quite sophisticated, are integrated into a transversal chain that forms the tourism destination. Subsequently, if tourism actors improve their relationships, it optimizes the value of the chain as well as the tourism supply as a whole within a specific area.

An interesting aspect is that every element of the framework feeds another element. Defining the borders of a LTS (spatial concentration) implies identifying tourism actors (SMEs) and the links with their local environment — length of time established, sharing of identity — (Cumulativeness degree). This piece of information (cumulativeness degree) is the foundation of mutual economic and social relationships and determines the sense of the system implementation (strategic means display). The strategic means are displayed if actors are aware that they are part of a system (systemic consciousness). The awareness of their similar objectives is partly based on the destination as a whole and, consequently, to the territory. As a consequence, this implementation can be considered as an exponential process.

The ID framework helps to highlight some specificities of a LTS. The difficulties to build such a system reside in the fact that tourism gathers a vast range of actors. Tourism, for some actors (such as shops, café, restaurants, etc.) requires a lot of efforts in return for relatively small profits. Consequently, the implication of actors varies and cannot be viewed as equal, which intricates the implementation of a system.

The fact that tourism actors are so diversified implies that they have to be very dynamic in order to create one coherent product. At this stage, various kinds of tourism systems can be distinguished. There is the LTS, as described before, and the reticular tourism system, defined as the implementation of relationships among tourism actors that share competencies. For the reticular tourism system, the spatial proximity is of no significance at all. This raises the question of the tourism propensity to be structured as a reticular system, rather than as a localized system.

Two actors that are aware of the necessity of having a comprehensive view will appeal to others for creating a bottom-up dynamic. Relationships will bring information that is important to feed local systemic tourism implementation.

With the aim of studying the significant factors for implementing a coherent tourism supply, the ID represents a plausible framework to evaluate systemic tourism from a spatial viewpoint and allows producing a multidimensional analysis by integrating all tourism actors. The endogenous development is increasingly considered as a guarantee for the sustainability of a project. To understand the specificities of partnership building in tourism, various factors have to be analyzed. The framework presented some of them in order to analyze a destination through the features of the LTS with the aim of having an all-embracing view, integrating all tourism actors.

## Acknowledgments

I would like to thank my PhD directors, Claire Billen and Jean-Michel Decroly for their support and research guidance.

# References

Becattini, G. (1990). The Marshallian industrial district as a socio-economic notion. In: F. Pyke, G. Becattini, & W. Senbenberger (Eds), *Industrial districts and inter-firm co-operation in Italy* (pp. 134–141). Geneva: International Institute for Labour Studies.

Becattini, G. (2001). *From Marshall's to the Italian industrial districts, A brief critical reconstruction.* Mimeo.

Becattini, G., Pyke, F., & Sengenberger, W. (1992). *Industrial districts and inter-firm co-operation in Italy.* Geneva: International Institute for Labour Studies.

Brusco, S. (1982). The Emilian model: Productive decentralisation and social integration. *Cambridge Journal of Economics, 6*, 167–184.

Capron, H. (2002). Aides publiques, infrastructures et développement régional. In: C. Vandermotten (Ed.), *Le développement durable des territoires, Collection Aménagement du territoire et environnement.* Belgique: Université Libre de Bruxelles.

Carbonara, N., Giannoccaro, I., & Pontrandolfo, P. (2002). Supply chains within industrial districts: A theoretical framework. *International Journal of Production Economics, 76*(2), 159–176.

Cingano, F. (2003). Returns to specific skills in industrial districts. *Labour Economics, 10*(2), 149–164.

Conforti, J. (1996). Ghettos as tourism attractions. *Annals of Tourism Research, 23*, 830–842.

Guerrieri, P., Iammarino, S., & Pietrobelli, C. (2002). *The global challenge to industrial districts. Small and medium-sized entreprises in Italy and Taiwan.* Cheltenham: Edward Elgar.

Guerrieri, P., & Pietrobelli, C. (2003). Industrial districts' evolution and technological regimes: Italy and Taiwan, *Technovation, 24*(11), November 2004, 899–914.

Henderson, D., & Morgan, K. (2001). Regions as laboratories: The rise of regional experimentalism in Europe. In: D. Wolfe, & M. Gertler (Eds), *Innovation and social learning*, New York: Macmillan.

Jansen-Verbeke, M., Lievois, E., Laureyssen, I., Boogaarts, I., & Vanden Bossche, L. (2000). Cultuurtoerisme en stedelijke revitalisatie. *Leuvense Geografische Papers* 11, Heverlee.

Markusen, A. (1996). Sticky places in slippery space: A typology of industrial districts. *Economic Geography, 72*, 293–313.

Marshall, A. (1896). *Principles of economics.* London: Macmillan.

Marshall, A. (1920). *Industry and trade.* London: Macmillan.

Obiol Menero, E.M. (1997). Turismo y Ciudad: El Caso de Valencia. *Estudios Turísticos, 134*, 3–21.

Park, S., & Markusen, A. (1995). Generalizing new industrial districts: A theoretical agenda and an application from a non-Western economy. *Environment and Planning* A, *27*, 81–104.

Pearce, D.G. (1998). Tourist districts in Paris: Structure and functions. *Tourism Management, 19*, 49–65.

Pearce D.G. (2001). An integrative framework for urban tourism research. *Annals of Tourism Research, 28*(4), 926–946.

Priestley, G.K. (1996). City tourism in Spain. In: C.M. Law (Ed.), *Tourism in major cities* (pp. 114–154). London: Thompson International Business Press.

Ruffino, M. (to be published in 2006). Les systèmes touristiques locaux vus en termes de processus d'apprentissage: Quelques points de repères. In: J.M. Decroly, A.D. Delbare, A. Diekmann, & A.M. Duquesne (Eds), *Tourisme et société mutations, enjeux, défis.* Bruxelles: Université Libre de Bruxelles.

Teo, P., & Huang, S. (1995). Tourism and heritage conservation in Singapore. *Annals of Tourism Research, 22*, 589–615.

Unioncamere. (1995). *Imprese e istituzioni nei distretti industriali che cambiano.* Milan: F. Angeli.

Chapter 4

# The Destination as a Local System of Innovation: The Role of Relational Networks

Jaume Guia, Lluís Prats and Jordi Comas

## Introduction

Over the last few years, the use of the term innovation has augmented in the tourism liter-ature, and more and more, tourism firms, destinations and public administrations are aware of the need to adopt new and more innovative policies in the management of tourism.

Nonetheless, in the tourism academic literature little research can be found on the man-agement of innovation and its repercussions on the competitiveness of firms and destinations. The fact that innovation has not been a major issue or not even present in much of the tourist industry, does not mean that innovation is not important or even necessary for the competi-tiveness of firms and destinations. It is, in fact, of prime importance (Hjalager, 2002).

The evolution of the literature on competitiveness has shown the relevance of innova-tion and innovative capabilities as the main factors in explaining the sustainability of the competitive position of firms (Teece, Pisano, & Shuen, 1997; Carneiro, 2000) — micro level — and also of regions and nations — macro level — (Porter, 1999a, b).

In the last decade, the literature on innovation has emphasized the role collective inter-active processes have on the acquisition and combination of knowledge and learning. In this context, a vast literature on the important role national and regional systems of inno-vation play in sustaining the competitiveness of firms and regions has been developed (Lundvall, 1992; Nelson, 1993; Braczyk, 1998; Asheim & Isaksen, 2002). Nevertheless, there is little account of studies focusing on the local level.

This fact can be explained because in most industries the local level might have an insignificant effect on the issue. However it is not the case in the tourist industry, where local knowledge can play a major role in the configuration and evolution of the destination as a tourist product.

The aim of the paper is, thus, the conceptualization of a *local system of innovation* (LSI), and the analysis of its applicability to the case of tourist destinations, and its rele-vance for their competitiveness.

The conceptual framework we propose displays all the actors in the local destination, relevant for its configuration as an LSI (public bodies, private sector, research and academic institutions and local community), and how they should be organized in order to achieve sustained competitiveness.

In what follows we will first present the background literature on innovation, competitiveness and tourism, then will proceed with the systems of innovation literature, and finally display the conceptual model of an LSI in tourism and highlight the relevance of the role relational networks play in it.

## Innovation and Competitiveness

In the literature on strategic management, several authors have highlighted the key role innovation plays in explaining competitiveness. Some examples read as follows: "firms gain competitive advantage through innovation" (Porter, 1999a), or "the competitive advantage of nations depends on the innovative capabilities of their industries" (Porter, 1999b), or "it's likely that in service sector intensive economies, the lack of innovative activity will negatively affect their competitive positioning and their productivity growth rates" (COTEC, 2001a).

Economic actors can obtain competitive advantage by being more efficient in the production and delivery of goods and/or by differentiating the products so that they are more attractive for the potential customers (Porter, 1980). However, from a more dynamic point of view, whatever advantage they have can be eroded by the innovative behavior of other competing firms, especially when this behavior brings about more efficiently produced and attractive goods. Protecting the resources that are the basis of a firm's competitive advantage does not seem to be the best strategy anymore, as resource-based theories of the firm defended (Wernerfelt, 1984; Peteraf, 1993). Strategic resources and capabilities might be difficult to copy or imitate, but nothing can impede the birth of new and still better resources and capabilities that erode the value of the older ones. This is, then, why innovation is key in explaining sustained competitive behavior by economic actors.

Dynamic capabilities are now at the forefront of factors that give competitive advantage to firms (Teece et al., 1997). It is now important to explore: where do dynamic capabilities come from? Do they come from individual actors? Or are they the outcome of collective processes in which interaction between actors makes learning and the emergence of new meaning possible? (Stacey, Douglas, & Shaw, 2000; Guia & Prats, 2004).

If we assume innovation as a collective process — as we do — the understanding of what configurations of actors make this process more feasible is paramount. Some academic literature focused on the analysis and study of industrial districts (Becattini, 1979; Camisón & Molina, 1998) and clusters (Porter, 1990) as collective entities, or institutions that provide participating firms with unique social and cultural routines. Initially, most of this literature aimed at explaining the advantages in efficiency that industrial districts provide to participating firms. Recently, their interest has shifted to explore the role of these institutions in the dynamic competitive processes in which firms compete. Therefore now, proximity and the common language and shared institutions available to firms in clusters and industrial districts form the basis of the processes by means of which firms learn and innovate.

# Innovation in Tourism

The academic literature on innovation in tourism is very limited, and most of it has been developed to deal with types of innovations in tourism and other rather descriptive issues (Hjalager, 2002; Jacob et al., 2003).

As for types of innovation, for example, we can distinguish product innovations, process innovations, marketing innovations, organizational innovations and institutional innovations. Another issue also dealt with in the literature is the sources of innovation. COTEC (2001b) identifies six different sources of innovation in tourism: managers, customers (questionnaires, complaints, etc.), employees (empowerment, etc.), competitors (benchmarking, imitation, etc.), suppliers (suggestions, etc.) and commercial fairs.

Poon (1990, 1993) has analyzed both, technological innovation and their diffusion in tourism, as well as the growth of small and flexible tourism firms. Innovation emerging in networks has been studied by Sundbo (1998) and Jensen (2001). Later, Hjalager (2002) made an important contribution to this literature by defining a theoretical framework in which the relevant issues can be analyzed in a systematic way. She takes a relational approach to innovation and highlights the relevance of interaction, cooperation and networks for the creation and diffusion of knowledge. And most importantly, she describes four categories of sources of innovation in tourism and explains where the main obstacles to innovation are and why they exist. Finally, from her conclusions we can deduce that the best way to overcome those obstacles is through networking and cooperation in the tourism local destinations.

Finally, more recent articles by Stamboulis and Skayannis (2003) and Grant (2004) deal with innovation strategies and technology for experience-based tourism, and the process of innovation in tourism planning, respectively.

# Systems of Innovation

In order to catch the trend of analyzing competitiveness in dynamic terms, new concepts have been coined to define a dynamic agglomeration of firms: from innovative industrial districts or clusters, to *milieux innovateurs*, and later to national systems of innovation. In this paper we focus on this last term.

Lundvall (1992) defines a system of innovation as a collection of actors and their inter-relations that interact in the production, diffusion and use of new and economically viable knowledge. Previously, Nelson (1993) had already used the term to define the collection of institutions that determine the innovating actions of firms from their interactions. Both authors agree in that the systems of innovation encompass institutions and organizations that search for and explore new technologies and knowledge. Nelson (1993) also argues that a system of innovation is not the result of a pre-designed plan of a particular actor, but of all the participating actors through interaction. Therefore, relations are at the core of the systems of innovation concept, like in the industrial districts and cluster literatures.

Three types of systems of innovation should be distinguished according to their geographical scope: national, regional and local systems of innovation.

Probably, the first academic definition of a national system of innovation is Freeman's (1987) who presented it as the network of public and private institutions, whose activities and the interaction among them, are directed to initiate, import, modify and diffuse new technologies. It is, however, Lunvall (1992) who is known as the father of the literature on national systems of innovation. In stricter terms, he defines a national system of innovation as the organizations and institutions involved in searching and exploration activities, like R&D departments and universities within a nation. And in broader terms as all the parts and aspects of the economic and institutional structure of a nation that affects education and research. He argues that the idiosyncratic character of each nation is reflected in the organizational structure of its firms, the relations between them, the role played by the public sector, the organization of the financial system, the role of R&D organizations and the intensity of their research activities.

A strong national system of innovation is one that has systemic ties between the different sources of knowledge production (universities and R&D organizations), the public administration and firms.

Following the development of the concept *national systems of innovation*, a similar concept but focused at the regional level was later coined (Braczyk, 1998; Cooke, 2001). The regional level was thought to be of great importance because there is not always institutional uniformity within nations or states. In some cases, these diversity within a nation can be as great as or even greater than differences between two different national systems of innovation (Olazaran & Gómez, 2001). This is, for example, the case of Catalonia in Spain. Some authors find an equivalence between the concept of regional systems of innovation and the *cluster* concept introduced by Porter (1992).

Furthermore, it is believed that most of the strong ties between the actors of a system of innovation exist at the regional level. Proximity, then, seems to play an important role in the systems. From this argument, the local level would be even stronger in terms of providing closeness and tie strength between the actors (Kirat & Lung, 1999). However, the problem of the local level is that it does not always have the variety and quantity of actors (for example, universities) required in a system of innovation.

At the local level, the system of innovation is made up of a network of local actors and the interactions between them. Not all local production systems can be considered as innovation systems. In fact, a lot of local industrial districts lack the required horizontal cooperation between firms, and between firms and the public local agencies, and/or lack research organizations embedded in the district. But, when they have the required elements become real *incubators of innovation* (Aydalot, 1982). All actors can participate more closely in the decision-making processes (including local communities) and, thus, make easier the implementation of innovations.

## The Destination as a Local System of Innovation

If we take any conventional tourist destination at the local level, we can identify different categories of actors intervening in the configuration of the tourist product.

There is some literature concerning this issue (Gunn, 1997; OMT, 1999) in which the private sector (firms), public administrations and research institutions (universities, etc.) are considered to some extent. They, though, are not concerned with innovation issues. Recently, some efforts have been made in order to define the tourism industry as a functional system and include local communities in the framework (Prats, 2003; Prats & Guia, 2003).

Local-destination residents are gaining more and more importance and are becoming relevant actors in determining the success of particular models of tourism development (Andereckt & Vogt, 2000). The growing public interest in environmental issues or in the social accountability of firms has produced important campaigns against urban developments in protected areas and other activities with negative impacts on local social and environmental systems.

In this context, the existence of all the relevant categories of actors and the type of relations between them, will determine the capacity of the local destination for innovation, as displayed in Figure 4.1.

According to this framework, we can state that a local system of innovation in tourism (LSIT) is based in a specific local area or local tourism destination, in which there are multiple tourism-related actors that, with the support of ancillary industries and external actors, relate and interact. As a result of this interaction and the characteristics of the local macro-environment in which they operate, knowledge can be created and diffused and thus, the capacity for innovation enhanced. With this capacity, local destinations will be ready to sustain advantageous competitive positions, and to generate sustainable collective wealth.

## The Relevance of Relational Networks

Even though all the elements of the framework are important in explaining the innovativeness and competitiveness of a local destination, in this last section of the paper our aim is to vindicate the relevance of relational networks.

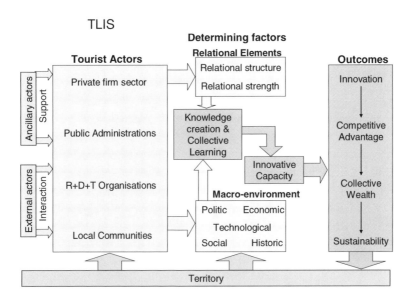

Figure 4.1: Tourist local innovation system model.

Figure 4.2 shows an example of different clusters or local destinations with the connections among relevant actors within clusters and between clusters.

For its part, Figure 4.3 presents a causal model depicting the relationship between relational networks and the competitiveness of local destinations.

As can be seen, there are two characteristics of the relational networks in a cluster or local destination to be considered: the centrality of each cluster in the global system and the internal structure or cohesion of the clusters.

As for centrality of the cluster (see top half of Figure 4.3), we assume that the clusters with more direct contacts with external clusters and actors will be more active in communication activity in the global system, and thus, will have more of the information and knowledge flowing through the whole system. Nonetheless, even though a cluster has a small number of direct links with external clusters, it can still play an important intermediary role between different clusters in the system (Guia, 2000). In Figure 4.2, cluster D is the only one who links the clusters on the right of the figure with the ones on the left, and thus, it has the most timely and exclusive access to the knowledge available in the system, that is, the most brokerage power.

Therefore, the more central the cluster, the more its potential to develop new tourist products in that it has advantages in identifying and assimilating the new knowledge available in the system; or in other words, the more potential absorptive capacity (Zahra & George, 2002).

Now, if we look at the bottom half of Figure 4.3, we see the role the cohesion of the internal network of the clusters play for its innovativeness and competitive capacity (Guia, 2000). The more cohesive the cluster, that is, the more actors are connected between them, the more trust and social norms will develop, and the more the efficiency in coordinating and controlling the collective actions carried by the group. Therefore, the more embedded in the local environment the actors in the clusters are, the lower the transaction costs of the collective activities of transforming the available knowledge and exploiting it in the form of new product development and marketing; or in other words, the more realized absorptive capacity (Zahra & George, 2002).

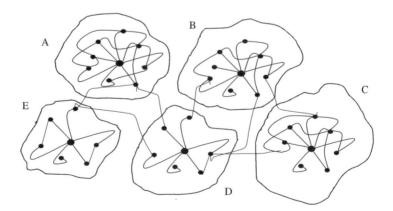

Figure 4.2: Connections between and within local destinations.

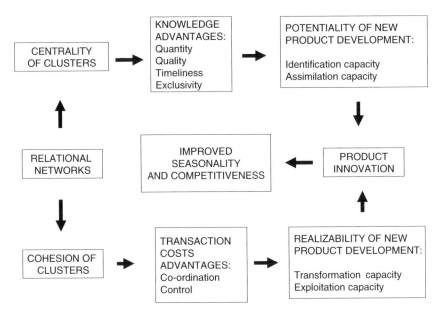

Figure 4.3: Relational networks, innovation and competitiveness.

The two circumstances (centrality and cohesion) have to coexist in order to improve the innovative capacity of the local destination. Actors cannot possibly exploit knowledge without first acquiring it; similarly, they can acquire and assimilate knowledge, but might not have the capability to transform and exploit it for profit generation.

## Conclusions

Briefly, due to the special characteristics of the tourist products we argue that the unit of analysis for the strategic study of these products is the local destination. Each local destination can be framed as a complex system in which every actor plays particular roles. The use of a framework for a LSIT as the one proposed above should prove relevant for the understanding of innovation processes and innovation deficits in the tourist industry and destinations.

Additionally, we highlight the particular relevance of relational networks in explaining the innovative capacity of a local destination. The centrality of de-destination in the global network of contacts between actors will determine its potential for new product development and innovation, in that, it will affect the quantity, and quality of knowledge to which it has access to. For its part, the cohesiveness of the internal network of contacts within the local cluster or destination will determine the "realizability" of the potential for new product development, in that it will affect the capability for transforming and exploiting the knowledge to which it had accessed.

Nonetheless, this paper is just a first exercise of translating the concept of systems of innovation to the tourism industry, and to the local level, which had not been done previously in the literature. The framework is, thus, a starting point for further research, as well on theoretical issues, as on applications to particular local destinations in order to assess their innovative capacity, or to compare their innovative capacity with the capacity of other local destinations.

# References

Andereck, K.L., & Vogt, C.A. (2000). The relationship between residents' attitudes toward tourism and tourism development options, *Journal of Travel Research, 39* (1), 27–36.

Asheim, B.T., & Isaksen, A. (2001). Los sistemas regionales de innovación, las PYMES y la política de innovación. In: M. Olazaran, & M. Gómez (Eds), *Sistemas regionales de innovación. Zarautz: Servicio editorial de la universidad del país vasco.*

Aydalot P. (1982). *Milieux innovateurs en Europe.* Paris: Economica.

Becattini, G. (1979). Dal settore industriale al distretto industriale. Alcune considerazione sull'unità di indagine dell'economia industriale. *Rivista di Economia e Politica Industriale 1,* 7–14.

Braczyk, H.J., Cooke, P., & Heidenreich, M. (1998); *Regional innovation systems: The role of governances in a globalized world.* Londres: UCL.

Camisón, C., & Molina, F.J. (1998). Distritos industriales y recursos compartidos: Un enfoque integrador. *Revista de Economía y Empresa, 32*(12), 65–82.

Carneiro, A. (2000). How does knowledge management influence innovation and competitiveness? *Journal of Knowledge Management, 4*(2), 87–98.

Cooke, P. (2001). Sistemas de innovación regional: Conceptos, análisis y topología. In: M. Olazaran, & M. Gómez (Eds), *Sistemas regionales de innovación. Zarautz: Servicio editorial de la universidad del país vasco.*

COTEC. (2001a). *Innovación en servicios.* Madrid: COTEC.

COTEC. (2001b). *Estudio exploratorio sobre innovación en el sector turístico balear.* Madrid: COTEC.

Freeman, C. (1987). *Technology policy and economic performance: Lessons from Japan.* London: Pinter.

Grant, R.M. (2004). Innovation in tourism planning processes: Action learning to support a coalition of stakeholders for sustainability. *Tourism and Hospitality: Planning & Development, 1*(3), 219–237.

Guia, J. (2000). *Implicaciones del capital social para la ventaja competitiva de la empresa en un contexto evolutivo.* Unpublished PhD disartation. Castelló: Universitat Jaume I.

Guia, J., & Prats, L. (2004). Innovation as institutional change: A complexity approach. *Research workshop management of innovation,* (7–8 June), Roskilde: Roskilde University (Denmark).

Gunn, C.A. (1997). *Vacationscape: Developing tourist areas.* Washington, DC: Taylor and Francis.

Hjalager, A.M. (2002). Repairing innovation defectiveness in tourism. *Tourism Management, 23*(5), 465–474.

Jacob, M., Tintoré, J., Aguiló, E., Bravo, A., & Mulet, J. (2000). Innovation in the tourism sector: Results from a pilot study in the Balearic Islands. *Tourism Economics, 9*(3), 279–295.

Jacob, M., Tintoré, J., & Simonet, R. (2003). *Innovación y turismo; en El papel social de la ciencia en Baleares.* Un homenaje a Javier Benedí, Universitat de les Illes Balears, Palma de Mallorca.

Jensen, C.F. (2001). *Innovative behaviour in experience intensive firms. A strategic perspective in tourism.* Report 01:2. Roskilde: Roskilde University, Centre of Service Studies.

Kirat, T., & Lung, Y. (1999). Innovation and proximity: Territories as loci of collective learning processes. *European Urban and Regional Studies, 6*(1), 27–38.

Lundvall, B.Å. (1992). National systems of innovation: Towards a theory of innovation and interactive learning. London: Pinter.

Maillat, D., & Perrin, J.C. (1992). *Entreprises innovatrices et développement territorial.* Neuchâtel (France): EDES (Editions de la Division Économique et Sociale).

Nelson, R. (1993). *National innovation systems.* Oxford: Oxford University Press.

Olazaran, M., & Gómez, M. (2001). *Sistemas regionales de innovación. Zarautz: Servicio editorial de la universidad del país vasco.*

OMT. (1999). *Desarrollo turístico sostenible: Guía para administradores locales.* Madrid: OMT.

Peteraf, M.A. (1993). The cornerstones of competitive advantage: A resource-based view. *Strategic Management Journal, 12,* 95–117.

Poon, A. (1990). Flexible specialization and small size — the case of Caribbean tourism. *World Development, 1,* 109–123.

Poon, A. (1993). *Tourism, technology and competitive strategies.* Oxon: CAB Intenational.

Porter, M.E. (1990). *The competitive advantage of nations.* London: The MacMillan Press.

Porter, M.E. (1992). *Els avantatges competitius de Catalunya.* Barcelona: Generalitat de Catalunya.

Porter, M.E. (1999a). *Ser competitivos: Nuevas aportaciones y conclusiones.* Bilbao: Ediciones Deusto.

Porter, M.E. (1999b). Ser competitivos: Fronteras en expansión. *Hardvard Deusto Business Review, 91,* 34–37.

Prats, L. (2003). Competitivitat i turisme: El paper rellevant del territori. *Cicle de conferències sobre competitivitat i territori,* (18–25 February), Universitat de Girona.

Prats, L., & Guia, J. (2003). *Aproximación a la competitividad de la industria del turismo: una propuesta de indicadores.* (21–25 October), Ministerio de Educación Superior de Cuba: Universidad de Matanzas.

Stacey, R., Douglas, G., & Shaw, P. (2000). *Compelexity and management: Fad or radical challenge to systems thinking?* London: Routledge.

Stamboulis, Y., & Skayannis, P. (2003). Innovation strategies and technology for experience-based tourism. *Tourism Management, 24*(1), 35–43.

Sundbo, J. (1998). *The organization of innovation in services.* Copenhagen: Roskilde University Press.

Teece, J.T., Pisano, G., & Shuen, A. (1997). Dynamic capabilities and strategic management. *Strategic Management Journal, 18*(7), 509–533.

Wernerfelt, B. (1984). A resource-based view of the firm. *Strategic Management Journal, 5,* 171–180.

WTO. (1999). *Desarrollo turístico sostenible: Guía para administradores locales.* Madrid: WTO.

Zahra, S.A., & George, G. (2002). Absorptive capacity: A reveiew, reconceptualization, and extension. *Academy of Management Review, 27,* 185–203.

Chapter 5

# Do Clusters and Networks Make Small Places Beautiful? The Case of Caramulo (Portugal)

Zélia Breda, Rui Costa and Carlos Costa

## Introduction

The growing increase in international and inter-regional competitiveness, associated with the apparent shortcomings of traditional regional development models and policies, are some of the reasons that have triggered the interest of academic and researchers for studying clusters and networks. Research in this area suggests that economies tend to develop through the emergence of clusters. In fact, the development of clusters contributes significantly to the world's economies and provides paths to developing national and, in particular, regional economies. Several examples of regional clustering provide evidence that even as competition and economic activity globalize, competitive advantage can be localized. Having in mind the reality of the tourism sector, which is mainly constituted by micro and small enterprises, the advantages of working together are enormous. Physical proximity, investment in R&D and cooperation between firms enhance information exchanges, thus leading to knowledge spillovers and generating (technological) innovation, which are pointed as essential factors in promoting economic growth. Partnerships and strategic alliances in tourism and hospitality were classified among the 10 most important world tourism issues for 2004 (Edgell, 2004). According to several authors, the strategic positioning of peripheral regions can be accomplished through the identification of product clusters, the establishment of public–private partnerships and the creation of networks.

## New Approaches to Tourism Planning

Tourism in Europe is dominated by small and medium-sized enterprises (SMEs), most of them in the form of family-owned businesses. This type of enterprises plays an important role in the economy of countries, and in particular, in the growth and development of

Tourism Local Systems and Networking
Copyright © 2006 by Elsevier Ltd.
All rights of reproduction in any form reserved
ISBN: 0-08-044938-7

tourism destinations, because of their ability to create new jobs, their capacity to stimulate competition and the higher multiplier effect. Globalization has led a growing pressure on this type of tourism enterprises, which are having difficulty to form a unique destination and to distribute their products widely. Traditional tourism destinations are also facing fierce competition. According to several authors (Inskeep, 1991; Mill & Morrison, 1992; Murphy, 1985), tourism policies should take into consideration social, economic and physical characteristics of destinations. In fact, it is through these characteristics, sometimes unique, that clusters of products emerge and create alternative forms of tourism in mature destinations.

On the other hand, globalization can also be seen as an opportunity to benefit from the open world market. In order to cope with the threats of global competition and develop strategic positioning, tourism destinations should encourage the emergence of tourism clusters, the establishment of networks and strong partnerships, among private sector operators, but especially between the public and the private sector.

Indeed, new directions (paradigms) that are emerging in the tourism field suggest that the efficiency and effectiveness of tourism planning comprises not only advances in tourism planning theory and practices but also improvement in the organizational framework within which decisions are designed and put into practice (Costa, 2001). The socio-economic changes that have occurred in the world during the recent past (globalization, information and technology, the development of more flexible economic activities) have boosted research in an attempt to look for alternative ways of putting forward the planning and organizational systems. Increasing interest and research studies on network, collaboration and partnership theory show how academics are becoming more sensitive on this matter.

Undoubtedly, an area which is pointed out in the literature as offering an alternative framework to adjusting organizations to the challenges brought about by recent events is that of networks. To Cook and Morgan (1993, cited in Costa, 1996) networks will acquire a new dominance in the field of industrial organization. In their view, this new paradigm seems to be flourishing on the basis of the shortcomings associated with markets and vertical hierarchies, primarily because of changing technologies, demands, products, etc.

According to Thorelli (1986, cited in Costa, 1996), networks are organizational structures whose philosophy may be placed between markets and hierarchies. The term network refers to two or more organizations involved in long-term relationships. In addition to this, he also argues that the entire economy may be viewed as a network of organizations with a vast hierarchy of subordinate, criss-crossing networks.

Jarillo (1993, cited in Costa, 1996) defines network as a set of companies that work together toward a common goal, in which coordination is not achieved by mergers and acquisitions, but through the creation of a 'strategic network' of companies, working together toward the same goals.

> Networks allow firms access to specialized services at lower cost, Clusters attract needed specialized services to a region. Networks have restricted membership, Clusters have open "membership". Networks are based on contractual agreements, Clusters are based on social values that foster trust and encourage reciprocity. Networks make it easier for firms to engage in complex production, Clusters generate demand for more firms with similar

and related capabilities. Networks are based on cooperation, Clusters require both cooperation and competition. Networks have common business goals, Clusters have collective visions. (Nordin, 2003, pp. 13, 14)

Interest in regional clusters and their role in economic development has grown substantially over the last years among academics, politics and professionals. "One reason for the enormous interest in regional clusters is the simple fact that 'they are there'" (Enright, 2001).

Historical investigation suggests that economies tend to develop through the emergence of regional clusters. In fact, an industry emerges around some natural resource, market need, or local skill. As the industry develops, new firms in the industry are founded. Soon suppliers emerge to provide inputs and services, and new industries are formed through spillovers and transferred knowledge (Caniëls, 2000; Holbrook & Wolfe, 2002; Kim, 1999; Porter, 1990; Simmie, 1997).

According to Porter (1998), clusters are geographic concentrations of interconnected companies and institutions in a particular field, linked by commonalities and complementarities. The difference between clusters and other forms of cooperation within a network is sometimes difficult to see.

> The cluster concept focuses on the linkages and interdependencies among actors in the value chain in producing products and services and innovating. Clusters differ from other forms of co-operation and networks in that the actors involved in a cluster are linked in a value chain. The cluster concept goes beyond 'simple' horizontal networks in which firms, operating on the same end-product market and belonging to the same industry group, co-operate on aspect such as R&D, demonstration programs, collective marketing or purchasing policy. Clusters are often cross-sectorial (vertical and/or lateral) networks, made up of dissimilar and complementary firms specializing around a specific link or knowledge base in the value chain. (OECD, 1999, p. 12)

The diffuse and fragmented nature of tourism development has long been recognized. In few situations does one company or organization control all the components, or all the stages and decision-making processes in the creation and delivery of the tourism product. Vertical integration is not a hallmark of most tourism operations. Equally, horizontal integration is relatively rare: single ownership of all the airlines, hotels or other forms of tourism product is unusual, even in one region.

The importance of involving diverse stakeholders in tourism planning and management is thus receiving growing recognition. This has led to increasing attention being directed to partnerships that bring a range of interests in order to develop and sometimes also implement tourism policies. "The term partnership describes regular, cross-sectorial interactions between parties based on at least some agreed rules or norms, intended to address a common issue or to achieve a specific policy goal or goals." (Bramwell & Lane, 2000, p. 1).

> A key reason for the growing interest in partnerships in tourism development is the belief that tourist destination areas and organizations may be

able to gain competitive advantage by bringing together the knowledge, expertise, capital and other resources of several stakeholders (Kotler et al., 1993 cited in Bramwell & Lane, 2000, p. 2).

According to Costa (1996), the importance of networks and partnerships for tourism seems enormous. Firstly, they offer planners an organizational framework in which more comprehensive, inclusive, participatory, informed and democratic approaches may be put forward, because policies are not exclusively designed by planning agencies but are, instead, supported by a wider range of participants.

Furthermore, they bring destination areas the assurance that development is no longer viewed from a short-term economic approach; instead, the planning and development of resorts are viewed from a wider perspective, which comprises the surrounding natural, social and economic environment, and, therefore, takes into account notions such as uniqueness, carrying capacity and sustaining growth.

In addition, they bring the tourism industry the hope that economic growth is viewed not only in the short term but also in the medium and long terms. By conveying more stability and competitiveness to the web, networks also bring more safety and profitability to private sector investments.

Finally, networks transmit governments the advantage that the development of tourism is viewed with respect the natural and social patrimony; that development takes into account the economic structure of every place; and also that, by stimulating the inter-organizational coordination of policies, the indirect and induced economic impact produced by tourism are maximized.

## Regional Tourism Networking in Portugal

The regional tourism organization in Portugal is under the responsibility of tourism boards, which are constituted by representatives of municipalities and of public and private sector organizations. However, the country is not fully covered by boards, since there are several municipalities, which have decided either not to join a board or to include their tourism departments in local organizations called Tourism *Juntas* and Municipal Commissions for Tourism. There are also other situations in which there is no particular tourism department responsible for tourism affairs, either at regional or local level.

Generally, it is recognized that tourism boards may play an important role in the regional tourism organization by stimulating and coordinating the tourism development process within their regions. However, according to a study conducted by Costa (1996), their small size; limited budgets; lack of qualified staff; little attention paid to planning and development; excessive spending on administration and on ineffective promotional activities; incapacity to coordinate the large spectrum of organizations and to bring together the amalgamation of interests; and excessive influence of political parties on their activities, explain the poor capacity demonstrated by tourism boards in assuming a leading role within regional tourism organization.

The study of the strength of tourism boards in a network, in order to examine whether organizations are in practice linked together, helped to show what sort of business or administrative relationships are established among them or, alternatively, whether they just result from a package of legislation issued by the government.

Using the example of the Rota da Luz board (located in the coastal central region and being constituted by 14 municipalities), it can be observed that there are four nodes which are linked to the network by just one arch (see Figure 5.1), showing that these organizations are only connected to the network by the tourism board, which means that after disconnecting it, four actors lose their ties to the network (see Figure 5.2). This might indicate that some organizations are associated with the network just because a law was enacted with the objective of including them in the web, thus not existing in practice a network of relationships among the organizations that make part of the tourism board.

Results of the study indicate that, despite including a number of members, the administration of tourism at regional level is dominated by a few organizations, such as tourism boards, regional planning agencies and the municipality where the board has its headquarters. Generally, this cluster accounts for over 50 percent of the total connectivity. It was also found that, within the regional tourism organization, partially as a result of their small size, private sector organizations have few links to other organizations, lower levels of prominence and little capacity to influence decisions, thus assuming a peripheral role, even if their importance to the tourism organization is recognized. Private sector and also

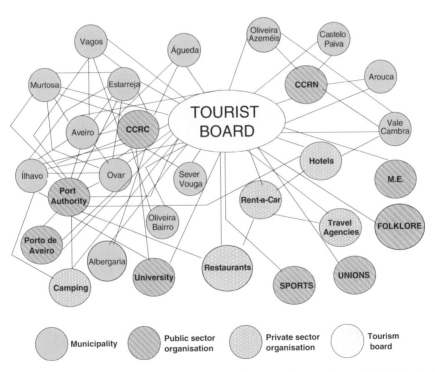

Figure 5.1: Network of relationships established among the members of the Rota da Luz tourism board (RTRL).
*Source*: Costa, 1996.

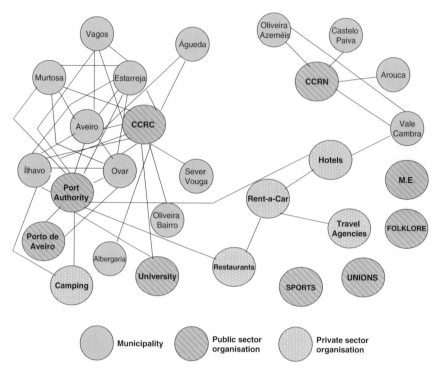

Figure 5.2: Network of relationships established among the members of the Rota da Luz
tourism board (RTRL) in the absence of the board.
*Source*: Costa, 1996.

medium-size public sector organizations (especially located in the interior areas) have low
levels of connectivity within the network (less than 10 percent); therefore, they tend to
operate much more on an individual basis.

Moreover, findings led to the conclusion that the importance of planning and environmental agencies within the tourism organization depends on the level of tourism development of the region; that is, planning and environmental organizations assume greater
importance in areas characterized by higher levels of tourism development. Since
Portuguese tourism is excessively bound to coastal areas, most regions located in the interior have little influence in the decision-making process, which brings strong imbalances
of power into the administration.

Despite their small size, most boards prefer to work in isolation instead of setting up
strategic alliances, or even mergers, with other boards capable of boosting their power and
capacity to intervene in the development process. In addition, there is poor coordination
with the national government, as well as the horizontal coordination of tourism policy and
strategies set up by other departments are very difficult to achieve. It was also found that
tourism boards operate in isolation from their members, resulting in regional policies that
offer poor quality and little capacity to represent all interests and groups associated with
the tourism sector, and have led to the fragmentation of regional administration.

Santos (2000) has also identified that the lack of cooperative culture and the absence of networking structure make the different agents to act on the basis of a set of individual strategies developed internally by each sector, this constituting the major limitation of the regional institutional structure in Portugal. It is argued that these Portuguese weaknesses can only be overcome if inter- and intra-regional cooperative relationships were reinforced.

Networks may bring significant improvements not only to the planning process but also into the administrative structure in which the planning activity is carried out. As seen previously, the way in which Portuguese regional tourism administration operates is based on an informal networking of organizations, though very weak. Their functioning discourages participation of many participants, since policies are set up in a formal and top-down way, resulting in fragmented and uncoordinated actions set up in the field.

When questioned about whether or not the bureaucratic way in which tourism boards are run in Portugal should be replaced by horizontal forms of administration based on the network philosophy, the vast majority of the organizations linked to regional tourism organization showed their willingness to accept tourism networks in substitution of the present administration. Although recognizing their theoretical importance, it was further suggested that networks could be difficult to put into practice because of opposition to change, unwillingness to share information, lobbying, lengthy decision-making process, disputes and conflicts, among other reasons.

However, the benefits pointed out by the same participants far outnumbered the problems that could emerge from the establishment of tourism networks in Portugal. The most important advantage is the better horizontal coordination of policies; that is, by giving an effective voice and empowering all participants, networks are able to strengthen the communication channels among organizations in order to lead to stronger commitments and to improve the inter-sector coordination of policies. Furthermore, it would lead to the establishment of better-informed policies and better management of tourism resources. Networks could also bring more efficiency and effectiveness to the operation of the regional tourism administration, new dynamics into their functioning, and make them more powerful and stronger for influencing national policies.

The study, thus, revealed that as a result of the characteristics and potential offered by networks, they present a credible alternative for the way in which regional tourism administration should move forward in the future. It also concluded that, if the government stimulates the establishment of tourism networks at the regional level in Portugal, they can be a reality since the vast majority of regional tourism organizations showed great willingness to join.

## Challenges for Tourism in Peripheral Areas: The Case of Caramulo

It has been recognized by the European Union (EU) that it is essential to diminish the gap between peripheral regions and metropolitan areas. The 1992 Maastricht Treaty acknowledged for the first time the role of tourism in promoting economic and social cohesion, thus reducing regional disparities.

Literature began to draw its attention on tourism in peripheral areas after the international conference on this subject held in September 1997 in Bornholm, Denmark. Two special issues of journals (the *International Journal of Contemporary Hospitality Management*, *10*(5), 1998 — covering small hospitality businesses — and the *International Journal of Tourism Research*, *1*(5), 1999 — looking at the broader issues of tourism in peripheral areas), the proceedings of the conference (Brown & Hall, 1999) and one book (Brown & Hall, 2000) resulted from the contributions presented at the conference.

One main conclusion of the conference was that insular and peripheral areas has several common problems and can benefit from sharing experiences, avoiding previous mistakes. It was also demonstrated that those regions, which have not explored their tourism potential fully, emerge as new and innovative destinations, following the collapse of traditional activities (such as agriculture and some industries). Service sector activities are frequently advocated as being sympathetic alternatives to the existing primary sector economies. Tourism, leisure and recreation activities are thus regarded as a means to achieve competitive advantage and are expected to play a major role in the development and prosperity of those regions.

Although relatively small, Portugal is a very diverse country, with pronounced differences between north and south, and the coast and the inland region. As a consequence of geographic constraints to many economic activities in peripheral areas, underdevelopment has favored the preservation of unique landscapes, environmental features, culture and tradition, which are being re-valued in post-modern societies. Caramulo is located in the Portuguese central interior region (see Figure 5.3) and comprehends four municipalities (Águeda, Oliveira de Frades, Tondela and Vouzela). It is situated in a mountainous area, which confers it a peripheral position.

The territory of Caramulo is characterized by an ageing population, which until recently had in agriculture its means of living. In spite agriculture had always been the main economic activity, it has faced a sharp decline in favor to industry and services in the last decade (see Table 5.1). Tourism can therefore play an important role in local economy and

Figure 5.3: Location of Caramulo.

Table 5.1: Some indicative characteristics of the Caramulo area.

| | Year of reference | Caramulo | Águeda | Oliveira de Frades | Tondela | Vouzela |
|---|---|---|---|---|---|---|
| Area (km$^2$) | n.a. | 1038.60 | 333.50 | 147.45 | 366.00 | 191.65 |
| Population | 2001 | 102.550 | 49.016 | 10.519 | 31.152 | 11.863 |
| Population variation (%) | 1991/2001 | 3.4 | 11.3 | −0.6 | −2.8 | −4.9 |
| Population density (person per km$^2$) | 2001 | 98.74 | 146.97 | 71.34 | 85.11 | 61.90 |
| Isolated places (%) | 2001 | 4.2 | 4.8 | 7.2 | 2.2 | 3.9 |
| Places with more than 2000 inhabitants (%) | 2001 | 11.2 | 15.2 | — | 12.8 | — |
| Elderly population (%) | 2001 | 18.9 | 15.5 | 19.6 | 22.8 | 22.2 |
| Life surplus (%) | 2000 | | 3.2 | −3.0 | −5.2 | −4.2 |
| Illiterates (%) | 2001 | 7.4 | 5.9 | 9.2 | 8.7 | 9.0 |
| Population with higher education (%) | 2001 | 6.3 | 7.1 | 5.3 | 5.9 | 5.0 |
| Unemployment rate (%) | 2001 | 4.4 | 2.9 | 5.1 | 6.4 | 5.5 |
| Rate of dependents elders (%) | 2001 | 36.6 | 28.6 | 40.4 | 45.8 | 45.3 |
| **Primary sector** | | | | | | |
| Percentage of total | 2001 | 9.3 | 2.1 | 17.8 | 17.5 | 16.1 |
| Variation (%) | 1991/2001 | 297 | 784 | 571 | 405 | 591 |
| **Secondary sector** | | | | | | |
| Percentage of total | 2001 | 49.9 | 59.9 | 42.2 | 36.5 | 42.7 |
| Variation (%) | 1991/2001 | 42.8 | 9.3 | 62.9 | 17.0 | 184 |
| **Tertiary sector** | | | | | | |
| Percentage of total | 2001 | 40.8 | 38.0 | 40.0 | 46.0 | 41.2 |
| Variation (%) | 1991/2001 | 112.4 | 53.0 | 33.3 | 47.0 | 32.7 |
| Number of enterprises | 2001 | 11.236 | 5.679 | 1.235 | 3.105 | 1.217 |
| Tourism enterprises (%) | 2001 | 6.4 | 7.2 | 5.9 | 5.4 | 18.4 |

*Note*: n.a. = Not applicable.
*Source*: National Institute for Statistics.

in communities' development. Products are delivered by small and medium tourism enterprises (SMTEs), mostly in the form of family-run businesses, whose workers lack of specific training. For a number of reasons, but especially because of the lack of tourist infrastructures and of a strong positioning strategy, the study area had always been left out of the traditional tourist routes.

Nevertheless, the territory possesses an exceptional natural environment and a rich cultural legacy. The variety and diversity of assets from which to harvest tourism opportunities confer an enormous potential to Caramulo, which can transform itself in a regional honey pot.

However, it should be noted that tourism faces several constraints in peripheral areas, which usually are characterized as lacking the appropriate tourist infrastructure, skilled workforce, entrepreneurship and has having limited market opportunities, among other factors (Wanhill, 1997; Morrison, 1998; Wanhill & Buhalis, 1999; Nash & Martin, 2003). In accordance with the arguments presented before, the way Portuguese less-favored regions should deal with that kind of constraints should be through the strengthening of network relationships.

It is recognized that tourism needs development networks that exhibit both exogenous and endogenous features (Williams & MacLeod, 2004). While, endogenous development set within the local framework is particularly important from a perspective of tourism in peripheral areas, exogenous forces must also play a role in tourism development, as the area must be linked in some way to a global network.

The establishment of a milestone investment program in Portugal (as discussed in the next section), which was the driven force for a change in the way the tourism sector started to be viewed in many regions, constitutes an important tool for less-developed areas to promote economic development through the encouragement of sustainable tourism activities. The Caramulo region, as many areas in Portugal, took this opportunity to encourage several stakeholders to strengthen and enhance the existing informal network of relationships, which may bind tourism participants together. One of the main goals of this program is the establishment of formal networks, having as basis the already existing informal links, and the development of strategic guidelines.

## Regional Tourism Policy Program Anchored on Private Sector Investment

The case of PITER, a Regional Tourism Policy Program Anchored on Private Sector Investment, constitutes an innovative methodology intended to promote tourism development, thus breaking up with traditional forms of regulation, on which public sector's role was mainly that of controlling and enforcing the law. It aims to bring together both private and public investment, allowing and enhancing a close relationship between public and private organizations that operate within the tourism sector, thus constituting an important instrument for the development of regions which are in most cases remote and structurally weak (Costa, 2002).

In general, tourist organizations face several constraints in an attempt to plan for tourism, and the results are usually indicative plans. Some aspects of physical development can be enforced by regulation, but in most cases tourism planning lacks an adequate legislative base. This program is pioneer in Portugal in interconnecting these components and in allocating investment incentives.

PITER's philosophy can be materialized in five strategic key vectors (Inácio, Rocha, & Ferreira, 2001):

- The program has its foundation in the development of a tourism strategic and integrated vision of the territory, materialized with the identification of broad goals in accordance with national and regional policies and with the creation of a tourism development strategy.
- While analyzing both private and public sector investments, attention must be given to core projects that will materialize the tourism strategy, which has been developed for the territory. Those are defined as anchor projects, which supported by other complementary projects, should demonstrate economic and strategic synergies. There is a minimum limit of 15 million euros for the total of projects considered, 50 percent of which must be private investment.
- The materialization of this program presupposes the dynamization and consolidation of partnerships between private and public stakeholders, not only in the definition of strategic goals but also in the implementation of the tourism development strategy. The involvement of different partners require the existence of articulation mechanisms and an internal organization capable of coordinating all aspects, thus being important the establishment of a program leader.
- The implementation of several interconnected investment projects should be preceded by their economic impact assessment, in terms of income and employment generation at the regional and local levels. These projects should be able to demonstrate their effects throughout the local economy.
- The last vector is also innovative because the program has its own investment incentive system. This facilitates and encourages the development of tourism by the private sector through the provision of interesting investment incentives to facilitate new product development and the enhancement of existing products.

This program constitutes a paradigmatic example of how both public and private sectors can be brought together successfully and promote development within a legal framework. It should be outlined the way in which the Portuguese Government has decided to direct the tourism development process in two different, though complementary, ways. On one hand, the government is placing the message across that tourism investment should be underpinned on solid tourism strategies. On the other, the government is also stressing that both public and private sector investment should be brought together into the same package of investment because, in most circumstances, they complement each other.

The region of Caramulo, although comprising a large number and diversity of tourist resources, presents four main types of products (see Figure 5.4).

Those constitute the core of the cluster of products (see Figure 5.5), essential to create an image for the territory.

Nature tourism is the main product, constituting the support for other important types of tourism, like rural and active tourism. Cultural tourism is also an important product, alongside with gastronomy and, in a lesser extent, wine tourism.

This region is perceived as being peripheral. The PITER program is therefore seen as a mechanism to prompt investment in an area which often lacks opportunities, but possesses

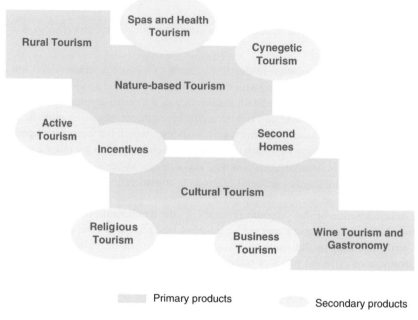

Figure 5.4: Main tourist products of Caramulo.
*Source*: Costa, 2005a.

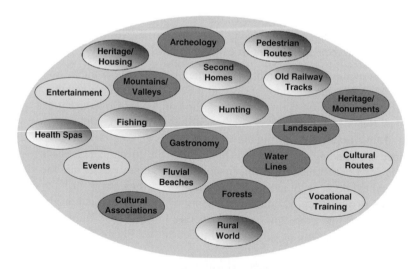

Figure 5.5: Regional cluster of products.
*Source*: Costa, 2005a.

a great potential for tourism development. The implementation of the tourism strategy consigned in the program presupposes a territorial intervention, which take action at several levels: physical, financial and institutional (see Figure 5.6). This intervention, aiming the implementation of the tourism development strategy, takes into consideration the interconnection between the object and the objectives of the program. The strategy itself focuses in four main areas: products (supply-side), markets (demand-side), socio-economic development (impacts) and the institutional structure.

Therefore, having as basis:

- the existence of a territory with many opportunities for tourism development;
- the existence of a potential demand market that can be attracted by the richness of the territory's resources, enabling the commercialization of tourism products; and
- the existence of resources that can be improved and of equipments that can be built or modernized, helping to consolidate the tourism supply basis at the regional level

three main areas of investment were identified in Caramulo according to the dynamics of tourists' attraction (see Figure 5.7).

Caramulo's tourism development strategy, which implies deepening the networking among local and regional actors, is supported essentially by private initiatives, through the establishment of a network of different types of accommodation and food and beverage equipments. The public sector is less directly involved in the development of tourism products; it assumes the role of equipment and infrastructure provider, is responsible for preserving and enhancing natural and historical attractions, for offering leisure and recreation

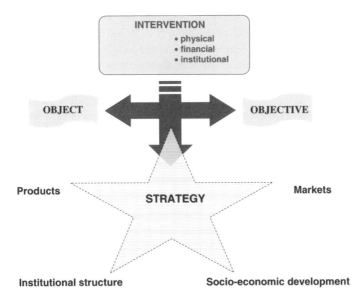

Figure 5.6: General framework concerning the implementation of the tourism strategy in Caramulo.
*Source*: Costa, 2005a.

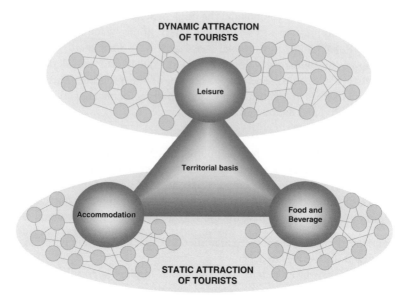

Figure 5.7: Dynamics of tourists' attraction.
*Source*: Costa, 2005b.

activities as well as it is critical to stimulating and facilitating private sector investment. The public sector is also responsible for the creation of a coordination body which will be responsible for monitoring the implementation of the whole program, producing events, developing promotional activities and a reservation center, as well as for creating an information network with demand and supply-side indicators. One of the main philosophies of the program is therefore the introduction of a new logic of coordinated and systematized support for investment within the tourism sector, thus putting an emphasis, not on individual projects, but rather on a group of investment projects.

As cooperation, rather than competition, will enable destinations to develop value chains and to achieve their strategic objectives, this seems to be a successful public–private sector partnership in tourism development at the local level. It intends to improve the destination's tourism attractiveness, and all stakeholders involved in the program are working closely and simultaneously for the same goal.

## Conclusion

Traditionally, the theories of clustering and the cluster concept have mainly been applied to the manufacturing industry. Despite this scenario is still dominating, the service sector, from which travel and tourism industry are an important part, is fast growing and showing a great future potential. Innovations in the field of tourism have, however, been a matter of limited research and political consideration.

The preponderance of small and micro enterprises together with the fragmentation of the tourism industry constitute a constraint to development, which may be helped by regarding each individual operator as a part of an integrated system. This holistic perspective aims to bring together both private businesses as well as government stakeholders at various levels in order to foster economic growth and development.

The role of the public sector is often pivotal in peripheral areas and it is common to assist a big reluctance of the private sector to invest. The involvement of commercial sector companies in tourism development is often undermined by the perceptions of these locations by investors. The problems inherent to peripheral areas and the small scale of most enterprises dissuade private sector investors from locating in some areas because of the perceived limited returns on investment.

The PITER program is considered to be a successful example of how to promote socio-economic development in those areas lacking opportunities, associating private and public sector investment in a harmonized effort to encourage tourism initiatives. The establishment of strategic partnerships is seen as a key factor to trigger potential investment, which will benefit from the outcomes of the projects already implemented, thus consolidating the tourism supply basis. All the projects to be implemented must be in accordance with strategic guidelines developed specifically for the area, which means that besides creating a pole of investment, this program intends the creation of sustainable forms of tourism, particularly important in areas which rely heavily in their endogenous resources.

The Caramulo area, suffering from a somewhat peripherality and having a little role in the tourism in the central region of Portugal, aims to achieve sustainable development through the implementation of several integrated projects, which will result in a very comprehensive network. This can constitute the foundation of a tourism cluster in the area, as a critical mass of enterprises, skills and supporting structures will be available, in a dynamic process.

# References

Bramwell, B., & Lane, B. (2000). Collaboration and partnerships in tourism planning. In: B. Bramwell, & B. Lan (Eds), *Tourism collaboration and partnerships: Politics, practice and sustainability* (pp. 1–19). Clevedon: Channel View Publications.

Brown, F., & Hall, D. (1999). Case studies of tourism in peripheral areas. *Proceedings from the international seminar on tourism in peripheral areas of Europe*, Research Centre of Bornholm, Bornholm.

Brown, F., & Hall, D. (2000). *Tourism in peripheral areas.* Aspects of tourism Series 2. Clevedon: Channel View Publications.

Caniëls, M.C.J. (2000). *Knowledge spillovers and economic growth: Regional growth differentials across Europe.* Cheltenham: Edward Elgar.

Costa, C. (1996). *Towards the improvement of the efficiency and effectiveness of tourism planning and development at the regional level. Planning, organisations and networks. The case of Portugal.* Unpublished PhD thesis. University of Surrey, Guildford.

Costa, C. (2001). An emerging tourism planning paradigm? A comparative analysis between town and tourism planning. *International Journal of Tourism Research, 3*(6), 425–441.

Costa, C. (2002). O Papel dos Sectores Público e Privado na Implementação de Projectos Estruturantes Regionais (PITER): Uma Proposta de Metodologia. In: IFT (Ed.), *Património e Turismo: Ciclo de Debates 1999* (pp. 143–163). Lisboa: IFT.

Costa, C. (2005a). (coord.), *PITER Terras do Vouga e do Caramulo.* Aveiro: GrupUnave/ Universidade de Aveiro.

Costa, C. (2005b). *New policies for the development of the tourism sector in Portugal.* Paper presented at the University of Aveiro, October 8th.

Edgell, D. (2004 May 26). Ten Important International Tourism Issues for 2004. TRINET Discussion list [online]. Available from : trinet-1@hawaii.edu.

Enright, M.J. (2001). Regional clusters: What we know and what we should know. *Paper presented for the Kiel Institute international workshop on innovation clusters and interregional competition,* November.

Holbrook, A., & Wolfe, D.A. (2002). *Knowledge, clusters and regional innovation: Economic development in Canada.* Montreal: School of Policy Studies.

Inácio, G., Rocha, M., & Ferreira, T. (2001). Desenvolvimento Turístico: O Papel Inovador da Administração. *Economia & Prospectiva, 17,* 99–108.

Inskeep, E. (1991). *Tourism planning: An integrated and sustainable development approach.* Van New York: Nostrand Reinhold.

Kim, L. (1999). *Learning and innovation in economic development.* New horizons in the economics of innovation. Cheltenham: Edward Elgar.

Mill, R.C., & Morrison, A.M. (1992). *The tourism system: An introductory text* (2nd ed.). New Jersey: Prentice-Hall.

Morrison, A.M. (1998). Small firm co-operative marketing in a peripheral tourism region. *International Journal of Contemporary Hospitality Management, 10*(5), 191–197.

Murphy, P.E. (1985). *Tourism: A community approach.* New York: Methuen.

Nash, R., & Martin A. (2003). Tourism in peripheral areas: The challenges for northeast Scotland. *International Journal of Tourism Research, 5*(3), 161–181.

Nordin, S. (2003). *Tourism clustering & innovation: Paths to economic growth & development.* Östersund: European Tourism Research Institute.

OECD. (1999). Boosting innovation: The cluster approach. *OECD Proceedings.*

Porter, M.E. (1990). *The competitive advantage of nations.* New York: The Free Press.

Porter, M.E. (1998). Clusters and the new economics of competition. *Harvard Business Review, 76*(6), 77–90.

Santos, D. (2000). Innovation and territory: Which strategies to promote regional innovation systems in Portugal? *European Urban and Regional Studies, 7*(2), 147–157.

Simmie, J. (1997). *Innovation, networks and learning regions.* Regional policy and development series n.18. London: Jessica Kingsley Publishers.

Wanhill, S. (1997). Peripheral area tourism: A European perspective in progress. *Tourism and Hospitality Research, 3*(1), 47–70.

Wanhill, S., & Buhalis, D. (1999). Introduction: Challenges for tourism in peripheral areas. *International Journal of Tourism Research, 1*(5), 295–297.

Williams, F., & MacLeod, M. (2004). Europe at the margins: EU regional policy, peripherality and rurality. *Proceedings from the international seminar on the role of peripherality in tourism development.* Angers: Regional Studies Association.

WTO. (2002). *Tourism in the age of alliances, mergers and acquisitions.* Madrid: World Tourism Organization.

WTO. (2000). *Public–private sector cooperation: Enhancing tourism competitiveness.* Madrid: World Tourism Organization.

Chapter 6

# Destination Governance and Contemporary Development Models

Bo Svensson, Sara Nordin and Arvid Flagestad

## Introduction

Tourism is often identified as a future growth industry, and destination development has very much emerged as a key issue in local and regional development. Destination development is here understood as a process aiming at improving the attractiveness and functioning of places and regions as visiting areas. The argument in this chapter is that the governance perspective is well suited for improving our understanding of the dynamics as an alternative to both the traditional planning perspective and the management perspective on destinations. This belief is grounded on a handful of assumptions about tourist destinations and their development process. The assumptions are also relevant from a governance perspective:

(1) There is a *multi-actor complexity* of the destination that needs to be taken into account.
(2) It is also likely, that certain *resource dependencies* between the actors involved are important dynamic factors of the process and need to be understood.
(3) The *public–private dimension* of the destination may be important; i.e. the role of government vis-à-vis firms needs to be taken into account.

The governance perspective is well suited for handling these aspects of the destination. It draws attention to complex sets of organisations and their interactions, and usually implies that the public–private dimension of this interaction is a crucial component for understanding the policy process (cf. Rhodes, 1996, 1997). A governance perspective then implies that neither government nor business is in charge of the process but that the interdependency between them may be crucial. In line with the above argument, governance implies less control and predictability, no self-evident leadership and no given hierarchy.

In recent research into local and regional development, a lot of attention has been paid to partnerships, clusters and innovation systems as development models. The partnership model is common both in political science research into governance and in studies of tourist destinations. The cluster and the innovation system approach, however, have entered the

Tourism Local Systems and Networking
Copyright © 2006 by Elsevier Ltd.
All rights of reproduction in any form reserved
ISBN: 0-08-044938-7

field of tourism research only recently and rarely occur in studies on governance. The purpose here is to explore these models from a governance perspective in order to illuminate to what extent and how the governance perspective makes sense when dealing with these models in the destination context. As will be shown, the models draw attention to different features of governance and even suggest different forms of governance and government involvement. While the public–private partnership perspective draws attention to linkages between government bodies and private enterprise interests in particular, the cluster model deals primarily with business dynamics, and the innovation system model brings a more complex interplay between governments, firms and research into the centre of attention.

The three sections to follow deal with these models in turn. Empirical observations are drawn from recent research into the Swedish ski resort Åre and are used to illustrate certain points in this mainly theoretical effort.[1] The concluding section summarises the major arguments concerning the governance perspective on the basis of theoretical and empirical observations made on partnerships, clusters and innovation systems. It also discusses implications for empirical research into tourist destination development based on these arguments.

## Partnerships

As mentioned in the previous section, partnerships are commonly studied both in the governance literature and research into tourist destinations. This section will outline a conceptual framework for partnership analysis based on three features of partnerships — *inclusiveness, accountability* and *coherence*.[2]

Scholars have for more than a decade observed and been occupied with partnerships as a driving force for transformations of regional and urban governance (Bailey, 1994; Pierre, 1998; Stoker, 1998; Halkier & Damborg, 2000). Partnerships have become a label on ambitions to bring actors together in new constellations for the purpose of joint problem solving and policy-making.[3] Partnerships are made up of "people and organisations from some combination of public, business and civil constituencies who engage in voluntary, mutually beneficial, innovative relationships to address common societal aims through combining their resources and competencies" (Nelson & Zadek, 2000). The multi-actor nature is thus central to the partnership idea, although a partnership may refer also to arrangements involving only two partners. This brings us to the first feature of our framework:

- *Inclusiveness*, i.e. the capacity of partnerships to widen the range of actors involved in the processing of destination development activities.

Who participates, which roles do they play, and on what basis is access to the partnership decided? These are some of the questions relating to inclusiveness. In addition, the

---

[1] Cases in question are taken from research by ETOUR on the ski resort of Åre in Sweden, in particular Nordin and Svensson, (2005).

[2] Framework modified from Svensson and Östhol (2002).

[3] A range of terms has been coined for analysing what are basically aspects of the same phenomenon: policy networks (Marsh & Rhodes, 1992; van Waarden, 1992; Jordan, 1990; Conzelmann, 1995); development/advocacy coalitions (Sabatier & Jenkins-Smith, 1993); inter-organisational relations (Halkier, 2000; Hanf & O'Toole, 1992; Hanf & Scharpf, 1978); modern governance (Kooiman, 1993; Rhodes, 1996).

idea of partnership in the local and regional development context brings attention to the public–private dimension of governance. This is, of course, true also when destination development is the process in focus. One might on good grounds argue that tourism is even more sensitive in this respect, due to its high reliance on public sector investments and service to make a destination a well-functioning area for visitors.

A simple empirical reference may illustrate the sensitiveness of partnerships in this respect. In the Swedish ski resort Åre, partnership arrangements have been frequent throughout the years. The municipality and some key actors in the destination undoubtedly have had close ties, thus illustrating the importance of the public–private dimension of destination development. Today, the most significant example of partnership in the destination is the Vision 2011 group. It consists of members from the leading tourism companies, politicians and senior officers, who have selected themselves after position, influence or access to capital. The partnership is not formalised to any greater extent, has not been very open and caused controversies between insiders and outsiders in the destination at different occasions. In terms of inclusiveness, this must be considered a closed body, which might question its legitimacy. This brings us to the second feature of our framework:

- *Accountability* concerns the location of responsibility and the mechanisms through which decisions-makers may be held accountable.

This is a highly sensitive issue that might threaten the legitimacy of partnerships, and this is where the distinction between public and private is most evident, and also most controversial. Particularly important in a governance perspective is the relationship between partnerships and the elected bodies. This is, of course, something the public partners cannot neglect, while private actors are less sensitive to criticism of this type — it is simply not their immediate responsibility. When the issue of democratic legitimacy comes up, partnership defenders often refer to the broad legitimacy the multi-actor partnership derives from its members. Again the ski resort in question provides an example, as it was obvious at the last municipal election that the town mayor was replaced in office by the opposition leader after a debate and campaign that focused on the close ties between the mayor and leading business interests in the village, suggesting businessmen rather than politicians being in power.

In addition to questions about inclusiveness and accountability, the coherence of partnerships is necessary to deal with in order to understand what it actually accomplishes.

- *Coherence* refers to the ability to gain support for a common outlook on destination development and the mobilisation of common resources for implementation of agreed operations.

The presence of partnerships does not guarantee that they make a difference, let alone add value to the process. In terms of empirical research this leads to a focus on the way in which resources are mobilised and combined. The last point is crucial because it deals with the question of whether a partnership makes a difference, or not. Both dimensions of coherence suggested, the common outlook and resource mobilisation, are vital for ensuring that a partnership can make a difference in the policy process. Their existence, however, cannot be taken for granted; strategies may lose coherence if the partners involved pursue their own goals without taking those of others into account, and it is of course perfectly possible to devise grand strategic schemes without having the resources for implementing them.

Several types of resources may make a difference, whereof financial resources are perhaps the most prominent, but where also knowledge, know-how, information, authority and legitimacy can be of crucial importance.

The Vision 2011 partnership plays a central role in forming and implementing a destination-embracing strategy with common goals on how to develop the destination. It is also an arena for mobilising resources for public–private investments and large-scale projects that could not have been carried out without this kind of joint approach. A recent and very clear example of this is the Mix Megapol Arena, an event and congress hall, and an establishment that has been of vital importance in developing Åre into an all-year-round tourist destination.

When making empirical observations on coherence it is important to be aware that partnerships differ in purpose and function. The following categorisation makes distinctions between three types of partnerships(cf. Halkier & Damborg, 2000; Svensson & Östhol, 2001). *Strategic partnerships* involve a significant element of co-ordination of activities between different actors in issues of long-term importance for the development of a certain destination, most likely based on mutual trust and commitment between the involved. To be efficient, they need to include the key public and private actors in the destination. They may stand out as an ideal form in destination development; something policy-makers strive for and are encouraged to establish, but also risk falling short of in their attempts. *Institutional partnerships* are tied to individual development bodies, such as destination companies, where public and private stakeholders manifest their cooperation in a joint organisation. This type of partnership may symbolise a good environment for cooperation where new institutions tend to emerge, or be the consequence of attempts at overcoming cooperation problems. In this case, the partnership needs a certain decision-making autonomy and financial resources at its disposal to become efficient. *Project partnerships* are time-limited arrangements tied to hands-on local projects and motivated by common ideas and interests in a particular issue. They do not depend on a favourable surrounding structure, although public–private governance structures tend to be advantageous, neither do they presume any obligations besides, or in prolongation of, project completion. This type of partnership is likely to emerge where there are difficulties in agreeing on common visions and long-term goals for the destination, but still possible to find common interests in specific measures of significant importance.

Historically the ski resort Åre has been observed to be a destination shaped by different large-scale projects (Bodén & Rosenberg, 2004). The actor constellations around these projects can be categorised as project partnerships and the destination has been skilful in mobilising resources around such projects, including a cable car in the 1970s. The current launching of a strategy for developing the summer season seems to create limits to what can be achieved by the vision 2011 group. Hence new forms of governance seem to be in demand in order to continue to stimulate development. This is also the shortcoming of loosely linked and not formalised partnerships, which has led to a discussion of whether a more institutionalised partnership is needed in the destination.

As has been noted earlier, the partnership model of destination development goes well with the governance perspective. While there is a clear connection between partnerships and governance, that is not obvious for clusters and innovation systems. Nevertheless, such a perspective will now be adopted in an attempt to illuminate the relevance of the governance perspective in the context of these development models.

# Clusters[4]

The cluster perspective on destination development puts the interaction between firms at the centre of attention, but it also focuses on the environment in which the firms interact and the linkages to associated institutions such as universities. Cluster theory moreover suggests that cluster development contribute to the process of innovation and economic growth (Porter, 1990). In recent time a lively debate over the possibility of cluster-building as a means of reaching local and regional development has been taking place, as the number of cluster-based policies have increased worldwide. From this point of view, clusters are not simply the outcome of spontaneous business logic, but something that can be developed and supported through conscious strategies. To view clusters from the governance perspective clearly belongs to this latter approach.

A cluster view on tourism is interesting for a number of reasons. One is the obvious resource dependencies among the actors. Much of an individual tourism business' potential to achieve growth lies outside the power and the influence of the company, since the visitor will base his or her experience on the overall impression of the destination visited. On the other hand, it is evident that a well-working system of players can create added value. In accordance, cluster theory suggests that some of the key factors determining competitive advantages lie outside the boundaries of individual firms. The cluster model on destination development clearly rests on a multi-actor complexity that puts firms and their ties at the centre of attention.

Cooperation, at least to some extent, is present in basically all destinations, but far from all qualify for the level of cooperation found in clusters. One may on good grounds argue that the destination of Åre belongs to the category of regional tourism clusters. The destination has a clear concentration of tourism firms, it has a dominant actor in Skistar as a key driver of development during the ski season, it has plenty of complementary firms within the fields of outdoor equipment, design, ski and outdoor magazines, etc. and there is a close proximity of companies in a limited geographical area giving way for a flow of knowledge and information as well as human capital. There is moreover a very strong trademark and a clear vision for the future development.

Many destinations, however, lack a system dimension and do not have a shared vision or even common goals. In this context, an integrative governance challenge is to foster synergies and trust as well as promote civic entrepreneurs who can facilitate further development. Initiatives to promote clusters in early phases sometimes depend on public resources and involvement, even if their success eventually depends on firm performance. The boundaries of a cluster do not generally follow ordinary administrative borders such as municipalities, counties or even countries. This might be a problem when it comes to the public–private interplay and the role of government in particular at the regional and local level, due to regulations limiting the ability to look beyond traditional boundaries.

Cluster developments are also challenging the old traditional dividing lines between the private and public sector. Sölvell et al. state that in the emerging model of economic development: "The public sector lacks the knowledge to understand the priorities for individual

---

[4] This section is to a great extent based on the report "Tourism Clustering & Innovation – Paths to Economic Growth & Development", by Sara Nordin (2003).

clusters and it lacks the policy instruments to implement all necessary actions. The private sector, however, is not organized to engage in joint efforts in business environment upgrading and it, too, has control only over a subset of the relevant policy areas" (Sölvell, Lindqvist & Ketels, 2003). This calls for coordination and cooperation among public and private stakeholders. In the example of Åre, the local government has turned over some of their traditional decision-making to the local business association to make the process faster and easier to handle for the firms. This has created an open dialogue and a good relation between the public and the private sector.

In the network society, old forms of governance generally based on command and control forms of imperative orders appear to be increasingly ineffective, as there has been a decline in hierarchical or top-down methods for determining goals and means. The policy process required in a cluster-based economy needs to rely more on consensus building and inclusiveness.

Cluster theories have not only been praised, but also criticized. It has often been underlined that industry clusters identified in the "real world" have little resemblance to the ideal ones described in the literature. Reality is often more complex. For example, Stopford and Strange point out when discussing the role of government that Porter fails to recognise the importance of government and government composition in relation to clusters (Stopford & Strange, 1991). This may be of particular importance when dealing with tourism, where government interests are highly influential (Wolfe and Gertler, 2004 and Wolfe, 2004). This flaw is obviously something the governance perspective on cluster development may overcome.

The government sector at local, regional and national level can facilitate tourism cluster development by efforts in various areas. They can support or provide cluster management, identify market failures and improve policies that affect the tourism actors and provide specialised infrastructure that benefits the tourism environment as well as implement the appropriate training and education, offer extended financial instruments to support the growth of the cluster and provide meeting arenas in the form of platforms for networking and exchange of the latest information and knowledge. In cluster-based economic developments the government sector needs to be a partner in a collaborative process rather than the central power. Hence the focus should be on coordination rather than centralisation, as cooperation and coordination among individuals, firms and sectors for their mutual advantage is what clustering in essence is about.

The level of government involvement required to stimulate cluster development vary a great deal. So does the role of public policy. It is clear that the content of economic policy and the structure of the economic policy-making process are important issues. Long-term commitment is moreover a vital factor. Clusters generally exist within a unique system of regulations, laws and conventions governing its operation and affecting its access to research and development, capital and other factors of importance. However, the role of government remains pivotal. They set the stage for the necessary socio-economic conditions required to foster the growth of competitive clusters of firms. International best practice shows that early political support helps in developing clusters and that government stakeholders may play a critical role in supporting the process, but that private sector leadership must follow (see Figure 6.1).

This is also apparent from Åre where the firms are the central actors. In a regional cluster environment such as the destination of Åre the governance structure has supported the

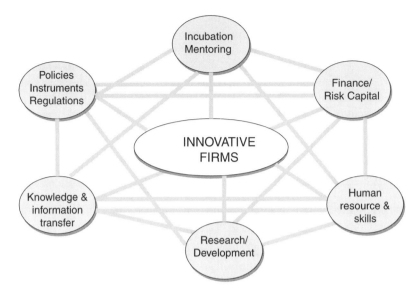

Figure 6.1: Cluster model (National Research Council, Canada).

development of collaboration as well as competition within the destination, but also worked to develop a broader industry base than one just focusing on tourism with a number of complementary industries. This has enabled skilled people to move to the destination and settle down on a long-term basis even if not all working family members are within the field of tourism. In turn, this has lead to a growing population, increasing job opportunities, high levels of investments, in for instance, housing and infrastructure and ultimately rising tax incomes in the community — all goals of the 2011 Vision.

The public–private strategy group also works hard to attract investors and get access to risk capital for new investments and innovative ideas. It is clear that the major company Skistar takes on an import role of a cluster animator and driver of innovation during the winter, but that a number of major establishments would never have taken place without the support of other industries and the public sector, emphasising the significance of public–private partnerships.

It is apparent that traditional government is declining in importance in the context of cluster-based economic developments. Instead, new forms of integrative governance are required. This means that new roles for the private and public sector are emerging. Private sector participants need to acknowledge the importance of being part of a competitive cluster of firms and get involved in the work. Public sector participants need to learn how to participate in the game rather than rule it. The governance perspective can contribute to our understanding of the preconditions for successful government involvement in cluster-building processes.

## Innovation Systems

The governance view on innovation systems more explicitly brings the role of knowledge institutions into the picture. Like clusters, the innovation system issue has in the 1980s and

1990s entered the debate on local and regional development with the general awareness that innovation is a crucial component in the renewal of economies, and that innovation is a process that may be supported with certain measures. The original debate on innovation systems is, however, usually occupied with national and more lately with regional innovation systems. Local innovation systems in terms of destinations as places have so far rarely entered the discussion.

The components, or actors, in an innovation system (Lundvall, 1992; Freeman, 1995; Spilling, 2002) may consist of individual firms, public authorities and institutions within education, research and development. The innovation system is by definition a multi-actor structure. The Triple Helix model of innovation points at the three components above, while the OECD model highlights the important centre point of knowledge dissemination. The distinctive element of the innovation system is the infrastructure of innovations, including research and research-funding institutions and universities (Östhol & Lembke, 2003).

Critical to the functioning of a system are relations, ability to create actions and interaction supporting a collective performance beneficiary to the actors, and the critical mass in terms of a system being sufficiently complete to create manifold synergies and complementarities. In the end, performance of an innovation system should be related to "effectiveness in producing, diffusing and exploiting economically useful knowledge" (Lundvall, 1992).

If we look closer at the key components of the system, their roles may be described as follows:

- *Commercial enterprises* constitute the great motivators and drivers for innovative actions in every aspect of the totality of the destination as well as within the enterprise itself. This statement is assumed to be valid for firms within tourism destinations as for other industries. Increased competitiveness through innovative actions is at the heart of every commercial entity. Competitiveness of the destination is ultimately measured through profitability of the commercial enterprises. Prosperity and wealth is governed by productivity and value created in the enterprises (Flagestad, 2002; Hjalager, 1994, 1998, 2002; Lundvall, 1992; Nelson, 1993).
- *The political system* is responsible for creating opportunities and laying down limitations for actions within enterprises. Attitudes and actions of public authorities have great impact on the innovative climate in a destination, by for instance, facilitating an interactive learning process, influencing type of destination leadership and organisation, institutional structures, creation of a vision for the destination, etc. (Bieger, 1998; Flagestad, 2002; Hjalager, 1994, 1998, 2002; Lundvall, 1992). This point at the importance of governance processes also in innovation systems.
- *Knowledge* institutions: A key success factor for innovation is the ability to build knowledge and develop learning processes. Creation of institutionalised learning processes and feedback systems for knowledge accumulation is crucial. Most likely destination-specific learning systems should be developed and the ability to release a collective innovative capacity and tacit knowledge should be emphasised (Bellandi, 1994; Hjalager, 1994, 1998, 2002; Lundvall, 1992; Lundvall & Johnson, 1994.)

According to this categorisation, the roles of different actors are relatively clear-cut and the necessary resource-dependencies between them are obvious. Do tourism enterprises see research-based knowledge as important for their innovative capacity? Do research bodies produce knowledge that is perceived as relevant to the tourism industry? And to what extent do government bodies support these linkages? These are relevant questions that deserve attention in future tourism research (see Figure 6.2).

In the ski resort of Åre, as being our case for empirical reflections, the careful observer might sense something reminiscent of an embryonic innovation system emerging. Some of the private enterprises in the destination certainly recognise knowledge as central to further development of the destination. The most recent, and perhaps clearest, example of this is related to the already mentioned effort to develop the ski resort into an all-year-round destination. Prior to formulating the strategy, Åre gathered research-based knowledge through a project that looked into North American and Alp resorts that seemed to have managed this transformation. Research findings were thereafter discussed in workshops involving key actors in the destination and researchers, followed by a study trip to one of the studied destinations. The research effort was jointly financed by private and public sources, and local and regional government bodies obviously saw their role in supporting further interaction between the tourism industry and their knowledge support bodies.

In general, however, the innovation system requirements for the above components might be hard to meet when interpreting the typical innovation system definitions given in the literature. The population of *enterprises*, dominated by small and medium-sized

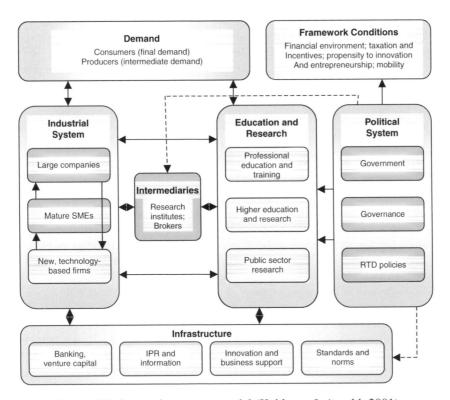

Figure 6.2: Innovation system model (Kuhlman & Arnold, 2001).

enterprises (SMEs), is often limited both in numbers and size, which means that the critical mass might be weak. In addition, knowledge is not always perceived as a key driving force within the tourism industry, rather it is often described as a low competence business in terms of staff education level. The capability of tourism enterprises as motivators and drivers of innovation therefore needs to be considered with great caution — it cannot simply be taken for granted. If these doubts about tourism enterprises are motivated they may indicate a more significant role for local and regional *public authorities* in innovation processes. Their role in facilitating the early phases of the innovation process may need to be more active and driving than in more mature business environments.

In addition, the importance of the public sector actors in innovation might also be underlined by the situation concerning *knowledge institutions*. Also these might be relatively weak in relation to the tourist destination. Universities and research institutes might be only at a distance and not naturally part of the local destination environment, which calls for government support in the creation of formal and informal institutional frameworks or arenas for knowledge management as the most critical element for the functioning of a destination innovation system. Governance in this context is perhaps more intricate in comparison with other industries and both government bodies and research bodies face great challenges in a system where the private actors might be less concerned with knowledge as a production factor.

The innovation systems' dependency on the interaction between private enterprises, knowledge institutions and government bodies again motivates the governance perspective. This is underlined by the presumed central role of government in facilitating the emergence of an innovation system. Understanding the dynamics and the role of various actors in the innovation system may help destinations in developing innovative processes, even if they cannot be regarded as fully fledged innovation systems.

## Concluding Remarks

The relevance of the governance perspective for studying destination development has been argued and illustrated in this article. It has also argued and illustrated the relevance of the perspective for studying not only partnership processes, but also clusters and innovation systems. The tourism industry is in many respects a highly political business, which motivates further research into the role and scope of government action. Better understanding of the governance process surrounding destination development is one important and often neglected field of research in this area. The policy relevance of such research is obvious, given the often high ambitions and expectations governments at different levels often express.

Governance was in the earlier sections of this article discussed with reference to three development models: the partnership model, the cluster model, and the innovation system model. The partnership model is relevant in most destinations. It is even hard to imagine a destination without any type of partnership linked to its development. It would have to be an area with one or a few businesses and basically no public interest involved in the destinations' development. There are different types of partnerships and the same destination is likely to house more than one partnership, which the governance perspective is well suited to illuminate.

The cluster model is less common in tourism research, even if this is changing, and is rarely dealt with from a governance perspective. The section on clusters illustrated the relevance of the governance perspective also in this model, by underlining the potential importance of public–private interaction in cluster development. It also suggested that tourism clusters might be more dependent on public–private interaction than clusters in the manufacturing industry, thus further motivating this approach. However, since clusters primarily are about business dynamics and competitiveness one has to be careful in drawing to far-reaching conclusions about the importance of government involvement. Governance is, however, an issue under any circumstances also in the cluster model.

The same caution in judging the role of government is motivated in the innovation system model. Government was here described as important in supporting linkages between business and knowledge production in, for example, universities and research institutes. In relation to a business like tourism, certain incentives for both business and research might be necessary in order to trigger the innovation system dynamics of a certain destination. One might wonder about the relevance of the innovation system in relation to destination development, but the idea is definitely challenging both for tourism developers and tourism researchers. It may actually raise the importance of tourism research and it should definitely be a useful reflection to make for those in the trade. The question is simple: Can tourism research support innovation?

It may thus be that all three models are worth keeping in mind when discussing destination development and also that they deserve a research interest. The governance approach is one way of entering this effort. The different models discussed here are, of course, more or less relevant in different destinations. While basically every destination qualify for partnership studies, fewer are likely to qualify for the cluster model and very few, if any, for the innovation system model. The latter models may make sense in what might be labelled "advanced" or "sophisticated" destinations. The innovation system model even requires a destination with the ambition to be a leading destination of its type. For this last mentioned type of destination, all three models bring out a specific understanding of some feature of the destination, which means that they may very well be combined in studies of destination development in general and destination governance in particular.

# References

Bailey, N. (1994). Towards a research agenda for public–private partnerships in the 1990s. *Local Economy*, 8, 292–306.

Bellandi, M. (1994). Decentralised industrial creativity in dynamic industrial districts. In: *UNCTAD/ITD/TEC/11, Tecnological dynamism in industrial districts: An alternative approach to industrialisation in developing countries?* United Nations, New York, Geneve (pp. 73–87).

Bodén, B., & Rosenberg, L. (2004). *Kommersiell turism och lokal samhällsutveckling. En studie av sex svenska fjälldestinationer*. ETOUR report R:2004:15. Edita: Västerås.

Conzelmann, T. (1995). Networking and the politics of EU regional policy: Lessons from the North Rhine–Westphalia, Nord-Pas de Calais and North-West England. *Regional and Federal Studies*, 5(2), 134–172.

Flagestad, A. (2002). *Strategic success and organisational structure in winter sports destinations*. Ph.D. dissertation, University of Bradford, UK. Vetenskapliga Bokserien, Etour, Sweden.

Freeman, C. (1995). The "National System of Innovation" in historical perspective. *Cambridge Journal of Economics, 19,* 5–24.

Halkier, H. (2000). Regional policy. An inter-organisational approach. *Regional and Industrial Policy Research Paper Series* (p. 37). EPRC, University of Strathclyde.

Halkier, H., & Damborg, C. (2000). Development bodies, networking and business promotion – the case of North Jutland, Denmark. In: M. Danson, H. Halkier, & G. Cameron (Eds), *Governance, institutional change and regional development.* Aldershot: Ashgate.

Hanf, K.I., & O'Toole, L.J. (1992). Revisiting old friends: Networks, implementation structures and the management of interorganizational relations. *European Journal of Political Research, 221,* (1–2), 163–180.

Hanf, K.I., & Scharpf, F.W. (Eds). (1978). *Interorganizational policy making: Limits to coordination and central control.* London: Sage.

Hjalager, A.M. (1994). Dynamic innovation in the tourist industry. *Progress in Tourism Recreation and Hospitality Management, 6,* 197–224.

Hjalager, A.M. (1998). Environmental regulation in tourism – impacts on business innovation. *Progress in Tourism and Hospitality Research, 4,* 17–30.

Hjalager, A.M. (2002). Repairing innovation defectiveness in tourism. *Tourism Management, 23,* 465–474.

Jordan, G. (1990). Sub-governments, policy communities and networks. Refilling old bottles? *Journal of Theoretical Politics, 2*(3), 319–338.

Kooiman, J. (1993). *Modern governance: New government–society interactions.* London: Sage.

Kuhlman, S., & Arnold, E. (2001). *RCN in the Norwegian research and innovation system.* Background Report No 12 in the evaluation of the Research Council of Norway, Fraunhofer ISI and Technopolis.

Lundvall, B.Å. (1992). Introduction. In: B.Å. Lundvall (Ed.), *National systems of innovation. Towards a theory of innovation and interactive learning* (pp. 1–19). London: Pinter Publisher.

Lundvall, B.Å., & Johnson, B. (1994). The learning economy. *Journal of Industry Studies, 1,* 23–42.

Marsh, D., & Rhodes, R.A.W. (Eds). (1992). *Policy networks in British government.* Oxford: Clarendon Press.

Nelson, J., & Zadek, S. (2000). *Partnership alchemy – new social partnerships in Europe.* Copenhagen, Denmark: The Copenhagen Centre.

Nelson, R. (Ed.) (1993). *National innovation systems: A comparative analysis.* Oxford: Oxford University Press.

Nordin, S. (2003). *Tourism clustering & innovation – paths to economic growth & development.* Örnsköldsvik: Ågres Tryckeri.

Nordin, S., & Svensson, B. (2005). The significance of governance in innovative tourism destinations. In: P. Keller, & T. Bieger (Eds), *Innovation in tourism: Creating customer value.* AIEST: St Gallen (Switzerland).

Östhol, A., & Lembke, J. (2003). *Strategies and partnerships for biotech regions. The regional innovation and partnership project.* Stockholm: ITPS A2003:005.

Östhol, A., & Svensson, B. (Eds). (2002). *Partnership responses – regional governance in the Nordic States.* Stockholm: Nordregio R2002:6.

Pierre, J. (Ed.) (1998). *Partnerships in urban governance: European and American experience.* London: Macmillan.

Porter, M.E. (1990). *The competitive advantage of nations.* New York: The Free Press.

Rhodes, R.A.W. (1996). The new governance: Governing without government. *Political Studies, XLIV,* 652–667.

Rhodes, R.A.W. (1997). *Understanding governance: Policy networks, governance, reflexivity and accountability.* Buckingham: Open University Press.

Sabatier, P.A., & Jenkins-Smith, H.C. (1993). *Policy change and learning: An advocacy coalition approach*, Boulder: Westview Press.

Sölvell, Ö., Lindqvist, G., & Ketels, C. (2003). *The cluster initiative greenbook*. Stockholm: Bromma Tryck.

Spilling, O.R. (Ed.) (2002). *NyskapingsNorge*. Bergen: Fagbokforlaget.

Stoker, G. (1998). Public–private partnerships and urban governance. In: J. Pierre (Ed.), *Partnerships in urban governance: European and American Experience*. London: Macmillan.

Stopford, J., & Strange, S. (1991). *Rival states, rival firms, competition for world market shares*. Canada: Cambridge University Press.

Svensson, B., & Östhol, A. (2001). From government to governance: Regional partnerships in Sweden. *Regional & Federal Studies, 11*(2), 25–42.

Van Waarden, F. (1992). Dimensions and types of policy networks. *European Journal of Political Research, 21*, 29–52.

Wolfe, D.A. (2004). *Social capital and cluster development in learning regions*, www.utoronto.ca/progris/recentpub.html, March 2004.

Wolfe, D.A., & Gertler, M.S. (2004). Clusters from the inside and out: Local dynamics and global linkages. Paper prepared for a special issue of urban studies.

Chapter 7

# Tourism Industrial Development and Multinational Corporations: A Case of Productivity Spillovers in Malaysia

Kong-Yew Wong and Tom Baum

## Introduction

In many developing countries, the most important reason for a country to attract tourism foreign direct investment (FDI) is perhaps the prospect of acquiring modern technology, interpreted broadly to include product, process, and distribution technology, as well as management and marketing skills, which are often scarce or unavailable in developing countries. There are various ways in which nations can benefit from the presence of tourism multinationals affiliates. For example, local firms may be able to improve their productivity as a result of forward and backward linkages with tourism multinational affiliates; local hotels may imitate or benchmark their operation with tourism multinational corporation (MNC) operation strategies; or they may hire workers trained by tourism multinationals. The increase in competition that occurs as a result of foreign presence may also be considered a benefit, in particular if it forces local firms to increase productivity and improve efficiency. This form of benefit can be categorised as 'productivity spillovers'. Another group of benefits that contribute to the more positive attitudes towards tourism FDI can be categorised as 'market access spillovers'. Tourism MNCs often possess strong competitive advantages from their image as international brands, experience and knowledge from previous international operations, established affiliation with other sectors within and between the industry, and existing loyal customers (Dunning & McQueen, 1982). As a result of their own international tourism marketing operations, tourism MNCs may pave the way for local firms to enter the same markets. For example, a new schedule or an increase in frequency of flights to the host country may be created by tourism MNC; or when a tourism MNC fails to retain the business of his own customer's next visit or recommendation. However, it is worth noting that these processes are desirable for developing countries, but not necessarily desirable for multinational tourism firms.

**Tourism Local Systems and Networking**
**Copyright © 2006 by Elsevier Ltd.**
**All rights of reproduction in any form reserved**
**ISBN: 0-08-044938-7**

The diffusion of proprietary knowledge to local hotel companies and hotel personnel is inevitable unless there is complete refusal to have any local business partner or total exclusion of locals in management (Go & Pine, 1995). In many cases, this can only be the desirable action in the short run. As noted by Kuin (1972) and Livingstone (1989), total exclusion of locals in management is very disadvantageous to the long-term development of the firm in the local environment.

After all, employment of locals in management and establishing local supply networks both backward and forward brings benefits to foreign multinational firms. This is because local managers are more aware of the domestic operational environment. This includes the local authority, community culture, and business networks. Similarly, using local suppliers enables goods and services to be imported or obtained and delivered with minimum interruption. This is important because by nature many tourism products have relatively short elapsed time from production to delivery. As a result, multinational firms will experience greater customer satisfaction, lower operational costs, and greater local support, which contribute to a more sustainable long-term profitable operation.

Academic research, both conceptual and empirical, has confirmed the need of foreign multinational involvement in tourism destination development, its significant impact (Behrman, 1974; Billet, 1991; Dunning, 1993; Caves, 1996). Researchers also identify the changing pattern of non-equity involvement as opposed to equity type of involvement (Rugman, 1982; Dunning & McQueen, 1982; Go & Pine, 1995). Thus indicates the important of diffusion of technology (Pine, 1992; Armstrong, 2000). It is the objective of this paper to advance this body of knowledge by examining the degree of productivity spillovers in local industry.

Diffusion of technology or 'technology transfer' by itself will not lead to sustainable industrial development. It is hypothesised that evidence of strong positive productivity spillovers is an essential criterion for long-term sustainable industrial development. In addition, from the perspective of industrial policy, to achieve sustainable industrial development, one should match the appropriate policy strategy to stimulate or prevent negative productivity spillovers. This critical condition was broadly discussed by Dunning and McQueen (1982), Jenkins and Henry (1982), and Britton (1982) in early 1980s and was further revisited by Dunning (1997), Dieke (2000), and Kusluvan and Karamustafa (2001). However, it remains conceptual and less specific in terms of policy implications.

## What are Productivity Spillovers?

Before further discussion on the productivity spillovers effect, it is important to introduce the term conceptually and analytically so that it gives operationable quality to the study. When companies establish affiliates abroad, they differ from existing firms in the host country for two reasons. One is that they bring with them some amount of the proprietary technology that constitutes their firm-specific advantage, and allows them to compete successfully with other MNCs and local firms that presumably have superior knowledge of local markets, consumer preferences, and business practices.

In industries with rapidly changing technologies (and, more generally, in developing host countries), the competitive assets of MNCs are likely to be related to new products and processes. In mature industries, MNCs may base their competitiveness more on marketing skills or organisational advantages, such as the ability to specialise across international borders, in order to exploit the local comparative advantages of various host countries. Another reason is that the entry and presence of MNC affiliates disturb the existing equilibrium in the market and force local firms to take action to protect their market shares and profits. Both these changes are likely to cause various types of spillovers that lead to productivity increases in local firms.

Generally, productivity spillovers are said to take place when the entry or presence of MNC affiliates leads to productivity or efficiency benefits in the host country's local firms, and the MNCs are not able to internalise the full value of these benefits (Blomstrom, Kokko, & Zejan, 2000).

### *Identifying Spillovers from MNC Activities*

**Contagion and demonstration effects**    This section discusses contagion and demonstration effects that result from the presence of international hotel chains in host destinations. Activities by MNC affiliates in a host country with potential productivity spillovers can be broadly classified into two categories: (i) within the host destination and (ii) between destinations.

(i)  Within the host destination, MNC affiliates engage in internal operations as well as external linkages with suppliers both forward (coach operators, local travel agents, theme park operators, MICE operators, etc.) and backward (F&B suppliers, sanitation service providers, hotel's architects, etc.). The uniqueness of the tourism industry or more specifically the hotel industry is where both forward and backward linkages are of equal importance (Dunning & McQueen, 1982).

Therefore, more often than not, high-quality goods and services are expected by the MNC from its supplier, because the MNC's major competitive advantage is its established brand name that is associated with perceived international quality standard by international travellers. Therefore, local suppliers will have to meet these detailed specifications of products, produce, and services set by international chain hotels. It is from these rigorous processes and requirements that we would expect to have initial evidence of productivity spillovers.

The evidence can be witnessed when, for example, local suppliers that have increased their goods and service quality according to 'international standards' are able to supply identical goods and services to local hotels. This new technology that a local supplier obtains as a result of its affiliation with international chain hotels is therefore available to the local industry and may also experience economies of scale (Go & Pine, 1995; Blomstrom et al., 2000). This may not have been possible earlier for a number of reasons: the costs could be too high for local hotels to initiate the use, the technology is not required given the competitive environment before the presence of foreign multinational hotels, and local firms have limited information about costs and benefits of the new technology. However, as a result of the presence of multinational hotels, the industry competitive equilibrium has been disturbed (Caves, 1996) and local firms have more information about new technology from MNC affiliates

(Blomstrom et al., 2000). Therefore, adaptation or change becomes necessary and less risky at the same time (Caves, 1996).

When local hotels' market position is being threatened by the presence of foreign hotels, this implies that existing technology used by local hotels is relatively inferior to their foreign counterparts. Local hotels are believed to be weaker in relative terms in their knowledge of international traveller's wants and needs, international affiliation with tour operators, airlines and also other foreign international hotel chains, and possibly experience in operating in and developing a destination (Dunnings & McQueen, 1982). Foreign multinational hotels enter the host industry with the technology that they already own and have established, and expect to yield additional returns (Caves, 1996; Rodriguez, 2002). This is also known as rent-seeking activities by multinational firms (Chrystal & Lipsey, 1997).

However, what this study is interested in is how the local hotel industry or the wider tourism industry can potentially benefit from the presence of this superior technology. First of all, multinational affiliates' operations in the host industry will create opportunity for local employees to learn and to be trained in international hotel management skills that eventually will add value to their career development (Go & Pine, 1995). As Pine (1991) suggests specifically in relation to the hotel industry, this process is known as technology transfer. However, unless this employee leaves the multinational firms and successfully utilises his or her skills and knowledge in a local hotel, the industry will not experience productivity spillovers.

(ii) On the other hand, multinational affiliates in the host industry will closely link their corporate operational activities with the corporate home or regional office. Activities such as central purchasing units, sales and marketing promotion, reservation systems, corporate training, and corporate alliances and affiliations, give them a leading edge or comparative advantage in both technology know-how and cost efficiency (UNCTAD, 1997). These activities will directly and indirectly benefit the host industry and the destination. Examples of a direct benefit are activities such as sending local employees offshore for corporate training programmes or to a new assignment in another destination (Go & Pine, 1995).

Another dimension of how MNC's activities could potentially benefit the host nation is that it develops the host nation as an international destination. This means that the host destination becomes more accessible, gaining positive publicity and welcoming international trade of goods and services. Multinational corporations are influential in establishing new air and sea routes to destinations. Besides, tourism promotion has the tendency to boost the positive aspects of a destination rather than projecting negative attributes. Destinations will begin to develop links with international distribution networks for goods and services. Once this is in place, the destination industrial environment will become more conducive to trade and therefore will attract more foreign investment and trading partners to the destination. This means, more international brand hotels will establish operations as well as international food chains, tour operators, airlines, and car rental companies. Within the wider service sector, we should also expect to see new international ventures such as banking, finance, and insurance in the destination.

This industrial multiplier effect, whether intentional or unintentional, will occur in a matter of time. This also explains how a destination gains its equity over time.

Destination equity, used in this study, refers to the significant level of knowledge and information that a traveller has about a particular destination in making his/her choice and whether international brands are essential for a comfortable and safe stay. This is based on the argument that

> foreign hotel accommodation as an 'experience good' often purchased in an unfamiliar environment where the trademark of the MNE hotel chain guarantees a standard of service with the characteristics demanded by tourists (principally business tourists) from the principal tourist generating countries. (Dunning & McQueen, 1982, p. 89)

This level of knowledge and information can be accumulated by a traveller's own experiences, recommendations by friends and relatives, and information gathered from mass media such as television, printed material, internet, etc. Therefore, if there is evidence that suggests an increasing positive level of destination equity is occurring, one should expect greater spillover presence in the industry. This suggests that the destination is relatively less dependent on the presence of foreign international hotel chains.

**Competition effect**   It does not matter which specific determinant is in place, in terms of ownership, location, and internalisation advantages as described in Dunning's (1979) eclectic theory of international production, for an MNC to enter host industry. Whichever, it will create competitive disequilibrium in the host industry (Caves, 1996). It raises the level of market concentration in the host industry or spreads oligopolistic markets from the developed industry (home country) to the less developed industry (host country) (Hymer, 1960). The presence of rent-seeking MNCs imposes pressure on local firms to increase productivity and to improve efficiency either by using existing technology, acquiring new technology, or by innovation.

Of course, foreign entry may also force local firms out of the industry or to take over existing local oligopolistic firms, and thereafter, monopolise the industry. Hence, the presence of competition-related spillovers between local and foreign multinationals is essential in any industry. Hypothetically speaking, the level of competition-related spillovers can be determined by technology gaps that exist between local and foreign operations and vice versa.

However, since the hotel industry serves various categories of guests, whether segregated by social economic or geographical criteria, there may not be direct competition between hotels in a destination. Dev and Klein (1993) argues that luxury hotels often attempt to establish a unique market position in an effort to stay competitive, which includes branding and promotional efforts. This means allowing them to operate in an enclave environment (Jenkins, 1982; Blomstrom et al., 2000) and establishing both vertical and horizontal integration to sustain this position (Claves, 1996). Thus, since competition exists only when two or more hotels are targeting the same segment of the market, there will not be any direct competition. Other explanations of the need for market positioning will be the presence of competition so that hotels of different classes are forced to focus on other specific markets (Dev & Klein, 1993). This could mean that, in this study, local hotels have no alternative but to forego the market segment that they used to enjoy before the advent of direct competition from or presence of a foreign multinational hotel chain.

From the traveller's point of view, the pull factor, it could be that brand and perceived international quality will influence the choice of a specific brand regardless of which geographical region they are from. These travellers are either non-frequent travellers or are price insensitive and luxury oriented (Dev & Klein, 1993). Therefore, hotels in a destination have to establish their brand equity to attract this specific group of travellers. This means that competing on the grounds of brand equity is unavoidable.

As a result, it is problematic to attempt to draw a line between hotels in order to segregate the competition environment in the market. Therefore, in this study, competition-related spillovers are indicated by the level of productivity of local hotels as a result of productivity spillovers from foreign hotels. This is based on the assumption that hotels are competing based on productivity, which is determined by efficiency in production.

**Market access spillovers**    This study next discusses a conceptual phenomenon where empirical evidence is scarce. However, the acceptability and validity of this phenomenon should not be jeopardised by the lack of empirical evidence alone. The barrier that prevents the collection of empirical data related to this factor is caused by the complexity of the tourism industry, and limited and non-standardised statistical data between nations.

The concept of market access spillovers refers to the direct and indirect efforts by multinational firms to transfer technology and establish networks, at international level, in the host industry (Kusluvan & Karamustafa, 2001). This leads to increases in international visitors that would not have been possible without the presence of the multinational's affiliates in the host country (Dunning & McQueen, 1982). As Blomstrom et al. (2000) suggest, being competent in manufacturing is not enough to become a successful exporter. Companies need to learn to manage international marketing, distribution, and servicing of its products. Because these tasks are often associated with high fixed costs, few local firms, particularly those in developing countries, have the skills and resources to take on all these challenges on their own (UNCTAD, 1997).

In the context of the tourism industry, the statement above still fundamentally holds. A majority of tourism firms in many developing destinations have no technical know-how with which to break into international markets (Jenkins & Henry, 1982). The issue of penetrating into new international markets is a complex discussion topic. It involves questions of who pays or how should the cost be shared? — doubts between tax receiver and tax payer, and between sectors; questions of which market segment? — regions, social classes, interest groups, etc.; what tourism product should be offered? — the issue of sustainable tourism, alternative tourism, etc. (Burns & Holden, 1995).

For the purpose of this study, the focus concentrates on how the presence of foreign multinational hotels impacts on local hotels positively in terms of the number of foreign guests. If the assumption of superior knowledge of international tourism markets possessed by foreign multinational hotels holds, the time dimension is important in discussing the impact. Initially, a destination needs international brand hotels to attract tourists from abroad. Presumably, international hotels will disproportionately attract tourists from their home country, e.g. Nikko Hotel will attract Japanese tourists and Hilton will attract North American and European tourists. As more international hotels open and there is an increase in international tourist arrivals to the destination, the local industry will have exposure to the technology in providing service to and accessing various market segments by geographical boundary (country and regional), class of travellers (business, leisure, etc.), and tourism products (shopping, adventure, nature, etc.). International tourists and travellers are now aware of the standards of local hospitality service providers, and therefore, will depend less on international brands (Dieke, 1993). Local hotels will use technology know-how from the distribution network established by international multinational hotels to access these markets.

This process takes time, and the length is highly dependent on the rate of productivity spillovers of both contagion and demonstration effects, as well as competition effects. Therefore, one may suggest, market access spillovers are a product or evidence of positive productivity spillovers. This is a characteristic of developing host industries.

## Absence of Productivity Spillovers

Primarily, it is important to emphasise that productivity spillovers are not what multinational firms would like to see or at least are not their objectives in operating in the host industry. Unlike technology transfer, productivity spillovers do not benefit multinationals in operational efficiency or productivity and in fact can be a threat to multinational affiliates. The lesser the competition and larger the technology gap between foreign and local hotels the lower the pressure for foreign hotels to be innovative in securing their rent-seeking behaviour (Blomstrom et al., 2000). As a result, it is in the interest of foreign multinational hotels to secure competitive advantageous positions by reducing the rate of productivity spillovers. Evidence to support this is that foreign multinational hotels often pay higher wages and benefits to reduce turnover of management personnel, especially with respect to locals (Go & Pine, 1995).

Low productivity spillovers may also come from within the attributes of the host industry. When the technology gaps between two firms are too large, they form a barrier for local hotels to imitate the newest and most profitable technologies used by international counterparts (UNCTAD, 1997; Blomstrom et al., 2000). High barriers can be explained by high market concentration, scale economies, high initial capital requirements, intensive advertising, and advanced technology (UNCTAD, 1997).

Absence of productivity spillovers is a cause of considerable economic development losses and disadvantage. As Dieke (1989) highlights, the danger of the industry being dominated by foreign firms could lead to a loss of development direction. Other issues involve leakages and poverty issues (Britton, 1982). Large and powerful multinational firms are able to avoid taxation through transfer pricing, and repatriate significant amounts of profit from the host industry. This is when local governments have little control due to industry over-dependence on foreign inputs. This is raised by Held, McGrew, Goldblatt, and Perratan (2001) as the phenomena of corporate power versus state power.

To summarise, it is clear from the above discussion, that there are a number of important tourism industrial attributes, which are necessary for positive productivity spillovers. These are labour skills, linkages within and between sectors and industry, competitiveness of local firms and destination equity. Labour skills refer to the basic skills that local employees must have in order to learn and to be trained successfully. This may involve language proficiency and level of education or vocational training. In addition, strong backward and forward industry linkages are essential for productivity spillovers, especially contagion and demonstration type of spillovers. The ability to compete and to secure a market share in a competitive environment is, by no means, the most important criteria that local hotels must have to achieve sustainable industrial development. Lastly, destination equity is an asset that a destination can build upon over time, and can serve as a lubricant to stimulate the overall process of productivity spillovers.

As a result, quality knowledge of the state of development of such variables in the host industry is essential in policy decision processes. However, a precise indication of such information is often vague. In this paper, we have adopted a qualitative approach to capture evidence of productivity spillovers in the Malaysian hotel industry. An elite group of interviews were conducted with key officers and personnel in government institutions, hotel associations, and other related organisations.

## Setting the Scene

The hotel industry in Malaysia is different from many developing countries, in that monetary capital is merely not a barrier to development. The majority of the hotels in the country are privately owned by Malaysians. More often than not, hotel investors' core business is not primarily tourism related. Over the last two decades, developers see the opportunity of building and owning hotels merely for their financial potential (i.e. operation profit, appreciation of property value, goodwill) rather than growth of the hotel industry's resources *per se*. There are negative implications of such motivations, which involve an influx of foreign managers into the industry and mismatch of policy and industrial development direction.

Because of the potential of the Malaysian tourism and hospitality industry, large corporations have been attracted to build luxury hotels. They invite established hotel brands and management groups to fill in the technology capital gap as a partner (equity form of involvement) or contractual base arrangement (non-equity form of involvement). This, by no means, is the fastest way to obtain superior technology and, thus, competitive advantage against its local counterpart. The technology that multinational hotel corporations (MNHCs) have to offer includes their international brand image, skilled personnel, production knowledge (i.e. purchasing, servicing, hotel architecture, etc.), alliances, and customer base.

Without doubt, it would be expected that MNHC would want to hold-up to its technology and be assured of its effective implementation. This point is particularly true in the initial stage, when its MNHC will send a group of managers to its foreign affiliates to merely act as a bridge of information and control. There is little concern at this idea by the owner, as long as their financial objectives are delivered. However, as in many other countries in the developing world, requirements were also set that all hotels should involve more locals in countries in middle and top management position.

It is generally accepted that international managers monopolise key positions in the hotel sector in many developing countries, at least in the infancy phase. It is also hypothesised that as the industry develops, more local managers will learn and develop and intimately replace the role of foreign international mangers. This is achieved as more locals are employed in foreign MNHC and receive the training and experience needed for its daily operation of the hotel.

All interviewees agreed that this is the way forward. However, there was still significant evidence of the domination of foreign international managers in the Malaysian hotel industry after almost three decades of growth. This case study reviews some of the reasons that contribute to the continuing reliance on foreign managers. Figure 7.1 represents the various actors that are directly and indirectly responsible for this, and is derived from the interviews undertaken for the research.

## Findings

To engage in the hotel business, especially luxury hotels, involves high initial monetary capital. Owners turn to financial institutions (supporting industry — Figure 7.1) to capitalise their project. Financial institution will then assess the feasibility of the project. It is well known to the industry, as expressed by interviewees, that an important criterion that financial institution considers is the operating management group and brand as an indication for future success. Not surprisingly, international management hotels with a strong brand and management score highly in this evaluation process. This would seem to be a lack of recognition from financial institution, a clear indication of the lack of confidence in local management skills in the hotel industry.

Even though there are pressures from the OECD (1992) and also initiatives from MNHCs themselves to move towards polycentrism, its implementation is ineffective. Human resource capital in Malaysia has reduced in real term. Human resource capital is arguably a lower standard than the 1980s and early 1990s. The number of local managers

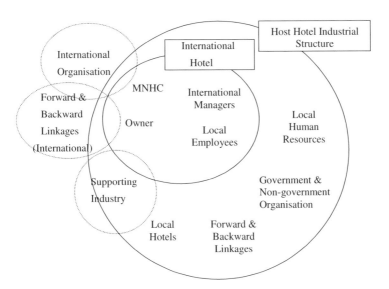

Figure 7.1: Host hotel industrial structure.

in the industry may have increased over time but it does not necessarily indicate higher capability of local managers. As indicated by the President of Malaysian Hotel Association, over-promoting is an issue that the industry has to acknowledge and rectify. This issue is largely due to significant numbers of jobs at managerial and supervisory level, which were available during early to mid-1990s, when many new hotels had been built. Since the skills ready to run a hotel is by rank-and-file and is developed through time, it is difficult for MNHC to find suitable local managers in a pool of 'over-promoting' managers for key positions.

An issue such as English language proficiency among the Malaysian workforce is something that needs addressing. What used to be an advantage is increasingly a disadvantage in Malaysian hospitality industry. As noted by Gladwin and Walker (1980), the American MNC have been more successful in engaging locals in higher positions due to ease of finding locals who are fluent in English. The workforce in Malaysia, especially in the 1980s, was known for their English proficiency. However, the medium of education has been changed from English to Malaysian language (National language) in the mid-1980s. The resulting decline of English proficiency has led to many problems in training and development of local human resources.

Another concern, as expressed by interviewees, is the willingness of international managers to train local managers. This is particularly the case when local managers are perceived as a threat to their organisational position. This is consistent with Go and Pine's 1995) view that where local managers excelled and demonstrated potential, MNCs will retain these local managers by offering promotion opportunities, which are often positions in larger operations of the MNCs in other host countries.

What is surprising is that despite the lower level of English proficiency, the local workforce prefers to be trained by foreign managers. The skills delivered by international managers are perceived to be international. However, according to an interviewee of an MNHC, there is no doubt that language is the biggest barrier when it comes to the issue of training and development. In addition, work ethic has changed immensely. The young workforce is less service oriented than before. The friendly and hospitable culture is missing in the younger generation. The Malaysian hotel industry's previous success was mainly due to its service-oriented culture. Today, however, the workforce is less keen to work at operational levels, while attention increasingly focused is on promotion opportunities from within or amongst other hotels, which are abundant.

A final issue to consider is that while government is known for its role in imposing pressure to have more local managers in key positions, which indirectly contribute to the issue of 'over-promoting', government is also responsible for the pronounced use of international managers in hotels. An example would be the policy to promote local culture and arts in hotels. Hotels are encouraged to employ local artists to perform in their premises. As there was resistance from hotels in the implementation process who, argued that the choice of performance should be customer driven, local authorities approached individual hotels. Local hotels or local managers were the initial point of approach in the process. Perhaps, they are local and, therefore, should have the initiative and responsibility to promote local culture and arts. This is one example of pressure to local managers, which cause more hotels to use international managers in the process.

## Conclusions

The findings in this paper exhibit the learning process and maturity of the Malaysian hotel industry, particularly human capital. There were evidences to suggest various forms of obstacles facing the industry in promoting higher degree of productivity spillovers. However, indication for potentially positive productivity spillovers in the industry is relatively strong. Thus, this paper draws attention for a more integrated tourism planning approach to ensure sustainable tourism industrial development.

## References

Armstrong, H., & Taylor, J. (2000). *Regional economic and policy* (pp. 65–88). London: Blackwell.

Behrman, J.N. (1974). *Decision criteria for foreign direct investment in Latin America.* New York: Council of the America.

Billet, B.L. (1991). *Investment behavior of multinational corporations in developing areas: Comparing the development assistance committee, Japanese, and American corporations.* New Brunswick, USA: Transaction publishers.

Blomstrom, M., Kokko, A., & Zejan, M. (2000). *Foreign direct investment: Firm and host country strategies.* New York: Macmillan.

Britton, S.G. (1982). The political economy of tourism in the third world. *Annals of Tourism Research, 9,* 331–358.

Burns, P., & Holden, A. (1995). *Tourism, a new perspective.* New York: Prentice Hall.

Caves, R.E. (1996). *Multinational enterprise and economic analysis* (2nd ed.). Cambridge: Cambridge University Press.

Chrystal, K.A., & Lipsey, R.G. (1997). *Economics for business and mangement.* Oxford: Oxford University Press.

Dev, S.D., & Klein, S. (1993). Strategic alliance in the hotel industry. *The Cornell HRA Quarterly,* (February), 42–45.

Dieke, P.U.C. (1989). Fundamentals of tourism development: A third world perspective. *Hospitality Education and Research Journal, 13*(2), 7–22.

Dieke, P.U.C. (1993). Tourism and development policy in the Gambia. *Annals of Tourism Research, 20,* 423–449.

Dieke, P.U.C. (2000). *The political economy of tourism development in Africa.* Elmsford, New York: Cognizant.

Dunning, J.H. (1979). Explaining changing patterns of international production: In defence of the eclectic theory. *Oxford Bulletin of Economics and Statistics, 41,* 269–296.

Dunning, J.H. (1993). *The globalization of business: The challenge of the 1990s.* London, New York: Routledge.

Dunning, J.H. (1997). World Investment Report, Transnational Corporations, Market Structure and Competition Policy. New York: United Nations.

Dunning, J.H., & McQueen, M. (1982). Multinational corporations in the international hotel industry. *Annals of Tourism Research, 9,* 69–90.

Gladwin, T.N., & Walker, I. (1980). *Multinationals under fire.* New York: Wiley.

Go, F. M., & Pine, R. (1995). *Globalization strategy in the hotel industry.* London, New York: Routledge.

Held, D., McGrew, A., Goldblatt, D., & Perratan, J. (2001). *Global transformations: Politics, economics and culture* (281 pp.). London: Blackwell.

Hymer, S.H. (1960). The international operations of national firms: A study of direct foreign investment. Ph.D. dissertation, Cambridge, MA: MIT Press (1976).

Jenkins, C.L. (1982). The effects of scale in tourism projects in developing countries. *Annals of Tourism Research, 9,* 229–249.

Jenkins, C.L., & Henry, B.M. (1982). Government involvement in tourism in developing countries. *Annals of Tourism Research, 9,* 499–521.

Kuin, P. (1972). The magic of multinational management. *Harvard Business Review,* (Nov./Dec.), 92–100.

Kusluvan, S., & Karamustafa, K. (2001). Multinational hotel development in developing countries: An exploratory analysis of critical policy issues. *International Journal of Tourism Research, 3,* 179–197.

Livingstone, J.M. (1989). *The internationalization of business.* Oxford: Macmillan.

OECD. (1992). *The OECD declaration and decisions on international investment and multinational enterprise: 1991 review.* Paris: Organization for Economic Cooperation and Development.

Pine, R.J. (1991). *Technology transfer in the hotel industry.* Ph.D. thesis, The University of Bradford.

Pine, R.J. (1992). Technology transfer in the hotel industry. *International Journal of Hospitality Management, 11*(1), 3–22.

Rodríguez, A.R. (2002). Determining factors in entry choice for international expansion. The case of the Spanish hotel industry. *Tourism Management, 23,* 597–607.

Rugman, A.M. (1982). *New theories of the multinational enterprise.* London, Canberra: Croom Helm.

UNCTAD. (1997). World investment report 1997: Transnational corporations, market structure and competition policy. *United Nations Conference on Trade and Development,* New York: United Nations.

# PART 2

# TOURISM LOCAL SYSTEMS: MANAGEMENT APPROACHES

Chapter 8

# Tourism System Dynamics: A Multi-level Destination Approach

Enrico Bonetti, Clara S. Petrillo and Michele Simoni

## Introduction*

A review of the late literature on local tourism development highlights a number of issues recently covered, such as: (1) the territory, meant as a bundle of resources to be preserved and developed over time, in line with environmental, social and economic sustainability criteria; (2) the tourism system, meant as a territorial dimension capable of enhancing the surplus value which can be generated by a destination as a whole (an incremental surplus value vis-à-vis the one which can be created by the individual stakeholders); (3) the forms adopted by the system and denoting how resources interact; (4) the tourism product, meant as the mix of tourism resources which defines the value proposition of a specific area vis-à-vis a specific target; (5) the evolutionary process which makes it possible for a specific area to modify its vocation over time and express it by generating new products.

The aim of this paper is to highlight the links among these issues, suggesting a unifying framework. The intention is to find a key; a conceptual model that represents more interacting levels where:

- The territorial system is seen as the generative context within which relationships among the various players generates over time a tourism system

---

*Even if this paper is the result of a common vision and an intense and constructive collaboration, among authors, the authorship of the paragraphs is shown by the following:
Enrico Bonetti: The level of centralisation of the system governance functions, The four ideal types of tourism systems, The Process.
Clara S. Petrillo: The Territory.
Michele Simoni: An overview of destination classification models, The level of interdependence among the actors, The tourism product.
Introduction, The model and Conclusions have to be assigned to all the authors.

- The tourism system, in its various forms, generates offers capable of creating value for specific market segments
- The tourism product, through the interaction with clients, determines their perception of the territory (global tourism experience)
- The process guides the evolutionary paths by dynamically linking the various levels.

In this way a conceptual model is suggested which facilitates understanding the various phenomena related to tourism development and, consequently, the studies and research works in this field.

## The Model

The economic development of a specific territory from the tourism point of view is a complex area of study, because of a number of reasons, including: the wide range of resources involved, the heterogeneous interests of the various actors managing the resources, the many inter-dependences linking the subjects involved. When trying to find the key concepts it is convenient to have an interpretation model, which unifies the various streams of thought, while simultaneously highlighting the relationships among these concepts.

The model suggested is built by breaking down the territorial area into different hierarchical units of analysis; each unit of analysis is identified so as to have aggregates characterised by "strong" within-block interactions, mutually linked by "weak" interactions and capable of evolving according to different time scales. Quoting Simon's words (1995) *"what this means from a dynamic standpoint is that: if the variables in a block are disturbed from equilibrium, the equilibrium among them will be restored rapidly; over any longer span of time each block will appear to move in a rigid fashion, the variables remaining close to equilibrium in relation to each other. Over some still longer period of time the weaker interactions among different blocks will establish equilibrium of the entire system. The weaker the between-block interactions compared with the within-block interactions, the smaller will be the ratio of the time required to restore within-block equilibrium to that required to restore between-block equilibrium"*.

From this perspective, assuming the territorial area as a starting unit of analysis, we can state that a tourism system does exist when all resources involved in the tourism activities are mutually linked by stronger relationships, compared to other territorial resources with different economic purposes. Within the tourism system it is then possible to categorise a further level of analysis, which enables to identify the sub-systems represented by the individual tourism products. Once again, in order to make this breaking-down process meaningful, the condition is a higher intensity of the relationships among actors supplying the same product, compared to that of the relationships with actors supplying other products within the same tourism system.

To summarise, the analysis made in this paper will be sub-divided into three different reading keys (Figure 8.1):

- The territory, meant as a generative context within which a tourism system is developed as a result of the close relationships established over time among the various actors
- The tourism system which, in its different forms, generates offers capable of creating value for specific market segments

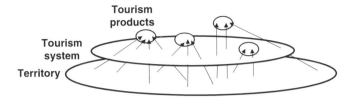

Figure 8.1: The analytical model.
*Source*: Our data processing.

- The tourism product which, by interacting with clients, determines their perception of the area (global tourism experience).

The model also includes a description of the processes, which drive development paths, by dynamically connecting the different levels of the system.

## The Territory: Resources, Competences and Sustainability of the Competitive Advantage

Studies and empirical analysis on the tourism industry recently focused on Destination Management: the research unit of economic-business disciplines progressively shifted from firms to territorial areas, meant as supply networks rendering services to customers.[1] Some authors maintain that destinations cannot be viewed as autonomous competitive entities; this because of a number of reasons including, for example, lack of a univocal territorial delimitation, intangibility of property rights, impossibility of a centralised management (Socher & Tschurtschenthaler, 2003). Conversely, the prevailing theory maintains that the unifying factor — that makes a competitive territorial area an autonomous entity — is its economic and cultural homogeneity, as perceived by clients, not its political border. Then each territory "autonomously" competes at the global level to get the scarce resources required to develop and support its firms, promote development and, ultimately, improve the quality of life of the local community" (Cercola, 1999).

On the one hand, the substantial increase of tourism flows world-wide highlighted the high fragility of environments: actually the risks linked to a gradual depletion of environmental resources because of excessive tourism consumption and to the progressive loss of the local identity because of globalisation are quite high. Priestley and Mundet (1998) highlighted that only a development respectful of the environmental sustainability principle can block the negative impact on environmental resources generated by the constant increase of tourism, typical of the development stages. Moreover, this principle can allow to avoid the following stagnation and decline stages which, according to Butler (1980) are the inevitable destiny of mature tourism destinations, such as the Mediterranean ones.

The increasing environmental awareness of the tourism industry and of the general public, combined with the tourists demand for nature and authenticity, are all factors which

---

[1] In Franch (2002) many interesting contributions on Destination Management can be found.

force the dissemination of a new concept of sustainable tourism: a form of tourism with a low environmental impact and respectful of both the territorial environment and identity.

Many initiatives have been promoted all over the world such as the United Nation *Environment Programme* (UNEP); the *Award for Tourism and Environment* of the European Union; the *Charter on the ethics of tourism and environment;* the *European Charter for Durable Tourism; The Ecotourism Society* (TES). In Italy, the creation of National Parks,[2] despite the high initial difficulties, was quite successful and resulted in the protection of over 10% of the national territory.

On the other hand, a sustainable territorial tourism development project — respectful of the natural and social environment — also guarantees the achievement of a competitive advantage against other competing destinations. In a Resource and knowledge-based approach,[3] the ability of a specific area to attract tourists mostly depends on the stock of factors at its disposal, i.e. its original local natural, historical-archaeological and social resources, its knowledge, capabilities, capital and infrastructures[4] (Smeral, 1998). However, even more than the static existing resources, a crucial role is played by the favourable conditions of a number of components and by the whole set of factors: the whole set of tangible and intangible values, such as inhabitants, culture, historical heritage, urban and artistic heritage, infrastructures, location and any other situation capable of increasing the overall value of the various components (Kotler, Haider, & Rein, 1993).

However, the competitive potential of a specific area is directly proportional to the customer's perception of the unique nature of the local resources: in other words, the advantage gained thanks to the local resources is sustainable provided that the resources on which it is based cannot be transferred and replicated. From this perspective, the resources of a specific area are its real source of competitive advantage; the higher the respect for local specificities, the more sustainable its competitive advantage. This involves not only

---

[2] *National or Regional Parks* are areas subject to special protection and management systems aimed at applying management and environmental rehabilitation methods, which guarantee man–nature integration and protection of local values and traditional activities. The second objective is to increase environmental awareness of youth by promoting education, training and scientific research activities. A similar approach characterises the UNESCO Biosphere Reserve, developed within Unesco Project Man and Biosphere in 1974. Protected areas play a more dynamic and experimental role as they have to monitor the environment identified not only from the naturalistic point of view, but also and above all from its social-economic features point of view, such as quality of life of the local community and bio-diversity level.

[3] The stream of studies, named Resource-based View of the Firm, developed in the 1990s, focused on the relationship between the competitive advantage of the firms and their resources and competence. For the firms to achieve higher performance, resources — defined as the factors owned and controlled by the firm — have to be heterogeneous, impossible to be transferred and hard to be imitated. A sustainable competitive advantage also results from the ability of the firms to combine resources. For a detailed analysis refer to R.B.V. cfr. Boschetti (1999).

[4] Smeral, applying the competitive diamond Porter's model (1991) to the tourism industry, identified the internal determinants of the competitive advantage: (a) conditions of the local factors; (b) conditions of the demand by residents and tourists; (c) local context, widely meant, namely prevailing culture, attitude towards tourism; (d) competitiveness of the supply or support industries; (e) strategies, structures and rivalry model among tourism firms. External determinants are: unexpected events, all factors which cannot be directly controlled by the destination (exchange rates and inflation, political situation and national stability, evolution of peace processes, natural events, weather conditions); the central or local government which can hinder or stimulate, promote and co-ordinate the local tourism development.

natural resources, geographical position, morphological features, but above all the assets represented by social resources which are the result of the traditions and habits of the hosting community (i.e. artistic and archaeological heritage, typical agricultural products, social, eno-gastronomic, handicraft traditions, and even general atmosphere, hospitality). These factors can be immediately used, hardly imitated and this can make the difference (Valdani & Ancarani, 2000).

In many cases these factors are unique, they cannot be reproduced and are linked to a specific site, a culture typical of a given area. These specificities cannot be invented, designed and implemented ex-novo; "the territory is a product with a strong 'vocation' ... this vocation has to be the starting and reference point for any marketing action, ... for any analysis of the customers" (Varaldo & Caroli, 1999).

Consequently, the bundle of local resources imposes the development path of a specific area and determines its possible use functions, "its vocation". However, these resources have to be at the very core of an organised system aimed at enhancing the area: it is only thanks to the organisational and innovative abilities of the local stakeholders that environmental and cultural resources can become attractive thus generating a tourism destination.[5] Vicari and Mangiarotti (1999) stress the need for turning local specificities into competitive attractive factors, an ability which, in its turn, is linked to the innovativeness level, namely to the relative rate of increase, improvement and specialisation of the resources themselves.

Harmonising the exploitation of the existing resources (while developing the deficient or not existing ones), and combining them it is possible to create distinctive competences, top-level management skills which in their turn guarantee a sustainable competitive advantage (Sicca, 1999). Ensuring a sustainable development of tourism and of the local resources it depends on the art of keeping the right balance between system coherence (convergence of visions) and flexibility (ability to adapt, generate new ideas and follow them through) (Tremblay, 2000).

Then, for a territorial area to develop and implement a sustainable development project two basic conditions have to be met:

- The project has to allow for the context
- The project has to integrate activities and resources.

The first condition can be met through a constant focus on resources, territorial specificities and traditional skills acquired over time (Ancarani, 1999). This guarantees to differentiate the tourism supply: the territorial area, by enhancing the value of its historical and inimitable heritage, provides a unique and distinctive product, a strong image which makes it "visible" and attractive to the various users. The development project then

---

[5] Paradoxically, a high number of natural resources might be a negative rather than a positive competitive factor when it stimulates inertial behaviours characterised by a mere exploitation of a situation rent and hinders the development of new creative and innovative capabilities. This is even more important if we consider that the situation advantage held by areas whose high tourism vocation is based on its many natural resources can be cancelled by areas lacking natural attractiveness; there are many examples of "artificial" attractions which turned a territory "built" from scratch into a successful tourism destination. For example the many Walt Disney's thematic parks, Santa Claus Village or even the city of Las Vegas.

becomes something which cannot be replicated nor imitated by competitors, and this will guarantee a distinctive positioning.

The second condition, supporting the first one, relates to the ability of the territorial area to make a combined use of these resources, by means of organisation processes for development. Adopting a functional and co-operative approach enables to maximise positive effects on the local community and minimise negative effects on the environment and local culture (Sautter e Leisen, 1999).[6] According to the concept of territory suggested here, the aptitude of each resource to create value is directly linked to its level of integration in the system and to the relationships among the various organisations, which guarantee the resources constant improvement and enhancement.

Crucial competences specifically relate to four critical dimensions of management[7]:

1. Innovation competences: the capabilities to discover and anticipate customers needs and desires and to invent a supply system that integrates local resources with services and attractions
2. Relationship competences: knowledge, capabilities and attitudes which make it possible both to link different factors and attractions crucial to clients and to manage the relationships with networks external to the territory
3. Interaction competences: ability to optimise relationships with clients both developing new procedure and replicating those that proved to be effective and created value for the customer
4. Communication competences: ability to highlight the value created for clients and include external elements and attractions in the product system.

Creating fruitful relationships is crucial: any actions implemented in the area become fully effective and efficient only if it is organised and managed by a partnership including the various local and external stakeholders (Weiermair, 1999).[8]

Each tourism destination is characterised by an "open-system" including many interdependent stakeholders — the various organisations interested and involved in its development — where the actions of an individual organisation have an impact on the other community members: no single organisation or individual can exert a direct control over the local development process (Jamal & Getz, 1995).

In this perspective, interests and wishes of the various local stakeholders have to be allowed for in a pro-active manner during planning and development stages.

---

[6] Conversely, within an economic-political approach, tourism is viewed as something, which imposes its own choices and the consequences of these choices on the local community, which is scarcely capable of influencing political groups or external groups.

[7] Because of the crucial importance of meeting customers needs and create a complete system of supply, we have added the innovation competence to the three suggested by De Carlo (2004), i.e. relationship, interaction and communication competencies.

[8] For example, the search for new customers implies collecting and selecting a huge amount of information, forcing the individual firms to incur into costs, which are often too high for them given their small size. Conversely, contracting-out these activities to an operator located out of the country of origin enables to get better outcomes at substantially lower costs.

The preliminary stage implies identifying and analysing the needs of the various internal (firms and resident citizens, local policy makers), or external stakeholders (users of goods and services provided by the area, investors or potential new clients). In the following stage, through the creation of profitable relationships among them, commitments, objectives, values and responsibilities will be fully understood and then included in the development strategic model.

In this way, a tourism destination becomes a sort of double network: the first level of relationships can be found within the local level; it links the actors to their territorial area and to all external economies — environmental, human and financial resources, knowledge, and infrastructures — which reinforce and give content to the entrepreneurial initiatives. However, at the same time, the competitive advantage depends on the extent of a second level of relationships, those established with the international system (Calvelli, Cannavale, & Canestrino, 2004). Thanks to the new information technologies, firms are always in touch with collaborators, suppliers and clients all over the world. The core of the current cross-national competition in the sector consists of large networked organisations including suppliers, organisers and intermediaries. The ubiquity and reversibility of these networks make it possible to have timely and reliable information flows, thus triggering a virtuous circle between information producers and users.[9]

A new network system is created with a different analytical value resulting from the existence of the relationships themselves; actually this system is a new individual operational unit with a competitive power different from the individual units analysed separately. The unit of analysis is no longer the single firm in relationship with its competitors within the same business area, but a network, a whole set of firms, establishing long-lasting co-operation relationships, regardless of their value chain stage (Lorenzoni, 1990). They are networked structures going beyond both the traditional network models consisting of central and peripheral points, and Porter's value chain where, through sequence-based activities and unidirectional relationships, value is assembled and made available to clients who (being external to the chain) get a pre-determined supply.

Conversely, within a simultaneous interaction framework, a relationship network is created; it can generate value through a system of relationships among interdependent economic actors co-producing value with constantly changing parallel relationships. From this perspective, value is co-produced by interfacing organisations. Customers are no longer passive purchasers/users of the supply, but are differently involved in its consumption (Normann & Ramirez, 1995). The model suggested better fits to a value creation process, such as the tourism one, which can be hardly pre-determined as it is jointly created and invented through interactions among producers and between producers and clients (Petrillo, 2001).

---

[9] Within a European scenario characterised by organised trips controlled by a limited number of Northern European tour operators, participating in international networks is crucial because of their scale economies and central position vis-à-vis the main tourism flows. Thanks to their wide range of action and high integration, they benefit of a stable network of suppliers with low costs and controlled quality, and of a selling network which is already rooted in the individual countries. In this way, they reinforce their powerful position by achieving scale economies and creating entry barriers.

# Systemic Frameworks: Interrelationships and Governance Body

## An Overview of Destination Classification Models

The latest literature on territorial tourism development analysed in detail local tourism systems with a specific view to dimensions such as network governance, impact of the network on tourists' perception, coordination mechanisms among stakeholders, role of technology as enabling factor, and intangible features of the systems.

Among the last mentioned field of research, the literature highlights many quantitative or qualitative interpretation and classification models. Within quantitative analysis, some authors (Bodega, Cioccarelli, & De Nicolai, 2004) suggest to focus attention on two aspects of the tourist network which can be more objectively measured (density and centrality degree of the network), highlighting four typical situations: the *governed model* (a low density model characterised by a high level of centrality); and the *corporative model* (where, while persisting a high level of centrality, a high level of density can also be found). When the degree of government functions decentralisation increases and density is low the *community model* is developed, while the *constellation model* corresponds to high levels of density.

Within qualitative analyses, some authors (Pencarelli, 2003), highlighting dimensions such as trust and willingness to co-operate, make a distinction between *casual tourism systems* and *tourism systems strictly meant*; the latter is sub-divided into those mainly characterised by self-organisation (*networks*) and those governed by a central body (*viable systems*[10]).

Within this framework, other authors (Flagestad & Hope, 2001), attaching more importance to the centralisation of the governance functions, maintain that tourism systems may have a configuration in-between the two end points of a continuum, named "Community Model" and "Corporate Model" respectively. The "Community Model", typical of the European areas, consists of specialised individual independent business units (service providers) operating in a decentralised way; no business unit holds a dominant administrative position or dominant ownership within the destination. Strategic leadership, which does exist, is characterised by a stakeholder-oriented management covering issues such as environmental sustainability, destination planning, product development, destination marketing, co-operation projects, etc. Management lies within the competence of the community political and administrative institutions (often the local government or a destination management organisation with local government participation or influence). In the "Corporate Model", typical of American areas, destination management is often represented or dominated by a business corporation. These corporations manage (for profit) a strategic selection of service providers incorporated by ownership and/or contracts; consequently, the local authority and tourism board play a marginal and support role compared to the corporation which is instead the process key player.

---

[10] The concept of Viable System originates from studies on business governance and management (Golinelli, 2000) and was effectively applied to territorial systems (Golinelli, 2002). Based on this approach a territorial viable system can be defined as an entity:

With its own objectives

Capable of expressing its own vocation depending on the characteristics of the territorial space in a given time

Characterised by a governance body capable of guiding its overall development

Object of strategic and operational decisions.

Jamal and Getz (1995) suggest some key conditions which have to be met in a joint-planning process to facilitate dissemination and implementation of ideas, integration of different views and solution of conflicts. For a *"community-based"* planning, co-operation requires participants recognising the high level of interdependence in the territorial planning and management, the benefits which can result from joint actions, a specific willingness to implement the decisions made by the community.

The authors highlight the need to involve some key players for a successful process — such as local government and other government organisations which have an impact on the local area, entrepreneurs and trade associations, organisations of citizens, as well as an experienced and recognised leader (whether private or public, individual or company) capable of involving the various stakeholders. Lastly, the success of the initiative strictly depends on the development of a shared vision and common objectives for a strategic planning, and on the creation of a stable co-operation organisation supporting and monitoring the development planned.

This short review synthetically illustrates a framework of studies and research works on territorial networks characterised by a high heterogeneity as to terminology and variables; this heterogeneity can be overcome only through an abstraction process aimed at identifying wider and unifying concepts including the various configurations.

### The Level of Interdependence Among the Actors

A classification is then suggested here allowing the various variables used to interpret the characteristics of the network and based on two synthetic dimensions:

- degree of interdependence among the system's stakeholders
- degree of centralisation of the system governance functions.

The degree of interdependence among stakeholders is meant as the degree of influence exerted by an individual player on one or more members of the system. The three variables identified by the literature as determinants of the intensity of the interdependence among the players of the territorial system are:

- density of the relationships, meant as the number of links among the organisations of the tourism system, against the total number of links which might be established
- degree of willingness, meant as players' awareness of their interdependence, and as intention to manage it
- degree of mutual trust (non-opportunistic behaviours).

Therefore, as long as the intensity of the three variables mentioned above increases, there is a shift from a configuration characterised by a low degree of interdependence to a configuration characterised by a high level of interdependence. In this way it is possible to position the tourism systems along a continuum of possible configurations (Figure 8.2), with two opposite positions at the two end points:

- low level of interdependence: organisations belong to the same territorial area but are only linked by proximity links and market relationships. This configuration is characterised by spontaneous and unaware interdependences, low degree of relationship density and low degree of mutual trust.

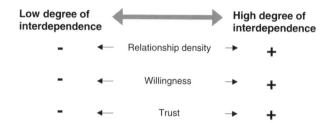

Figure 8.2: Interdependence among the organisations of the system.
*Source*: Our data processing.

- high level of interdependence: organisations, in addition to belonging to the same territorial area, have the same strategic objectives and a high level of co-ordination. This makes it possible for the system to present itself to the external world (and to be perceived by it) as a unitary entity. In this case the configuration is characterised by an aware planned and managed interdependence, high relationship intensity and high trust levels.

### The Level of Centralisation of the System Governance Functions

As to the second dimension suggested above, the degree of centralisation of the system governance functions can be meant as a measure of the distribution among all players of the formal and actual powers to influence the evolutionary paths of the system.

The three variables which mostly affect the centralisation level of the system governance functions are:

- recognition of the governance body: meant as the recognition by the organisations inside and outside the system of a body performing strategic functions to orient the system itself
- degree of strategy formalisation: meant as the degree of use of codified methods and tools when outlining the system development paths
- degree of centrality of the organisations: meant as the distribution of the relationships among the various players, and consequently, the degree of centralisation of the whole network.

Also in this case there is a continuum (Figure 8.3); when the intensity of the variables allowed for increases, there is a shift from a situation characterised by a low level of centralisation of the governance functions (distributed governance) to a high level of centralisation (centralised governance).

Specifically, the configurations which can be found at the two end points of the continuum are:

- low level of centralisation: internal and external organisations do not recognise the governance body, the level of strategy formalisation is low and centralisation level is low as

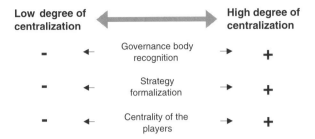

Figure 8.3: Centralisation of the system governance functions.
*Source*: Our data processing.

well. The organisations involved adopt decision-making mechanisms based on mutual adjustment; functions are equally distributed

- high level of centralisation: internal and external organisations recognise the governance body, the strategy formalisation level is high, and the degree of relationship centralisation is high as well. The organisations involved adopt hierarchy-based decision-making mechanisms; roles and functions are clearly defined.

### *The Four Ideal Types of Tourism Systems*

Crossing these two aforementioned dimensions, four ideal types of tourism system can be identified (Figure 8.4):

- Market cluster: it is a system where players, although located in the same area and belonging to the same tourism *filière*, do not establish co-operation relationships and do not recognise a unitary governance body. The system evolves following paths determined by exogenous factors, such as market dynamics and individual choices basically made as a result of mutual adjustments within a competitive approach.
- District: it is a system where, like in the market cluster, there is no unitary governance, but differently players try and establish long-lasting co-operation relationships and decision-making processes are jointly implemented. Evolutionary pathways imply co-evolution of the various players and individual choices are based on a multi-lateral adjustment (partnership like).
- Tourism local system: it is a system characterised by close relationships among players and the existence of a governance body capable of orienting development paths. Decision-making processes are then guided by a key player whose choices are amplified by the close interdependence among all organisations involved.
- Constellation: it is a system with a governance body having strong powers and acting as a core of the relationship network; then, while relationships among the various players are mere market interdependences, relationships with the key player are characterised by hierarchy. Decision-making processes are then guided by the key player, which determines the evolutionary paths the organisations will have to adjust to.

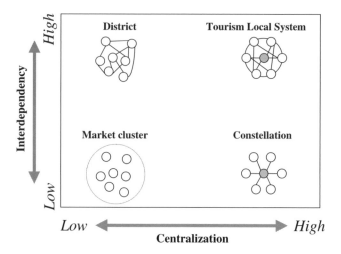

Figure 8.4: Possible configurations of the system.
*Source*: Our data processing.

With respect to the various tourism system configurations, in the literature there is a debate on the superiority of one configuration over the other ones (meant as capability of supporting the sustainable development of a specific territorial area). Actually, till date there is no study capable of producing univocal empirical evidences of such superiority. Conversely, it seems more meaningful to assume that the ability of a tourism system to generate competitive products is not only a function of its configuration, but also of the consistency between the configuration itself and a number of contingent factors related to the territorial area and the competitive system.

## The Tourism Product

The third level of analysis of the conceptual model suggested here is the tourism product; it is a further breaking down of the tourism system and can be viewed as the whole set of sub-systems, which have to meet the tourism demand attracted by the area. Into these sub-systems the resources are strictly inter-linked by constraints and scope economies to meet the needs of a specific typology of tourist are conveyed. These resources are then an idiosyncratic whole capable of contributing — in a unitary fashion — to tourists satisfaction level. Based on this approach the literature has developed many different notions of tourism product which can be sub-divided into four macro-categories based on two variables (Figure 8.5):

- the perspective from which the product is defined; actually a distinction can be made between the definitions referring to the product from the supply side, and the definitions referring to the product from the demand side

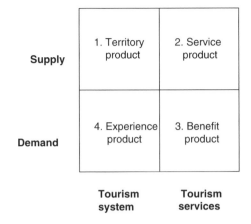

Figure 8.5: Different concepts of tourism product.
*Source*: Our data processing.

- the emphasis laid on the various elements making up the product; in this case a distinction can be made between the definitions which mostly relate to the individual tourism services and the definitions referring to the tourism system as a whole.

The combination of the two variables identifies four ideal types of tourism product:

• Territory product, related to Lewis's and Chambers's definition (1989), meant as a whole set of natural and/or anthropic attraction factors which a specific area can provide to a specific typology of tourist
• Service product, meant as a whole set of goods and services differently provided to tourists during their stay in the destination, in line with Borghesi's definition (1994)
• Benefit product, meant as the bundle of activities, services and benefits which contribute to determining the tourist satisfaction level (Medlik & Middleton, 1973)
• Experience product, meant as the tourists' overall experience of the destination resulting from their cognitive processes during their interaction with the area attraction factors. This definition was suggested by Rispoli and Tamma (1995).

While these four definitions differently emphasise the features of the tourism product, a number of convergent elements can be found in them.

Firstly, it is possible to highlight that, in defining the tourism product, all of them (although to a different extent) refer to the demand/supply interaction and to the unitary re-arrangement of the bundle of resources within the tourists' cognitive system. Actually, through their discretional actions, tourists make a selection of the available resources — choosing the ones which are more consistent with their way of thinking and their motivations — and link them within a unitary experience framework. The tourism product is then recognised as a product having a systemic nature and the capability of creating synergies resulting from the participation of the various resources in the same tourism enjoyment process. Lastly, the organisational dimension of the tourism product and the resulting value are considered by all approaches illustrated here as the joint result generated by the supply and demand process (Figure 8.6).

As to this point it is worth stressing that the ability of the tourism system to generate organised supply forms translating into a value added for the demand side is limited by some specificities related to the system stakeholders:

- High supply fragmentation; the number of firms involved in the tourism system is quite high and they usually are small-sized firms
- Limited scope of the business; firms have a short-term strategic vision and their scope of action is limited to their own *core business*
- High level of heterogeneity; firms are quite varied as to their main business and their legal status.

These features hinder inter-firm co-operation making the creation of spontaneous forms of tourism products quite complex.

In this field there is a wide scientific production which, adopting the point of view of small tourism firms, analyses their capability of establishing win–win relationships with other players within the system. Lowe (1988) focused on the composition of the systems and observed that the "extended family" approach, also described by Quinn, Larmour, and McQuillan (1992) and Lee-Ross and Ingold (1994) can be applied. The author maintains that firms view economically important subjects linked to them by social relationships (e.g. consumers, employees, distribution channels) as part of their family network; from this network other subjects are excluded, such as banks or accountants with which formal and rigid relationships are established.

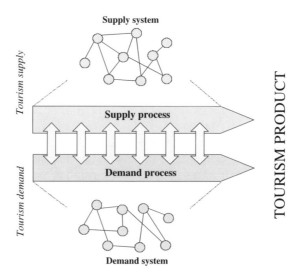

Figure 8.6: Origin of tourism product.
*Source*: Our data processing.

Adopting the small firm's perspective, Morrison (1994), focusing on the relationships between small tourism firms and product distribution channels, identified four typologies of organisations as potential partners (wholesalers, private sector retailers, public sector retailers, voluntary consortia) highlighting their costs, benefits and main implications in terms of power management.

Littlejohn, Foley, and Lennon (1996), analysing accommodation facilities consortia, identified a positive attitude of individual firms in creating networks with promotional aims and supporting the creation of new products. Conversely the authors highlighted that, also in case of high co-operation levels, limited effects on the business performance are produced.

As to the origin of the tourism product, the literature recognises three different modes through which it is generated (Rispoli & Tamma, 1995). The first one includes the organisational activity of the tourist who, taking care of what is necessary to organise his/her vacation, actually assemblies the product (point-point approach). Tourists devise their own vacation, select the individual operators, purchase the relevant services, plan the activities to enjoy the products and services provided, manage unexpected events.

The second mode of "genesis" recognises instead the existence of an organisation arranging the tourism product (e.g. a tour operator or a travel agency). This organisation deals with all most important issues linked to the management of the vacation in a specific destination (from planning to organisation, purchasing of the various product components, implementation of the actions required in case of unexpected events) providing tourists with a structured service package (package approach).

The third mode of "genesis" identifies in the mutual co-operation among local organisations the basic principle to facilitate the tourism activity. Through a multiple network of relationships, the various players differently contribute to defining joint marketing policies and/or joint tools to enjoy the services provided (network approach). By so doing tourists are given additional benefits compared to those provided by the individual services:

- Timely organisation of the vacation; e.g. by proposing a portfolio of ideas and options linked to the stay in the specific area
- Cost effectiveness, e.g. through discounts linked to the joint purchase of different services
- Facilitating service purchasing, e.g. thanks to joint telematic booking services
- Guarantee of the product quality, e.g. by using shared standards
- Facilitating payment of the services provided, e.g. by pre-paid *cards*
- Efficiency in visiting local attractions, e.g. by organising local mini tours.

These three different forms of aggregation of the local tourism resources generate a specific *value proposition* through which the territorial sub-system qualifies as tourism product. Simultaneously, the services which are part of it make the satisfaction level promised to tourists explicit.

Consequently the value proposition has to be: easily recognisable by tourists while organising their vacation and enjoying it; accessible from the space and time standpoint; usable in a way which is consistent with the tourist's expectations.

The different models originating the tourism product determine the different level of inclusion of the *value proposition* key attributes in the product (Figure 8.7). Actually, assuming that the tourist has self-organised the whole product, the value proposition might

| | Value proposition characteristics | | |
|---|---|---|---|
| | **Self-organised** | **Co-organised** | **Externally organised** |
| **High** | Recognisable | Usable | Accessible |
| **Medium** | Usable | Accessible | Recognisable |
| **Low** | Accessible | Recognisable | Usable |

Figure 8.7: Modes of product organisation and value propositions.
*Source*: Our data processing.

be highly recognisable, but the level of accessibility might be low and the level of use not always in line with the expectations. When the product organisation is made by a single operator (e.g. a tour operator) the value proposition might be highly recognisable and the level of accessibility quite adequate, but the level of use might be too full with constraints and then would not meet the tourist's needs.

Lastly, when operators co-operate to facilitate self-organisation, the level of use might meet the tourist's needs, the level of accessibility might be adequate, but the value proposition might not be very recognisable.

## The Process

As observed by some authors (Tinsley & Lynch, 2001), destination development is mainly analysed allowing for the geographical and/or physical increase of tourism infrastructures, disregarding intangible aspects, such as people's attitudes and values or the role played by inter-organisation relationships and their contribution to the territorial development.

Therefore, analysis of the development processes of a destination refers to the strategies implemented to introduce changes on the territory as a whole, making distinctions based solely on the evolutionary stage. Within these classifications different typologies of models explaining change can be found:

(a) prescription models, such as Butler's traditional life cycle (1980), which suggest a number of evolutionary stages the destination goes through following a pre-set path
(b) construction models, such as the ones founded on the application of the theory of chaos (Russel & Faulkner, 1999, 2004), which do not include pre-set paths and provide for the possibility of incremental and radical changes
(c) hybrid models, such as the Broad Context Model suggested by Weaver (2000), including different possible stages the destination goes through, which are not linked to a sequence-based path but to a number of paths, identifying a given number of possible evolutionary pathways.

On the contrary, to investigate the dynamic aspects of the model illustrated here the analysis will be focused on two main processes: the process which, starting from the platform of local resources, leads to the creation of a tourism system; the process which links, through a mutual interaction, the tourism products to the tourism system from which they are originated.

The first process is characterised by a high degree of homogeneity as to the nature of the macro-stages, and by a high level of heterogeneity as to the sequence of these stages.

Specifically, the main macro-stages highlighted by the empirical observation as constant stages of the process are (Figure 8.8):

- *Planning of the local resource development*: it is the stage when the framework of the actions required to adjust the local resources to the pre-set tourism development objectives is outlined.
- *Creation of a Destination Management Organization (DMO)*: in this stage a body is created charged with co-ordinating the activities implemented by the various organisations involved in the local tourism supply.
- *Searching for regulatory and financial tools*: it is the stage when financial resources are searched for and identified; the juridical-administrative conditions necessary to implement tourism development programmes are also created.
- *Marketing planning*: it is the stage when crucial marketing choices are made and the operational activities required to reach the local tourism development objectives are developed.
- *Innovation management*: it is the stage when processes of change are triggered concerning the relationships among the various operators involved in the design of the basic principles which will guide the development of the local tourism business.

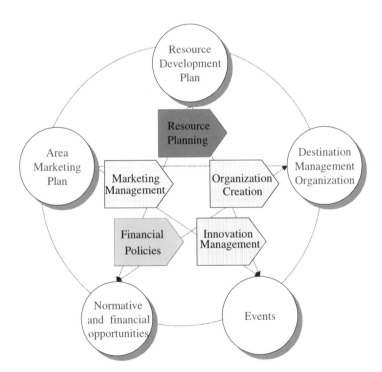

Figure 8.8: Territorial development plan (from Bonetti & Simoni, 2004).

Each of these macro-stages give rise to an operational activity aimed at implementing the decisions made and related to the various fields.

Actually, the process to create a local tourism system can start from any of the macro-stages mentioned above and have a different sequence (Figure 8.9).[11]

For example, from the empirical point of view, processes aimed at creating tourism networks are frequently started by the availability of financial resources aimed at promoting the local tourism development. Usually to catch this opportunity an organisation is created at the local level, charged with allocating these resources and co-ordinating the beneficiaries. The actions carried out by this co-ordinator and by the organisations involved by it translate into a more or less formal marketing plan, followed by a local resource development plan. The process is finalised by organising an event during which the new ability of the local area to position itself on the tourism market is illustrated.

In other cases a number of local operators, with an innovative strategic vision, develop a marketing plan aimed at catching new tourism markets, the outcomes achieved by these operators are a stimulus for public and private organisations to allocate higher financial resources, the use of which is decided by a local development plan and governed by an ad hoc DMO. Also in this case the process is finalised with an event aimed at promoting the potentials of the destination and of its "new tourism supply".

The processes shortly illustrated above highlight that financial and market opportunities are a trigging factor; however, the observation of concrete examples highlights how this role can be played by any of the other macro-stages.

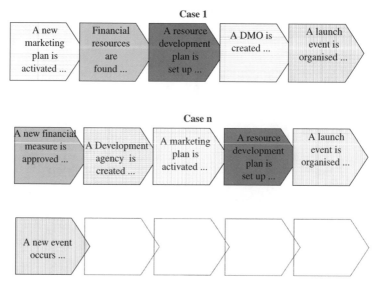

Figure 8.9: Examples of process configuration (from Bonetti & Simoni, 2004).

---

[11] An interesting case study about the dynamics of network creation is provided in Pavolvich (2003).

However, regardless of the sequence of the macro-stages, when these develop regularly, the arrival point is represented by a tourism system capable of enhancing resources and turning them into tourism products, thanks to:

- A coordinating organization capable of governing the system
- A resource development plan guiding the process aimed at improving local infrastructures
- A marketing plan guiding the creation, enhancement and commercialization of the tourism products
- A whole set of financial resources and administration tools enabling the implementation of the plans mentioned above
- A whole set of competencies allowing the system to evolve and to face future environmental and internal changes.

As to the relationships between tourism system and tourism products, the aggregation process of the tourism resources in order to create specific products is characterised by some specificities, which substantially differentiate it from the marketing process traditionally meant.

Specifically, to reconstruct the different rationales underlying this process two approaches (well established from the theoretical and practical point of view) have to be mentioned:

a) The first approach, short-term change-oriented, is basically aimed at making the local tourism offer more attractive to the segments of tourists usually served and to other segments not currently covered. This result is achieved by enhancing the capability of a specific area of "reshaping" its *value proposition*, namely by finding new configurations and mix of the available resources.

b) The second approach is medium-long term change-oriented, instead of increasing tourism flows in the short term. It is aimed at re-positioning the destination to catch tourism segments which cannot be currently covered. This result is achieved by radically changing the local resources and re-defining the local identity, thus making it possible for the area to develop fully new tourism products.[12]

Tourism development then starts from an approach based on a short-term competition and tourism offer strictly meant, to shift to a strategy requiring to make leverage on the creation of tourism-territorial distinctive competences, and on the ability to promote new, sustainable ideas convincingly.

A sustainable tourism development of a specific area is then increasingly a function of its ability to combine short-term strategies, capable of attracting substantial tourism flows, with medium-long term strategies which, by generating new knowledge, relationships and financial resources enable to increase the competitiveness of the area against other alternative tourism destinations.

More specifically, the first approach is a *market-driven approach*, aimed at identifying that mix of *available resources* capable of catching the contingent opportunities provided by the tourism market, while being consistent with the long-term tourism development strategy.

---

[12] These two streams of thought are often identified referring to the concepts of tourism marketing and territorial marketing; for the distinction between the two concepts also refer to: Caroli (1999); Borghesi (1997); Golfetto (1996).

Conversely, the second approach is a *resource-based approach*, aimed at identifying and developing the *necessary resources* to fill the gap between the current local tourism identity and its future identity, which will be a function of the possible evolutionary scenarios.

In the first case the existing resources are re-arranged and re-combined so as to give rise to new tourism products; in the second case existing resources are integrated with fully new ones so as to generate a new configuration of the tourism system, and, synthetically a new identity of the area.

These concepts are better explained by a number of key concepts included in the different theories developed with respect to large firms. More specifically, the methodological approach is split in two parts as a result of the *dual strategy* theory (Abell, 1994) where the firm development dynamics strictly depends on the co-existence of a short-term opportunistic change guided by the current context and a medium-long term change guided by the business vision of a "possible future".

Conversely, a simultaneous focus on supply and resources results from the strategic studies started in the early 1990s, highlighting a multi-level competition, making a distinction between product-based competition and ideas-based competition (Hamel & Prahalad, 1995; Grant, 1994).

Lastly, market-driven tourism development paths can be related, from the conceptual point of view, to the well-established studies on tourism marketing,[13] while those included in the second typology relate to the *resource-based view* (Grant, 1994) and to the studies on local development based on it. In a hyper-competitive environment tourism systems can be successful in the medium and long term provided that *destination management activities* achieve a balance between short and medium-long term processes.

Like in business strategy studies, these two processes are inter-related and unified (Figure 8.10).

The first process, in addition to achieving the main outcome — i.e. attracting tourism flows to the destination — generates two additional outcomes: (a) weak signals will be produced as to the points and of strength and weakness of the bundle of resources the tourism supply is based on, and/or as to the opportunities linked to specific development scenarios; (b) one or more local organisations will play the role of change promoters suggesting new visions to introduce changes in the area and create a new valuable function for it.[14] These *outcomes* are *trigging factors* of the medium-long term process which, in its turn, generates a change in the structure of the local resources and in the capabilities of the local players, and the possibility to exploit new market opportunities thus creating fully new tourism offers. Of course within a mutual link-based approach, these new or changed capabilities are the foundation to develop a new short-term oriented tourism marketing process.

Local resources then play a crucial role in linking the two processes as they are both the crucial *tool* used in short-term processes and the *object* of medium-long term processes.

---

[13] Refer to Baccarani (1999); Casarin (1996); Rispoli and Tamma (1995); Borghesi (1994).

[14] In this paper, by main output of the process we mean the result for which the process is implemented and for which qualitative and/or quantitative objectives have been set; for example the variation, in absolute or percentage terms, of the number of tourists in a specific are in a given period of time. By outcome of the process we mean instead not a sub-product, but a result for which no qualitative and quantitative objectives can be set during the design stage. Actually, we cannot think of setting as a process objective such as getting weak signals or having a player playing the role of change promoter.

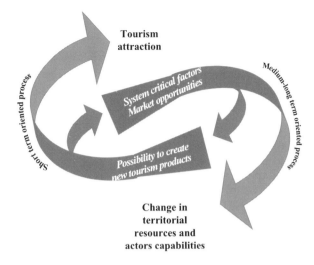

Figure 8.10: Interactions among the various time scales of the process.
*Source*: Our data processing.

## Conclusion

Local tourism development has been studied by many authors, as witnessed by the many papers written on this issue, the wide range of approaches suggested and the specific issues covered.

The territorial area, as a complex system, seems to be a field of study at the border of many disciplines, thus requiring a cross-fertilisation of the different knowledge domains involved. It is too early to know whether all these studies and research works will give rise to a new discipline; however, there is no doubt that, from the epistemological point of view, there is a need for systematising and linking the various streams of thought being developed so far.

This paper does not intend to provide any final answer; its aim is to participate in the current debate suggesting an interpretation model according to which the study of a territorial system requires its breaking down in various levels, each of them characterised by its own specificity in terms of problems, interpretation keys, evolutionary dynamics, functioning and governance approaches. Understanding the differences among the different levels of analysis is the only way to recognise the contribution provided by the various theories and to plan concrete and sustainable development processes.

## References

Abell, D.F. (1994). *Strategia duale: Dominare il presente, anticipare il futuro*. Milano: Il Sole 24 Ore.
Ancarani, F. (1999). Il marketing territoriale: Un nuovo approccio per la valorizzazione delle aree economico-sociali. *Economia e Diritto del Terziario, 1*.
Baccarani, C. (1999). Il marketing delle località turistiche. *Sinergie, 17* (49), 101–103.

Bodega, D., Cioccarelli, G., & De Nicolai, S. (2004). New interorganizational forms: Evolution of relationship structures in mountain tourism. *Tourism Review, 59*, n. 3.

Bonetti, E., & Simoni, M. (2004). Network creation paths: The role of sport, cultural and tourist events as trigging factors. In: J. Swarbrooke, & C.S. Petrillo (Eds), *Proceedings of the 12th Atlas International Conference, Networking & Partnerships in Destination Development & Management*, Irat-Cnr, Albano, Napoli.

Borghesi, A. (Ed.). (1994). *Il marketing delle località turistiche*. Torino: Giappichelli.

Borghesi, A. (1997). Dal marketing turistico al marketing territoriale. In: *Economia, società e istituzioni* (Vol. 9).

Boschetti, C. (1999). *Risorse e strategia d'impresa*, Il Mulino.

Butler, R. (1980). The concept of a tourist area cycle of evolution: Implications for management of resources. *Canadian Geographer, 24*, n. 1.

Calvelli, A., Cannavale, C., & Canestrino, R. (2004). The replication of the industrial district model: Cross-cultural issues. *Journal of Cross-Cultural Competence & Management, 4*.

Casarin, F. (1996). *Il marketing dei prodotti turistici. Specificità e varietà*. Torino: Giappichelli.

Cercola, R. (1999). Economia neoindustriale e marketing territoriale. *Sviluppo & Organizzazione, 172*, 65–78.

De Carlo, M. (2004). La formula imprenditoriale: Uno strumento per analizzare il profilo strategico. In: M. De Carlo (Ed.), *Management delle aziende del turismo. Letture e casi*. Milano: Egea.

Flagestad, A., & Hope, C.A. (2001). Strategic success in winter sports destinations: A sustainable value creation perspective. *Tourism Management, 22*, n. 5.

Franch, M. (Ed.) (2002). *Destination management. Governare il turismo fra locale e globale*. Torino: Giappichelli.

Golfetto, F. (1996). Un marketing per le città? Riflessioni sulla nascita di una disciplina. *Economia e Management, 5*.

Golinelli, G.M. (2000). *L'approccio sistemico al governo dell'impresa* (Vol. I). Padova: Cedam.

Golinelli, C.M. (2002). *Il territorio sistema vitale. Verso un modello di analisi*. Torino: Giappichelli.

Grant, R.M. (1994). *L'analisi strategica nella gestione aziendale*. Bologna: Il Mulino.

Hamel, G., & Prahalad, C.K. (1995). *Alla conquista del futuro*. Milano: Il Sole 24 Ore.

Jamal, T.B., & Getz, D. (1995). Collaboration theory and community tourism planning. *Annals of Tourism Research, 22*, n. 1.

Kotler, P., Heider, D.H., & Rein, L. (1993). *Marketing places*. New York: The Free Press.

Lee-Ross, D., & Ingold, T. (1994). Increasing productivity in small hotels: Are academic proposal realistic? *International Journal of Hospitality Management, 13*, n. 3.

Lewis, R., & Chambers, R. (1989). *Marketing leadership in hospitality*. New York: Van Nostrand Reinhold.

Littlejohn, D., Foley, M., & Lennon, J. (1996). The potential accommodation consortia in the highlands and islands of Scotland. In: *Proceedings of IAHMS Spring Symposium*, Leeds Metropolitan University, Leeds.

Lorenzoni, G. (1990). *L'architettura di sviluppo delle imprese minori*. Bologna: Il Mulino.

Lowe, A. (1988). Small hotel survival — An indicative approach. *International Journal of Hospitality Management, 7*, n. 3.

Medlik, S., & Middleton, V.T.C. (1973). Product formulation in tourism. In: *AIEST conference proceedings – tourisme et marketing, 13*.

Morrison, A.M. (1994). Small tourism business: Product distribution systems. In: *Proceedings of CHME Research Conference*, Napier University, Edinburgh.

Normann, R., & Ramirez, R. (1995). *Le strategie interattive d'impresa. Dalla catena del valore alla costellazione del valore*. Etaslibri.

Pavolvich, K. (2003). The evolution and transformation of a tourism destination network: The Waitomo Caves, New Zealand. *Tourism Management, 24, 2.*

Pencarelli, T. (2003). I rapporti interaziendali nelle reti turistiche: Collaborazione e conflitto. *Economia e Diritto del Terziario, 2.*

Pencarelli, T., & Civitarese, C. (1999). Marketing tradizionale, marketing relazionale e marketing interno nell'industria turistica: Verso un'integrazione. *Economia e Diritto del Terziario, 1,* 125–153.

Petrillo, C.S. (2001). *Risorse ambientali e sviluppo delle attività turistiche.* Monografie C.N.R. I.R.A.T., No. 10.

Porter, M. E. (1990). *The competitive advantage of nations.* London: Macmillan.

Priestley, G., & Mundet, L. (1998). The post-stagnation phase of the resort cycle. *Annals of Tourism Research, 25,* n. 1.

Quinn, U., Larmour, R., & McQuillan, N. (1992). The small firm in the hospitality industry. *International Journal of Contemporary Hospitality Management, 4,* n. 1.

Rispoli, M., & Tamma, M. (1995). *Risposte strategiche alla complessità: Le forme di offerta dei prodotti alberghieri.* Torino: Giappichelli.

Russell, R., & Faulkner, B. (1999). Movers and shakers: Chaos makers in tourism development. *Tourism Management, 20,* n. 4, 411–423.

Russell, R., & Faulkner, B., (2004). Entrepreneurship, chaos and the tourism area lifecycle. *Annals of Tourism Research, 31,* n. 3, 556–579.

Sautter, E.T., & Leisen, B. (1999). Managing stakeholders. A tourism planning model. *Annals of Tourism Research, 26,* n. 2.

Sicca, L. (1999). Le risorse e le competenze come fattori di sviluppo del territorio. *Rassegna Economica Banco di Napoli, LXIII* (luglio-dicembre), 2.

Simon, H.A. (1995). Near decomposability and complexity: How a mind resides in a brain. In: H.J. Morowitz, & J.L. Singer (Eds), *The mind, the brain and complex adaptive systems.* Reading, MA: Addison-Wesley.

Smeral, E. (1998). The impact of globalization on small and medium enterprises: New challenges for tourism policies in European countries. *Tourism Management, 19,* n. 4.

Socher, K., & Tschurtschenthaler, P. (2003). Destination management e politica normativa. In: H. Pechlaner, K. Weiermair, & C. Laesser (Eds), *Politica del turismo e destination management.* Milano: Touring Club Italiano.

Tinsley, R., & Lynch, P. (2001). Small tourism business networks and destination development. *Hospitality Management, 20,* n. 4.

Tremblay, P. (2000). An evolutionary interpretation of the role of collaborative partnerships in sustainable tourism. In: B. Bramwell, & B. Lane (Ed.), *Tourism collaboration and partnerships: Politics, practice and sustainability.* Clevedon: Channel View Publications.

Valdani, E., & Ancarani, F. (2000). Il marketing territoriale nell'economia della conoscenza. In: E. Valdani, & F. Ancarani (Eds), *Strategie di marketing del territorio.* Milano: Egea.

Varaldo, R., & Caroli, M.G. (1999). Il marketing del territorio: Ipotesi di un percorso di ricerca. *Sinergie, 17,* n. 49, 73–84.

Vicari, S., & Mangiarotti, D. (1999). Il marketing delle grandi città. *Sinergie, 17,* n. 49, 85–99.

Weaver, D.B. (2000). A broad context model of destination development scenarios. *Tourism Management, 21,* n. 3, 217–320.

Weiermair, K. (1999). Partnership in tourism as a tool for competitive advantage in tourist SMEs. CISET, *International Conference, From destination to destination marketing and management,* Venezia, 15–16 marzo.

Chapter 9

# Integrated Quality Management as Part of the Strategic Management of Tourism Destinations: A Systems Perspective

Francisco Manuel Dionísio Serra

## Introduction

> The tourism industry must meet the challenge of competitiveness. Quality has become a key element in Community actions aimed at the competitiveness of European tourism, a condition of growth, of job creation and thus of the sustainable and balanced development of the European Union. (Crauser, 1998)

The quality of tourism destinations is essentially a qualitative concept, resulting from a positioning or reputation earned in the market and usually reflected in its consolidated (organic) image. It is, thus, a perception based on the overall evaluation of the services delivered by the many tourist providers in a given destination, together with other inputs, like day-to-day information conveyed by the media, the security situation, perceptions of country development and political alignment, etc.

Integrated quality management, or IQM, is a European-led initiative aimed at encouraging the development and implementation of a sustainable and quality-oriented approach to tourism. A quality service only exists as much as the visitor, or consumer, perceives it to meet their expectations and requirements. It is important therefore to take into account all aspects of the visitor experience, from initial planning through travel, destination information, accommodation to the 'after-sales' care and communication.

The existence of feedback cycles is a major reference to those who believe that structures condition systems behaviour and that the way to change it is to understand how the structure is organized, since these feedback cycles determine the characteristics of the interrelations between variables of a given system or from different systems.

The principles of IQM take into account the whole of a destination's tourism system. It is an initiative that relies heavily on community involvement and participation and allows a form of integrated dialogue to develop between potential visitors, tourism stakeholders at local and regional levels, and sustainable economic and cultural development initiatives.

Quality management requires a continuous and dynamic process, not a one off initiative and as such the approach taken needs to be one that becomes reflected in all the normal activities undertaken by a destination: promotion, information provision, developing and improving product and so on (see Figure 9.1).

IQM is about delivering quality at all stages of the tourism experience. The deliverance of a quality experience will result in an increase in repeat visitors and those that visit through recommendation by others (see Figure 9.2).

Quality management of a tourism destination is achieved through working closely with the local communities and tourism stakeholders in the area. Working towards sustainable quality in tourism involves communication and monitoring, through

(1) understanding needs and meeting them;
(2) checking and communicating standards;
(3) training and business support; and
(4) monitoring impacts on local economy, community and environment.

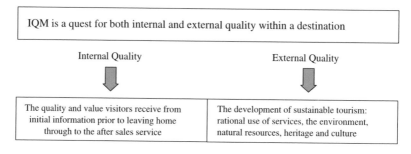

Figure 9.1: The IQM concept.
*Source*: University of Wales (online) 3/2004.

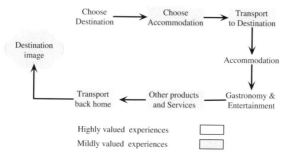

Figure 9.2: A tourist services chain.
*Source*: Author's own.

In its report *Towards Quality Rural Tourism: IQM in Rural Tourist Destinations (2000)*, the European Commission recommends that tourism destinations aiming to develop and implement a quality approach to tourism should adopt and adhere to 15 core principles of IQM at every stage of tourism planning and development. These principles offer a common sense approach to sustainable and integrated tourism, a realistic and achievable way to meet social, cultural and environmental needs while improving the competitiveness of the tourism destinations.

## Tourism, Integrated Quality Management and Sustainability

To evolve in accordance with the sustainability principles, tourism must operate in harmony with the local environment, community and culture, so that these become the permanent beneficiaries and not victims of tourism development. Achieving sustainability depends on a balance of private initiative, economic instruments and regulation, translating global principles into focused local action and new public–private sector delivery mechanisms. This may give birth to a new and necessary tourism culture that bestows more importance to the environment as a valid and valued raw material for tourism development, contributing to the positive reinforcement of the overall destination image which, ultimately, is the key variable used by the potential tourists to make their decisions.

According to these principles, tourism can be a driving force in the management of the involved resources, in such a way that we can fulfill economic, social and aesthetic needs while maintaining cultural integrity, essential ecological processes, biological diversity and life support systems (Murphy, 1994).

The dimensions incorporated within this definition are an example of the general multi-dimensionality and interdisciplinary concerns commonly addressed by the sustainability and the integrated quality movements.

The fulfilment of social obligations, means more than intergenerational equity, it means respect for other livelihoods and customs. Such variety and heritage is a major resource for tourism in a world that is fast becoming homogenized into a global economy.

A major component of environment and culture is their aesthetic appeal. While the focus has often been on international markers, such as world-renowned sites, the aesthetic qualities of regular townscapes and general landscapes should not be overlooked. These needs should be addressed within ecological parameters to sustain both the physical and human environments. The ecological process needs to be understood so that tourism intrusions will have the minimal impact, especially in sensitive coastal areas. The concern over maintaining our biological diversity is particularly germane to tourism, which thrives on the appeal of different flora and fauna along a distinctive sense of place.

Quality exists only to the extent that a product or a service meets the customer's requirements and expectations. Accordingly, the individual elements making up a strategy based on quality 'standards' have to be based on a thorough understanding of the customer. Total quality management systems are already part and parcel of the approaches that tourist service providers (tour operators, travel agents, hotels, restaurants, etc.) are developing.

As far as tourists are concerned, however, the satisfaction derived from staying at a destination does not just depend on their experience of tourist services, but also on more general factors such as hospitality, safety and security, sanitation and salubrity, traffic and visitor management. A large number of factors have an impact on tourists' perception of a destination, on their level of satisfaction and therefore on their willingness to return to the destination or to recommend it to potential visitors. The success of a destination in terms of tourist satisfaction is therefore shaped by a number of interdependent components. This underscores the need for strategic and integrated planning of tourist destinations, and for specific tools and techniques through which IQM (including quality control) can be put into practice in the destination.

According to Grahn and Johnson (2000), business are encouraged to register for ISO standards under the assumption that compliance with them will lead to improved processes, product/service reliability, relationships with customers and ultimately profits. It is possible to identify five key feedback structures (Cost Savings, Bureaucracy, Stakeholders Motivation, Quality Improvement and Investment) regarding the implementation of quality management systems. All of them are worth considering, be it a tourism destination concerned with the implementation of the IQM concept or an organization considering to register for an ISO standard.

(1) *Cost Savings*. When the reliability of products and services goes up, the internal and external failure costs (scrap, rework, warranty, etc.) should go down. However, there can be a delay in realizing these savings, because it takes time for the added standards to go up. The cost of compliance also goes up, owing to corrective actions, system maintenance, etc. This expense can increase cost pressures on the total system and take investment resources away from other opportunities. If this loop should begin to dominate, it would reverse any gains achieved from boosting customer retention and profits. In addition to improving processes, product/service reliability and customer relations, conforming to quality standards can lead to cost savings and money to invest in other opportunities.

(2) *Bureaucracy*. The increased level of compliance to ISO standards that occurs as audits continue over time can lead to more and more bureaucracy. Bureaucracy can in turn result in increased rigidity throughout the organization, whereby the firm becomes less adaptable to rapidly changing customer and market needs. Not surprisingly, lack of responsiveness to customers can severely damage customer retention over time.

(3) *Stakeholders Motivation*. Too much of a focus on "problems" (what is not working) as opposed to forward movement (what is working, or what we need more of to achieve our purpose) can seriously corrode stakeholders moral, motivation and willingness to embrace change. The primary focus of auditing (enforced compliance) is on finding what is known as "non-compliances". Third-party, professional auditors typically discover anywhere from a dozen to 50 or more non-compliances every time they perform an audit. Most auditors would not consider that they had done their job well unless they uncovered a "respectable" number of non-compliances.

Regardless of how hard a destination or a company, for that matter, may try to couch such "findings" in terms of opportunities, this kind of auditing is unavoidably problem-focused.

The relationship between auditors and audited ranges, very often, from wary to downright adversarial. Over time, this tension can drain the destination's positive energy, leading to lower motivation and damaged morale. If motivation and morale go down, customer service could suffer, which in turn could threaten customer retention (see Figure 9.3).

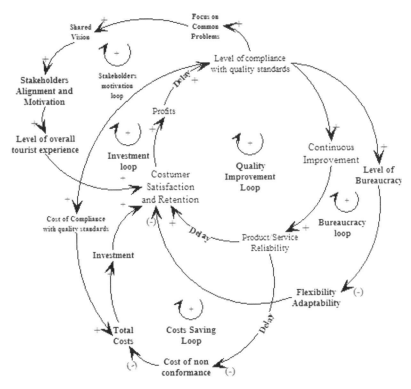

Figure 9.3: The five loops of quality implementation and its consequences.
*Source*: Author's own.

The positive reinforcing cycles of compliance to quality standards, improved customer/supplier relationships and cost savings may be balanced by the negative impacts of increased costs of compliance, a rise in bureaucracy and a focus on problems brought about by incessant auditing.

## The Systems Approach

The focus of most traditional quality management approaches is the individual tourist enterprise. For a destination, however, the number and range of actors involved necessarily requires a systems approach.

Tourism is an abstract, fragile, perishable, extremely diversified and fragmented "product". It requires a 'quality chain' made up of a number of links (operators): tour operators, travel agents outside the destination, passenger carriers, travel agents, hotels and other service providers in the destination. Visitors will also be faced with a set of stimuli within the destination which, although not specifically designed for them, will have an impact on their perceptions: security, the state of the roads, pollution of all kinds, local services (post, telephone), etc. For visitors, the service provided by the destination then takes the form of a global experience shaped by multiple, frequent and varied interactions between all the dimensions of the system. Account therefore needs to be taken of the whole of a destination's tourism system, from visitors initial planning to their return from their stay.

For a tourist destination, IQM can be seen as a systematic quest for internal and external quality (economic improvement in the short term and local development in the long term). Internal quality is the value that tourists receive throughout the chain of experiences characterizing their visit from the initial information that they receive prior to departure to the 'after-sales' service. This chain includes private links (private services purchased directly at market price) and public services such as destination's promotion, road maintenance, water management, public cleanliness, security, etc. Internal quality has short-term aims. External quality means the development of sustainable tourism with a rational and renewable use of resources such as territory, energy, water, natural resources, the heritage, etc., in order to prevent problems of congestion. The aim of external quality is one of long-term equilibrium.

## The Research Method

Traditional research in tourism has tended to use a reductionist approach in order to monitor certain flow variables, for instance, visitor numbers and their expenditure, or to measure discrete relationships, like tourist expenditures and employment, visitor numbers and social impacts, etc. It is important to recognize that tourism is not only realized through material flows, but mainly through *personal interrelations* (Sessa, 1988). Once this human element is introduced into the study of tourism, the limitations of mono-disciplinary approaches (economic, geographical, managerial, anthropological, etc.) recommend the adoption of a multi-disciplinary and holistic perspective (see Figure 9.4).

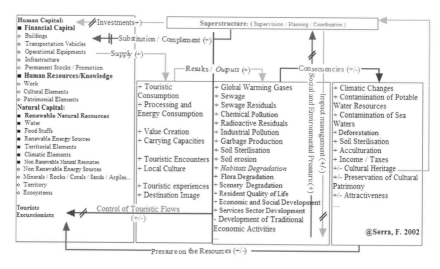

Figure 9.4: Input–Output model of the tourism system.
*Source*: Author's own.

One of the most important questions that arise in the context of integrated management (be it sustainable management, IQM or tourism destination management), is how it can be made effective and operational. In this matter, past research suggests that it can be achieved by (but not limited to) social dialogue, public administration's leadership, independent regulation, community participation or a combination of them. The results of such experiences show, however, that in most cases, the lack of an operative knowledge-based platform makes it difficult to achieve a shared vision and implement the strategies that derive from it, in order to give a real meaning to the qualitative (political) concepts mentioned above.

Systems Dynamics is a methodology that recognizes the interdependence and interrelatedness of all elements within a system and, although its origins are rooted in the General Systems Theory and its application was primarily in engineering, it has been progressively adopted by the social sciences as a method for understanding real-world phenomena, following the pioneering works of J.W. Forrester in the 1960s (Forrester, 1961 and 1973).

In the late 1960s it was recognized that the principles of General Systems Theory could be applied to a broad range of problems in the context of natural and social sciences and a considerable body of literature has since emerged on the theory and practice of systems methodology, particularly in the management sciences. Early positivist and functionalist approaches that characterized traditional systems thinking have given way to a more conceptual approach that can accommodate qualitative as well as quantitative factors.

For the purpose of tourism management a functionalist approach may be suitable in an operational sense, but many aspects of the tourism experience are also determined by perceptions of quality. It is therefore appropriate to use also the soft systems approach for the understanding of tourism.

In order to contribute to the continuing research effort and to find suitable answers, Serrra (2003), developed a dynamic model of the tourism system (MODISTUR) as well as a management experimental laboratory based on the mentioned model, which are summarised in this chapter. It is proposed that this model is a suitable choice to the understanding and management of tourism destinations because it includes the most important dimensions influencing the functioning of the tourism system. It can be used to manage the destination as a whole or just one of it's dimensions, with the advantage of having the model working and producing information from the whole system, showing the impacts of our decisions upon other dimensions that are not of prime concern now, but can be influent in the future, as the behaviour of the system is influenced by the existence of feedback cycles (see Figure 9.5).

A management experimental laboratory, also called Microworld in the Systems Dynamics literature, makes it possible to experiment with different management strategies and observe the impacts of those strategies, over time, upon the system's components. Hopefully, its use to support the building of consensus and the achievement of a shared vision facilitates the networking and partnership efforts that have to be made by the key stakeholders in the tourism destinations if they aspire to achieve a satisfactory level of integrated management.

## Systems Modeling and Tourism Development

A holistic approach has been used to conceptually study the impact of tourism development on society and ecosystems in some cases, namely in Mauritius (Lutz, 1994), Bali

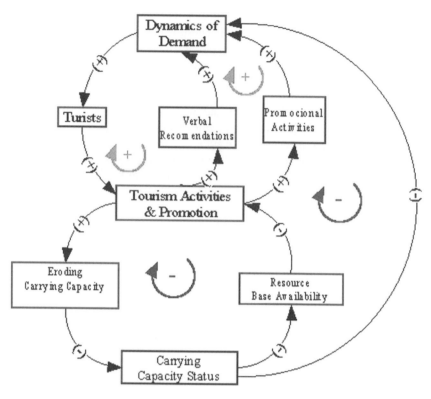

Figure 9.5: Example of feedback cycles (demand, promotion and carrying capacity).
*Source*: Author's own.

(Martopo & Mitchell, 1995), Greece (Van den Bergh, 1996) and Cyprus (Georgantzas, 2001). However, there are no empirically tested models of the tourism system, suitable for the integrated management of a tourism destination, as such.

The literature to date has been concerned with analyzing the results of tourism development, rather than understanding the process that transforms economic, social and environmental structures, partly due to the single sectored approach to research that has characterized the tourism literature, so far. The narrow focus on tourist flows and observable economic and social impacts have disregarded the more fundamental factors that underlie the functioning of tourism as a system. The systems approach offers tourism researchers, planners and destination managers a tool for understanding these factors more closely, a fact that is particularly relevant to small regions where the system as a whole can be modeled within more controlled limits and the relationships between the sub-sectors of the model can be more clearly defined.

If we can work together to create a theory about what might be happening in a system over time, we have the potential to influence its outcome in desirable ways. By creating a visual depiction, we can identify "leverage points" and, if necessary, perhaps alter the dynamic structure itself, so that it yields more positive outcomes.

The kind of diagrams explored offer a number of important benefits:

(1) *Heightened Awareness.* The creation of a causal diagram can help make people more sensitive to the issues of balancing the costs and benefits of IQM, avoiding the pitfalls of bureaucracy and red tape, managing structural behaviour and understanding the dangers of focusing on symptoms rather than concentrating on the root causes of the problems posed by unsustainable development patterns.

(2) *Action Planning.* After studying the causal diagrams, it is possible to understand the advantages of some specific policies (such as the maintenance of high service standards and good infrastructure) and to find ways to realize the potential benefits (cost savings of product, service and infrastructure reliability). Organizations can design strategies, for instance, to focus more energy on key areas that are working well and to simplify and minimize bureaucracy and paperwork, to avoid becoming overly internal-focused. If costs associated with complaints, rework, warranty and other wastes were carefully measured and analysed, they would certainly, in most cases, justify the above mentioned strategic orientation. Finally, visual tools, such as sensitivity analysis, life cycle dynamics or a Balanced Scorecard, can be set up to assess progress in the most sensitive action areas and measure cost savings (see Figure 9.6).

(3) *Visibility.* The idea that creating graphical representations of systemic behaviour can help us fine-tune a system for more positive outcomes is a powerful concept for any destination or organization seeking to improve the outcome of its business systems. Dynamic models are useful tools for visualizing complex dynamics, and its use for tourism management is thought to be a must, although real results only occur when people act on the insights gained from such tools.

## Anatomy of a Management Experimental Laboratory

Dynamic models running on a computer are, basically, compilers for the mental models that researchers (modellers) construct in their minds. MODISTUR is a dynamic model that results from a deep understanding of the real-world tourism system and its complex dynamics, based on the consolidated body of knowledge that exists, allowing people to test present assumptions and learn from experimenting with it by observing the future consequences of those assumptions upon the system's behaviour. In that sense, dynamic models are quite important, since they eventually contribute to change the mental models of their users, making it simpler to understand complex dynamic behaviour and, thus, better manage a real-world system's most sensitive parameters (see Figure 9.7).

Some management simulators do not expose their underlying model structure, hiding its inner workings from the user (black box simulators). MODISTUR, however, adopts a different principle: it is a transparent laboratory, one that lets the user access the model's structure and learn from it. This is an important distinction because the user can see how it works and what it depends on, so it is not a game, but rather a real educational and management tool.

As an educational tool MODISTUR stimulates users to learn more about the 'real-world' tourism system by revealing the internals of its fundamental structure. Educators are encouraged to expose the internals of MODISTUR to students in advanced tourism

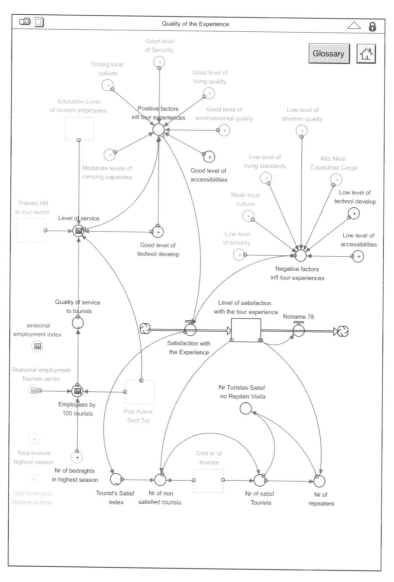

Figure 9.6: Partial diagram of MODISTUR. Structure of the tourist experience.
*Source*: Author's own.

studies because it contributes to their overall understanding of the system's functioning and helps significantly to achieve their learning objectives in many of tourism's area of knowledge. MODISTUR was not conceived for teaching people what to think. Instead, its main purpose is to help us learn, by developing systemic and strategic thinking skills that can be used to improve decision-making performance.

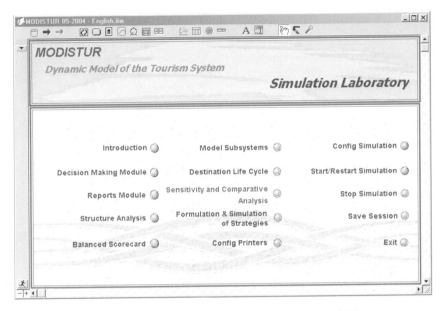

Figure 9.7: Main panel of the management experimental laboratory.
*Source*: Author's own.

## Learning and Managing Through Controlled Experiments

The management experimental laboratory is a programmed software interface that allows the user to perform simulations according with one (or several) management techniques. Policies can be designed to test conflicting goals, impacts of externalities, behaviour optimization and a number of other aspects, including structural reform, whenever possible (see Figure 9.8).

The simulation itself is just a method of playing the model's dynamics over time, to see the results of our expressed assumptions. The user can simulate the system countless times, using different sets of assumptions and time horizons.

The design of the laboratory has a lot to do with its intended purposes of use. MODIS-TUR, for instance, supports a number of different strategic management tools in order to cover a wide range of potential uses, although its main objective is to serve as a high-level platform for strategic management of tourism destinations. MODISTUR is presently working with several development scenarios, conflicting behaviours and goals. Anyone using it can set its own scenarios from scratch and develop them in any desired way.

MODISTUR has a medium for storytelling: Its power goes far beyond the boundaries of what the computer is able to simulate. One can tell stories about the different sub-systems, interacting between them to show their relatedness, test assumptions as the stories develop and make useful conclusions that may contribute to the user's learning.

MODISTUR is a fully transferable model that can be used for the management of any tourism destination, at any level (the world, a world region or a continent, a group of countries, a region within a country, a place). Of course, depending on the specifics of a

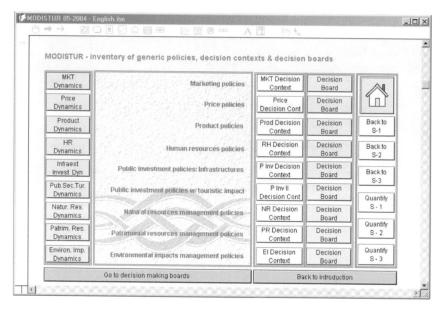

Figure 9.8: The centre for strategic decision making.
*Source*: Author's own.

particular level, some structures will need to be adapted and parameters have to be calibrated using data from appropriate secondary or primary sources. Also, scenario planning and strategy formulation is a unique process that any interested party would have to undertake, using one (or several) of the methodologies and techniques available for that type of work.

Two of the most important features that are included in the laboratory are the centre for strategic decision making and a balanced scorecard style panel.

## Conclusions

The following is a resume of the conclusions derived from the findings of the simulation runs of MODISTUR, in the application that was made to the Algarve, a tourist region in the south of Portugal, although they corroborate those of other studies mentioned in the text.

1. The problems of concentration and seasonality of tourism in certain areas and at certain times of the year show that there is a need for appropriate solutions in terms of IQM. The answers are to be found on the one hand in the type of products offered by the tourism destinations, through visitor flow management, the promotion of new tourist products and alternative forms of tourism, made possible by changes induced by governments in the social sphere; and on the other hand by changes in demand patterns, frequently linked to school and professional holiday systems.

2. The examples of concrete solutions for satisfying the needs and expectations of tourists showed that operators and public authorities were not yet fully aware of the importance

of quality for the competitiveness of tourism and that they still need to gain experience in this field, mainly in what concerns stakeholder responsibility, cooperation and strategy alignment.

3. The experience gained in quality management at business, sectoral and destination level is worth sharing in order to identify good practice, to analyse the success factors and identify the best working methods to be applied by operators and public authorities. The challenge of integration, driven by information society technologies has become one of the main domains of competitiveness. The use of the new tools provided by telecommunications networks and electronic commerce providers permits that both the supply and the demand sides to be accessed easily, and for all relevant information to be made available that allow choices of professional partners and tourist destinations to be made.

4. The users will obviously be very sensitive to the quality of information that appears on the screen of their computers. A company or a destination that does not build this element into its quality strategy starts off heavily handicapped. Unfortunately this is still the most common situation, even in highly developed tourism destinations.

5. The importance of sustainable management of natural and cultural resources in the development of a strategy aimed at the competitiveness of tourism, in particular from the point of view of quality, is globally recognized. In the long run, tourism is not possible without the integration of the economic, political, environmental and cultural dimensions. These are common objectives, and not ones to be pursued only by public authorities, although they might play a leading role.

6. Uncontrolled growth of tourism can have a negative impact on the cultural and human natural environment. The management of resources demands the involvement of all stakeholders and sensitivity to the question of the environment, particularly fragile in certain areas and cultural sites, must be promoted as part of a shared vision for sustainable development.

7. There are still some strategic issues regarding tourism planning and stakeholders motivation, besides tourism contribution for regional development. Consequently, destinations require a holistic approach to management, especially in their development and consolidated stages, to put together the necessary skills and management structure; this is a good example of the need of networking and cooperation for those who have responsibilities in the field tourism in any given destination.

# References

Crauser, G. (1998). *Speech of the director of directorate-general XXIII of the European commission.* European Forum on Integrated Quality Management of Tourism, Tyrol, DG-XXIII.

European Commission, Directorate-General of Enterprises, Tourism Unit. (2000). *Towards quality coastal tourism, integrated quality management of coastal tourist destinations.* Office for Official Publications of the European Communities, Luxembourg.

European Commission, Directorate-General of Enterprises, Tourism Unit. (2000). *Towards quality rural tourism of rural tourist destinations.* Office for Official Publications of the European Communities, Luxembourg.

Forrester, J. (1961). *Industrial dynamics.* Cambridge: MIT Press.

Forrester, J. (1973). *World dynamics.* Cambridge, MA: Wright-Allen Press.

Georgantzas, N. (2001). Cyprus tourism: Environment, profitability and sustainability dynamics, *Proceedings of the international system dynamics society 2001 conference*, Atlanta, USA.

Grahn, D., & Johnson, L. (2000). Visibility works: Implementing ISO/QS 9000, *The Systems Thinker, 11* (4), 9–11.

Lutz, W. (1994), *Population/environment/development:Understanding their interactions in Mauritius.* New York: Springer-Verlag.

Martopo, S., & Mitchell, B. (1995). *Bali: Balancing environment, economy and culture.* Department of Geography, University of Waterloo, publication series n. 44, Australia.

Murphy, P.E. (1994). Tourism and sustainable development. In: W. Theobald (Ed.), *Global tourism: The next decade.* New York: Butterwroth Heinemann.

Serra, F. (2003). *Modelización del Sector Turístico y Simulación de Estrategias Mediante Dinámica de Sistemas: Aplicación al Algarve Portugués.* Ph.D. thesis, University of Huelva, Faculty of Economic and Management Sciences, Spain.

Sessa, A. (1988). The science of systems for tourism development, *Annals of Tourism Research, 15*, 219–235.

University of Wales. (2004). *Integrated_quality_management.htm.* Available online at http://www.irs.aber.ac.uk/rsw, Accessed March 2004.

Van den Bergh, M. (1996). *Ecological economics and sustainable development: Theory, methods and applications.* Cheltenham, UK: Edward Elgar.

Chapter 10

# The Use of Relationship Marketing in Developing Network and Co-operative links within Tourism Product Marketing Groups (PMGs)

Catherine Gorman

## Introduction

Tourism in the Republic of Ireland has seen a considerable increase in the recent past with a doubling of overseas visitor numbers and more than doubling of total foreign tourism revenue in the period 1990–2003 (see Table 10.1).

In 2002, there were 140,000 people employed in the tourism sector in the Republic of Ireland. The industry is considered to be one of the most financially important industries within the state, and contributes significantly to the gross national product. This growth in the industry has been due to a number of factors. The allocation of significant funding from the European Union initially led to the investment in and development of the tourism product. Subsequent investment in marketing in the sector has helped the industry gain a competitive advantage, which is recognized by its annual growth during this period. More recently, due to a number of internal and external factors including increased competition from other destinations, the perceived high-cost economy and increased mobility by consumers has seen an erosion of this competitiveness. This has led to a greater need to become more market oriented particularly with a focus on identified market demand with respect to the product, and industry players have generally developed a more strategic approach to the marketing of their products. A reorganization of the structure of the statutory bodies within the industry (Bord Failte and CERT) in 2002 led to the creation of Tourism Ireland Limited (TIL) and Failte Ireland. Tourism Ireland Limited has sole responsibility for the marketing of the industry within both the Republic and Northern Ireland internationally and Failte Ireland is the domestic arm of the organization and has responsibility for servicing, training, product development and domestic marketing.

Table 10.1: Overseas tourism nos. and revue 2003 – Republic of Ireland.

| | Overseas visitors numbers (millions) | Total foreign revenue (billions € ) |
|---|---|---|
| 1990 | 3.0965 | 1.446 |
| 2003 | 6.178 | 3.228 |

*Source*: Tourism Ireland Limited (2004).

During the 1980s and 1990s, the availability of funding allowed the statutory bodies to develop a strategy that would develop an attractive product suited to both the resources of the country and to the expected demands of the international visitor. One of the resources that was recognized as being important to tourism were gardens. Gardens have played a significant role in the tourism product in other countries such as Great Britain, Italy and France and although they are transient in nature, they are often linked to features of heritage such as great houses and attract a significant number of visitors. Due to the diversity of geology, mild climate, geomorphic and social history, many gardens have been created throughout Ireland over time. The art of gardening arrived to Ireland with Christianity about 500AD with monks developing gardens, which focused on the cultivation of vegetables for food. In 1620, Lismore, County Waterford was created and is one of the earliest formal gardens, which still survives to some extent in its original form. The French, Dutch and English all had considerable influence over the subsequent centuries in garden design and development which resulted in numerous gardens. The introduction of many plants from around the world to these gardens were as a result of plant hunting expeditions undertaken particularly in Australasia during the nineteenth and early twentieth centuries (Lamb & Bowe, 1995). Today, many of these gardens are part of a tourism product marketing group (PMG) called Houses, Castles and Gardens of Ireland (www.castlesireland.com). This group, which is simply structured requires the payment of a membership fee which goes towards the employment of a part-time marketing executive and co-operative marketing activities. The decision on which activities to pursue, is made by a board of voluntary non-executive members all whom are part of the group. A representative from the Irish tourism board (Failte Ireland) also sits on the board and they meet once per month. Numerous interactions in the form of relationships building, networking and co-operative practices take place between the members of the group and between the members and external stakeholders. These webs of network interaction and relationships exist, developed to a greater extent by some gardens over others.

Gardens have been identified as being of significant importance to the heritage of Ireland, and as well as there being an identified market demand for such a product, this resource closely fits the image Ireland wishes to portray in the international tourism arena. Gardens attracted 438,000 overseas visitors in the Republic of Ireland in 2001 (Bord Failte, 2003). During the 1990s under the Operational Programme for Tourism, many of the gardens in Ireland availed of substantial funding through the Great Gardens of Ireland Restoration Scheme which was administered between 1996 and 2001 (Gorman & Reid, 2000). A dedicated manager, Ms. Finola Reid oversaw the management of this particular scheme.

In the mid-1980s tourism PMGs were initiated in the Republic of Ireland with a focus on activities and leisure pursuits. It was during a time that just preceded the rapid growth in overseas tourist numbers to the country and this co-operative marketing approach was part of an overall marketing strategy undertaken by the national tourism board (Bord Failte). In the accommodation sector in Ireland, common product groups have been in operation since the mid-1960s when Irish Farmhouse Holidays were set up to promote Irish Farmhouse accommodation to the visitor. The organization successfully operates alongside Town and Country Houses and the Irish Hotel Federation (IHF) as the main bodies promoting serviced accommodation in the Republic of Ireland.

The PMGs focused on bringing together a number of Small and Medium Tourism Enterprises (SMTEs) in identified sectors of the industry who offered a common core product to the visitor. The Gardens of Ireland was one of the first such PMGs and this was facilitated by Mary Nash of Bord Failte — the Irish Tourist Board of the time.

This chapter attempts to answer a number of questions that surround PMGs. These include:

- the extent and type of co-operation and relationships undertaken by tourism PMGS — this includes both inter-and intra-organizational relationships undertaken by members of a PMG;
- the type of marketing strategy and tactics utilized by members of a tourism PMG — considered in order to evaluate the type and degree of tools associated with relationship marketing that is being used by each group member;
- the consideration of the importance of value of the product; benefits and barriers in developing co-operative links; and
- an investigation into a number of variables which may have an impact on co-operation such as geographical loci, experience, qualifications, history and background of the development and maintenance of relationships within a marketing co-operative group.

The significance of the research is based on the fact that in order to be competitive, a strong marketing ethos is required within any organization. Li and Nicholls (2000) state that in order to remain competitive, co-operation is required with a range of stakeholders. According to Buhalis and Cooper (1998), SMTEs lack competitiveness. Many SMTEs are fragmented and lack structure either of the organization or in the way business is undertaken. Since the 1980s in Ireland, many SMTEs have become involved to a lesser or greater degree with co-operative marketing bodies. Some of these co-operative bodies operate efficiently, some do not.

Being funding led rather than market led has caused a problem with some groups struggling as funding has run out. Other groups focus on market-segmented areas and specific demand, e.g. angling and walking. Many of the co-operative bodies are involved in various forms of relationship management, which includes interaction with a variety of stakeholders including the traditional customer (visitor). Relationship marketing, although advocated by the national tourism board (Bord Failte, 1998) has been undertaken in many cases in an ad hoc rather than structured manner. A structured relationship-oriented approach, however, can help to create bonds and links between the group members and the various stakeholders.

Strong bonds, common vision, a structured approach and other variables are considered important to efficient networking. In identification of practises operating within a PMG, it is hoped that both best practise and deficits can be explored so that a more efficient and effective approach can be developed with a view to increase competitive advantage for SMTEs in this sector.

## Literature Review

It is necessary due to the breadth of the topic area that three academic disciplines be explored. These included organizational theory incorporating network/co-operative/alliance/collaborative theory and authors such as Gray (1985, 1989), Grabher (1993) and Stoel (2002); relationship marketing theory considering authors such as Gummesson, Gronoos (1997), Christopher, Peck (1990 to present), Kotler (2003) and Carson, Cromie, McGowan , and Hill (1995); and co-operative theory focusing specifically on the tourism sector and work undertaken by authors such as Palmer (mid-1990s to present), Morrison (1998), Drucke-Damonte (2000), Selin (2000), Jamel and Getz (1995), Caffyn (2000) and Tremblay (2000) had an input into the literature.

The definition of co-operation is based on that taken by Palmer (2002) as the 'bringing together of people and businesses to accomplish activities that would not otherwise be done'.

Parvatiyar and Sheth (1994) identify that relationship marketing is conducted through both a collaborative and co-operative effort. Kotler (2003) among others recognize that relationship marketing is only suitable where the long-term value of the relationship is important enough or valuable to maintain. In the tourism sector, this would mean relationships would be important to develop and maintain with some stakeholders such as competitors, suppliers (tour operators/tourist offices) that influence market (media) and local visitors rather than overseas visitors (tourist) who are considered the traditional customers of a tourist attraction. The relationship under investigation within this research includes both dyadic and network relationships. Consideration is given to Gummessons (1999) approach to relationships, whereby the focus of marketing goes from being marketing mix centric (4P's) to networking centric (30R's). This approach includes the following relationships:

- Customers, suppliers and competitors
- Non-market relationships
- Nano-relationships

Morgan and Hunt (1994), in their seminal work termed the phrase 'co-operate to compete' and in their research considered closely the different relational exchanges that occur both internally and externally to an organization with the firm being central to all relationships that are undertaken.

Zueldin (1998) went a step further and termed the word 'co-opitition' whereby competitive firms collaborate to compete within a market. More recently, Gummesson (2002) recognized that relationships networks and interactions are core values of any business and that relationship marketing can now be defined as marketing based on the interactions within networks of relationships (see Figure 10.1)

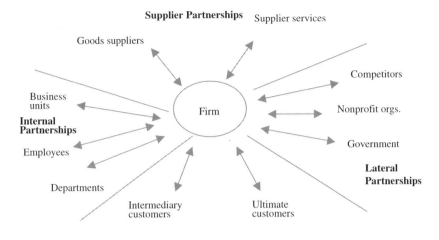

**Figure 10.1:** The relational exchanges in relationship marketing (based on Morgan & Hunt, 1994).

## Characteristics of Networking, Co-operative Marketing and Relationship Marketing

Some of the similarities and dissimilarities of characteristics of each form of interaction are explored and are illustrated in Figure 10.2. Those that are priority to each of the disciplines are considered separately under their disciplines. Those that are deemed to be common to each discipline are considered within the central zone. These are now discussed.

### Cohesiveness and Interdependence

Palmer, Barret, and Ponsonby (2000) in researching co-operative marketing organizations identifies that the cohesiveness within a group over time is helped by a number of factors such as similarity of work, group size, threats from outside, leadership style and common social factors such as age, race and social status. Tremblay (2000) identifies that economics has a part to play and that structures such as networks and partnerships allow high levels of interdependence and cohesiveness which provide an efficiency. He also suggests that networks are different from formal planning in the tourism sector as they involve continual investment in relationship capital. Grabher (1993) and Gray (1985) also recognize interdependence as an important factor to successful networking. Different forms of interdependence can occur: horizontal which was the most competitive form and members competing directly with each other for resources and the disposal of goods and services; vertical whereby different members act at different stages of production and symbiotic, where there is the least competition and organizations complement each other (Pennings in Hall, 1991).

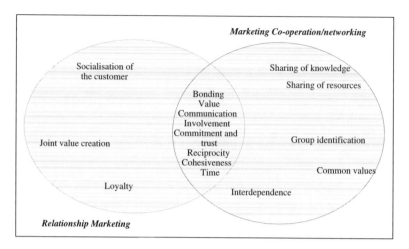

Figure 10.2: Characteristics of relationship marketing and marketing co-operation.

### Common Vision and Goal

Jamel and Getz (1995) in researching tourism planning and partnerships suggest the need to joint formulate a vision statement and tourism goals. As the nature of the industry is fragmented, there is a need to instigate methods that would help implementation, collaboration and facilitate consensus in order to achieve successful co-operation. The formation of a network may occur whereby there is a common vision of issues. The creation of any partnership arrangement requires vision and energy and is easier if the benefits are clearly seen (WTO, 2003). Vision and goals need to be clearly articulated and transparent.

### Involvement

Involvement and investment are part of any relationship and make up one of the key constructs discussed by Wilson (1994). To some degree this investment can be considered set along a continuum similar to that developed by Kotler (1996) whereby the relationship changes from being initially transactional through the stages to eventual partnership. Low involvement may cause ineffective relationships. A number of factors influence low levels of involvement and these are based on the value of the relationship to the stakeholder. Values can include utilitarian value, sign value — what the involvement indicates to others and pleasure value (Gordon, McKeague, & Fox,1998).

### Value

Wilson (1993) discusses the concept of value within the relationship and develops it along three dimensions: behavioural which includes social bonding, trust and culture; strategic which considers goals, time to market, strategic fit and core competencies, and economic with the inclusion of cost reduction and value engineering. In a study of behavioural analysis of co-operative marketing organizations, Palmer et al. (2000) saw a drift from business to social values as co-operation progressed over time. The production of a dynamic tends to be based on co-operation between firms who were at similar points within the value chain.

### Trust and Reciprocity

Numerous authors have written about the importance of trust in relationship marketing (Morgan & Hunt, 1994; Berry, 1995) and invariably it is taken as given that trust is required to a greater or lesser degree in relationship formation and management.

Grabher (1993) identifies reciprocity whereby there is mutual exchange of information and interdependence with long-term interaction leading to stability is an important element required for successful collaboration. Yau et al. (2000) also identifies reciprocity as a component of relationship marketing whereby it allows either party to provide favours for others within the relationship. Carson et al. (1995) develops this well within the small and medium enterprises (SME) sector when considering the importance of the exchange of information which itself requires a degree of trust. The initial communication leads to an information exchange upon which trust is built over time and there may also evolve a social and personal bond. A social bond can compensate for financial costs of the relationship. As Donaldson and O'Toole (2002) suggest a successful relationship goes from being passive to active over time.

### Bonding and Socialization

Levels of bonding within a relationship are important. Berry (1995) identifies three levels of bond within any relationship. These include price, social personalization and structural solutions. Whether the price be that which is offered to the traditional customer or that which is part of the cost of a co-operative membership creates a bond which forms a relationship and generates expectancy by the service/product provider. Personal socialization may develop over time. Sometimes a social bond may be there from the initial stages whereby a social similarity between stakeholders within a relationship exists, e.g. social or educational class. Structural solutions bonding emerges from the bonds that are created through the organization and the agreed contract by the active stakeholders within the group.

### Sharing of Resources

A sharing or combination of resources is a factor of unification in peripheral tourism organizations which enable effective marketing (Morrison, 1998). Telfer in Laws (2002) describe the Canadian Tourism Commission Product Clubs (www.canadatourism.com) which have been established to combine resources in order to offset seasonality, increase diversity and be more competitive.

### Geographical Proximity

This has been identified by Hall (1991) as an important factor in determining the level and frequency of interaction within an organization. Those who are geographically far apart may feel isolated, lack group identity and be less motivated to co-operate or network. More recently used technologies such as email and teleconferencing can help to offset the isolation felt by some members of a group.

### Communication and Marketing Techniques

The intensity of network communication and participation and the degree of integration is strategic to the decision-making process. Convergence through communication exchange allows organizations to learn from each other (Tremblay, 2000). The increased difficulty in finding the time to communicate with an increased number of people/stakeholders which is identified as part of relationship/network management process has an impact on the ability to establish and maintain the necessary contacts to successfully network. The frequency of contact is important to establish and maintain a relationship with any stakeholder within a network in order to strengthen ties. The World Tourism Organization (WTO, 2003) advocate open and frequent communication to capitalize on the synergies at all stages of a partnership from its formation through to ongoing management. The correct timing and frequency of this communication is imperative to sustain commitment. Communication with all stakeholders within a network is important.

Connell (2004) investigates the way in which visitor obtains information indicating the effectiveness of tools used for marketing communication with visitors. She found that word of mouth (WOM) was by far the most important source (83.4%) for information. This could be considered a referred personal approach that is dependant of visitor experience and product quality. She also found that the internet was the least important channel utilized for information with only 8.3% consulting the web. This may be a reflection of the older age group, which has a propensity to visit this type of tourism product. Frequent flyer programmes and hotel loyalty schemes would be two of the most frequently used techniques within tourism co-operatives to foster and maintain relationships with customer (Garnham, 1996).

### Group Identification and Size

Group identification and image are addressed by Stoel (2002) who saw group identification as an important factor to collaboration as well as frequency of communication. Group identification is defined by Kelly and Kelly (1994) as 'the desire of an individual to connect with other members'. Hall (1991) suggests that an increase in the number of organizations within a relationship affects dependences, domains, rewards and resources. Many ties may reduce the strength of each individual ties. Stoel (2002) suggests that the larger the group size, the weaker the group identification.

These are a number of issues that affect the interactions that are undertaken through the different types of relationships with a variety of stakeholders in tourism co-operative marketing and they gave direction to the questionnaire content which was administered as part of a semi-structured interview to the garden owners/managers.

## Research Description and Methodology

Owing to the nature of the research subject, it was decided to undertake a qualitative approach to the methodology. The type employed is based on the philosophy of interpretivism and within this the phenomenological approach was used whereby the interviewer attempts to understand the situation from the interviewee's perspective. An inductive approach with theory building occurred as interviews were being conducted. There was an element of deduction as existing theory was used to guide the questions at interview stage. The facts that emerged and their associated values are interdependent. There was also linkage between researcher and the subject matter that led to a degree of both knowledge and involvement. The researcher had worked in the National Botanic Gardens for seven years in the mid- to late-1980s and had been involved in a national organization which included a number of the respondents. The researcher subsequently worked in tourism marketing and had sat as a regional representative on the chosen gardens' element of the PMG — Gardens of Ireland in the early 1990s. Therefore, both access and historical knowledge had a bearing on the methodology. This also contributed to the pre-understanding of the subject area and to the working paradigm (Gummesson, 2000).

A basic conceptual framework was drawn up from the theoretical material (see Figure 10.3) and this together with experience in the area guided the question content used for the semi-structured interview process.

The method of a semi-structured interview was used as 'they are a resource that reflects the interviewee's reality outside the interview (Seale, 1999). Judd, Smith, and Kidder (1991) state that less-structured interviews are used to obtain a more intrinsic study of perception, attitude, finding out basic issues, how people conceptualize a topic and their level of understanding. The mix of both structured questioning to obtain specific information and less-structured questions was considered to be the best approach to this research.

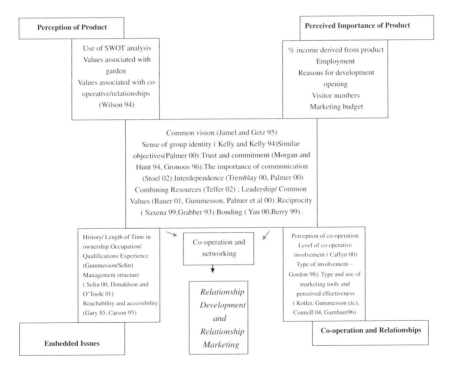

Figure 10.3: Basic conceptual framework.

Sampling was undertaken in a purposive manner with the chosen interviewees who are or were members of a marketing co-operative with a focus on a single product area — in this case: gardens open as a tourist attraction. The choice to focus on those who were members of a national co-operative structure allowed membership at least at one stratum and possibly other strata such as local, regional and county co-operative groups. The members of Great Houses and Gardens of Ireland own or manage a garden which is considered a tourist attraction. As mentioned before, they pay an annual fee to employ a part-time co-ordinator who markets and promotes the garden on their behalf.

Twenty-five gardens were contacted with information being derived for 21 gardens. Prior to undertaking the interviews with the gardens, three interviews were undertaken with individuals who had a significant impact/input into the product-marketing group. These included the marketing executive and the tourist board representative. The results of these interviews gave an insight into the function and operation of the PMG and aided with question refinement. The semi-structured questionnaire administered individually to the garden owners/manager constituted of 50 questions and the interviews took between 1.5 and 3.5 hours to complete. The questions were a mix of open and closed questions and the use of Likert scaling in closed questioning gave direction to the answers and managed the research process. Prompts and aids were used with the main aid used being the Six Market Model based on Payne (1997). This was used when participants required help in identifying the contacts and relationships that they were involved in marketing the attraction. The lack of specific knowledge in this area was apparent from pre-testing the interview and from general experience working within the SME tourism sector. The use of the model eased interviewee involvement. The Six Market Model was used as it has been successfully employed in over 50 organizations (Gummesson, 1999).

Areas of interviews explored:

- Non-sensitive classified information
- Embedded issues such as history, length of time in ownership, occupation, qualifications and experience
- Perception of the product using a SWOT analysis
- Importance and benefits of the product including economic, social and the use of different marketing tools
- Issues related to co-operation within the group — contacts, relationship development, identification of essential characteristics for success/barriers to success
- The use of monitoring, auditing and market research

Administration did not include the use of a tape recorder. This decision was made for the researcher at the initial stages when the first respondent did not wish to be interviewed by tape. Hence the decision was made that all interviews would be undertaken without the use of a tape recorder. Although Silverman (2000) advocates the use of a tape recorder, Wolcott (2001) and Yin (1994) state that it is matter of preference. It was found that the interviewees were very frank and candid in their responses and subsequent testing using a tape recorder with a respondent showed a marked difference in response by an interviewee with no comment cited as a response to several questions. The non-use of tape recorder was also used as a method of interview procurement in certain instances as it was emphasized that it was part of the confidential nature of the material.

In order to get the respondent to focus on the area in question in greater detail, the questions included the seeking of essential characteristics for successful co-operation in order to build a picture of the individual perception of the co-operative group.

Analysis started with the completion of the first interview. Three methods of analysis was utilized in thesis research based on Carson, Gilmore, Perry, and Gronhanig (2001). Axial coding identified the respondent. Selective coding identified themes that were common to the literature and this information was clustered using frequencies throughout the findings to provide material for discussion. The use of anecdotal evidence was used to illustrate certain points or extremes of viewpoint.

## Summary of Findings and Discussion

### Classified and Embedded Issues

Most of the gardens were in private ownership ($n = 14$). This has significance as they do not receive state funding or support. All of those interviewed were either the manager or the owner/manager of the garden and no information apart from the general nature of the research was given to them prior to the interview. More than half of the respondents had no formal qualification in marketing, business or horticulture or were from a non-related background and had therefore learnt 'on the job' ($n = 13$). The gardens ranged in size from 2 acres to 160 acres and attracted between 500 and 380,000 visitors per annum indicating to the substantial difference in product type and capacity. The larger gardens tended to have additional or complementary facilities thus being attractive to a broader market which could include children/families, general day visitors, tour groups as well as specialist plant lovers. Values associated by the respondents with their garden product included 'freedom', 'tranquillity', 'peaceful', 'unique' and 'therapeutic'. Most of the gardens ($n = 12$) considered their gardens as specialist rather than general gardens indicating a perception of uniqueness. The variety of backgrounds and experiences would not contribute to the cohesiveness of the group — lack of a common ground (Palmer, Barrett, & Ponsonby, 2000) and many of them had a wide ranging perceptions and understanding of what values the gardens bought to the market.

There were 105 full-time equivalents employed in the gardens ($n = 21$) though this did not include those employed in county councils, training schemes or students/summer placements. Conservation was the main reason for development and the opening of the garden to the public as minimal income was derived from the gardens with many citing a loss or minimal income ($n = 11$). Only one garden which had significantly diversified its product reported a 50% contribution of the garden to its overall income. Marketing budgets ranged from the subscription of the PMG alone to €80,000 per annum with many ($n = 10$) allocating less than €5,000 per annum to marketing or were not aware of their marketing expenses. The strengths, weaknesses, opportunities and threats of gardens as a tourism resource and product were discussed and are illustrated in Table 10.2.

All respondents were members of the national co-operative marketing groups with a third not members of any other marketing groups. Other co-operative marketing group involvement included those at county, regional and local tourism/marketing levels.

Table 10.2: A SWOT analysis of Irish Gardens as perceived by the owners/manager.

| | |
|---|---|
| Strengths | Climate, variety and diversity, history of the large house, range of plants |
| Weaknesses | No weaknesses; don't market ourselves; attracts elderly visitors; seasonality; roads and access |
| Opportunities | Tranquillity; local marketing; need to get Irish people to visit gardens; packaging |
| Threats | Commercialization; serious financial trouble; weather; lack of interest; low population in Ireland as a potential domestic market; fragmentation; price transparency; staffing issues |

The use and effectiveness of marketing tools was explored. All were or had been members of a co-operative marketing group with most finding it a very effective method of marketing ($n = 13$).

Advertising and brochure production were the most common tools used ($n = 15$) though there was a mixed reaction to their effectiveness. Only a third of the garden ($n = 7$) dealt with tour operators though some had tried this distribution channel with limited success. The size and capacity of some of the gardens would be a deterrent to working with the tour operator trade. Most of the respondents used the internet as a marketing tool ($n = 17$) though all have a presence on the House, Castles and Gardens website. There was a mixed feedback in relation to its effectiveness and only a few ($n = 3$) citing it as a very effective tool. Other forms of tools used (not prompted) included WOM, signage and the use of marketing students.

## Co-operation and Relationships Marketing

Respondents were asked of their thoughts on garden PMGs. Word association was asked for in the context of the phrase 'garden product marketing groups'. Five respondents indicated that either they had not thought about them or that they did not understand them. Other respondents used positive words or phrases such as 'a good idea', 'dedication', 'listen', 'should be effective', 'quality', 'communication' and 'togetherness'. Negative association included 'unfulfilled', 'poor', 'aging members', 'ineffective' and ' a lack of them'.

Interviewees were asked to define the meaning of the word co-operation and the following results are shown in Table 10.3.

The definition of co-operation included 'helping each other', 'pooling resources' and 'communication' with only one person citing a social element to co-operation or the fact that the group had similar products. This combination of resources and sharing is recognized in network unification by Morrison (1998). Much of the co-operation within this group involves joint promotion, which is undertaken by an executive and the compilation and distribution of a joint brochure.

It can be seen that there is an understanding of co-operation, though this understanding varies from a product focus, to a human/social focus to a financial focus.

Table 10.3: Frequency of words/phrase used to define co-operation.

| Words/phrases used | Frequency | Words/phrases used | Frequency |
| --- | --- | --- | --- |
| Joint marketing including promotion/brochure | 8 | Agreement | 2 |
| Helping each other | 5 | Cost efficiency | 2 |
| Communication | 4 | Similar products | 1 |
| Togetherness | 3 | Common policy | 1 |
| Pooling resources | 2 | Getting to know each other | 1 |
| Social | 1 | Something that should be done in the future | 1 |
| Sharing | 1 | | |

Values associated with co-operation focused on both information derivation and marketing. The need to seek information and to be in touch with what was going on spurred membership.

The essential characteristics were sought in relation to co-operative marketing. Different words, many of them commonly associated with a successful and efficient approach to co-operation, were used. They included leadership, active co-operation, intelligence, focus, interest, ability to deal with people, image definition, commitment, enthusiasm, sharing, dynamic and the need for training and a marketing background. These characteristics concur with such work undertaken by the WTO (2003) and Tremblay (2000). During the exploration of this particular area, a number of issues in relation to their involvement with co-operative marketing groups were mentioned and these included geographical location and infighting within the co-operative structure. One respondent said that they 'did not have a clue' in relation to essential characteristics required for successful co-operative marketing. However, there seemed to be a general understanding of what co-operation was about, and many of the phrases/terms used to define characteristics are considered essential requirements to successful cooperation (trust and commitment: Morgan & Hunt, 1994; reciprocity: Saxena, 1999; similar objectives: Palmer, 2000; and the importance of communication: Stoel, 2002).

## Relationship Building and Benefits

There was a marked difference in relationship between those who had either been through some form of education/training in business/marketing experience and those who had neither a great deal of experience or knowledge of marketing. Some of the larger gardens and those that attracted a greater number of people had a strategic view with them citing the different markets without the use of the Six Market Model and had a more planned and strategic approach to marketing.

Marketing co-operatives ($n = 10$), and tourism organizations ($n = 9$) were the most common contacts undertaken by the respondents with tourist offices, friends and family and business associates being the least-featured contacts ($n = 3$)(see Table 10.4). The benefits of relationship building had not really been considered in many cases. Communication and frequency of communication between the garden owners/managers and other stakeholders were probed. Although email was seen as an important support tool, it was the telephone and personal communication that was considered important by the more strategically minded gardens. Leaflet distribution between the gardens was also considered to be important. The development of a social element was mentioned by a number of the more successful gardens as an important factor though one garden mentioned that the members of the national co-operative had been broken down into cliques as 'there were some people that you got on better with than others'.

These benefits of relationship development and contacts made included confidence building, creating and maintaining awareness, generating a good rapport, leaflet and brochure distribution, increase in visitor numbers and strengthening and brand building. However there were a number of negative responses such as 'I'm defeated by it all — there is so much jealously and begrudgery', 'I don't want to travel to Dublin to meetings' and 'there is no need to meet'. These may indicate a general lack of understanding of the work of the co-operative and the objectives of the group and show a lack of group vision and direction. Group and individual responsibility also seemed to be unclear in many circumstances — for example, one respondent 'tour operators should contact you', though in relation to the co-operative marketing group, the same respondent stated 'it is yourself who is important — only you can help yourself'.

The aim was to get the respondents to identify problems about relationships/contact development without being too negative about one person or specific organisation. A number of respondents were positive 'no real problem', 'no negatives except standards'. The standards as an issue is interesting to pursue, as it emerged through several of the interviews. A number of problems did emerge and these included 'a fragmented approach with a number of groups doing the same thing'. Quite a number of the respondents alluded to the ongoing disquiet within the co-operative marketing groups, e.g. 'moaners wondering what they will get out of it' and 'many people seen as more important than others' and 'parochialism' on a county level. One respondent mentioned the important aspect of experience — those with experience vs. those without, and that this caused a problem in relation to the ability to develop contacts. One respondent suggested that 'the group was too large' and

Table 10.4: Present relationship/contacts (Six Market Model shown as prompt).

| Relationship/contact | Incidences | Relationship/contact | Incidences |
|---|---|---|---|
| Co-operatives | 10 | Other gardens/competitors | 4 |
| Tourism organizations | 9 | Media | 4 |
| Other products providers, e.g. B & B's. | 7 | Tour operators | 4 |
| Suppliers | 7 | Business associates | 3 |
| Customer | 6 | Tourist offices | 3 |
| Employees | 5 | Friends/family | 3 |

there was a lack of time to contact them all; however, this respondent said that 'it was mainly beneficial'. Time appeared as an issue by several respondents. Co-operation was 'a good idea but nobody to do it'. Lack of trust was also mentioned by a respondent. Money was identified as an issue — 'some get caught up in the financial aspects and do not have time to market'. This can be seen more prevalently among those who are close to the garden, i.e. private/family owners who may be relying on the garden as a source of income.

In summary, perceived barriers to relationship development included the lack of time, the size of the garden, parochialism among the group and group dynamics.

Methods used to develop contacts/develop relationships were sought as was frequency of contact. 'The creation of awareness and communication' was used as prompts if required. The responses ranged from the use of the usual marketing tools, such as brochures, familiarizations, better distribution, etc. to the need to be focused, creation of awareness through personal contact, creation of a bond, use of local co-coordinators and perseverance. Frequency ranged from once a year or 'not a lot' to once per month, with much of the contact being undertaken in a personal manner, i.e. by phone or meeting.

The thoughts of the respondents concerning co-operative marketing groups at the various different geographical levels, local, county, regional and national, were explored. No prompts were given here so as not to provoke a response in relation to a particular group. The general theme of each of the responses was considered and is shown in Figure 10.4.

One respondent who had studied co-operation in an academic context was wholly negative about the concept being used for the gardens as a tourist attraction as 'co-operatives and their structure attract altruistic people rather than business people'. The manager of the garden suggested that one should 'look at the underlying reasons why people join co-operatives', perhaps suggesting that there is a social rather than a business need. Palmer

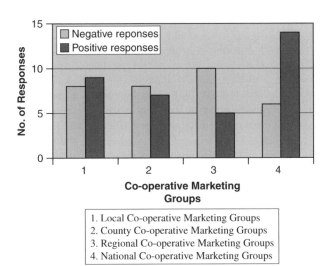

Figure 10.4: Thoughts on co-operative marketing groups.

et al. (2000) does state that this drift to a more social focus tends to occur as a co-operative relationship progress.

This introduction of a social element may help to strengthen ties and increase cohesiveness making it more difficult to leave the group if there is an element of social equity tied up with the group. The manager did, however, believe that 'the co-operative model will work, but only if there is continuous adherence to the co-operative principle and if the members have a serious commercial stake in the property'. A question has to be asked whether co-operative marketing structure is the most suitable method of marketing gardens as tourist attractions due to both the diversity of the product and the diversity of the values and vision of the owners/managers.

The garden managers/owners were generally more positive about national co-operative marketing groups though this is due to the fact that a third of them were only members of these groups and therefore could not make personal comment of the other strata of marketing co-operative group. There seemed to be little complaint in relation to geographical proximity, the fact that it was a national organization 'though it was recognized that core group of people did attend meetings and sometimes distance did prove a problem'. Other elements tie this core together, be it a passion for plants and gardens which was evident throughout many of the interviews.

The perceived value of both the product and of co-operative marketing groups was sought. This was done in an effort to establish whether there was commonality between the values perceived by the members. Most respondents applied the value concept of the product to their own garden and generally spoke of the tangibles, such as the plants and facilities, and the intangibles, such as ambience, space, tranquillity and sense of history.

Additional comments were sought and overall the respondents were very positive about the interview. Some of them said that it had prompted them to think about what they were doing. Others were very interested in the results and all of the respondents have asked for feedback in some form or other.

## Conclusion and Future Issues

A substantial amount of information has been gathered to date. This information has raised more questions than answers though there is an agreement in many instances with the existing literature on co-operation and relationship development. Many of the respondents are involved in different elements of relationship marketing and management and though proactivity is limited in most cases particularly in relation to the tour operator trade. The information shows that most of the members of the various co-operative marketing bodies are positive about their involvement. Are the levels of involvement, perceptions of value of the group similar and positive enough, and is there a significant amount of cooperation to develop effective group marketing and relationship marketing? It appears that a basic framework does exist on which to base a relationship and truly co-operative structure.

Thought and effort in relation to their involvement varies considerably from garden to garden. This is often linked to experience and training/education in the area of management. Not all tools of communication were used by members and their usage linked either to knowledge of marketing, specific objectives in relation to garden visitors or desired level of involvement. Level of involvement is important to a relationship (Wilson, 1993) and was impacted by geographical proximity to other members and to Dublin. Meetings do take place around the different gardens to allow each member an opportunity to the other gardens and to ease distance travelled.

Many of the respondents did not really identify with the group looking at it solely as a body to market the gardens overseas. Many could not cite a vision or objective. Group identification (Stoel, 2002) and vision (WTO, 2003) are essential elements of successful co-operation. The group in question is informal, loose, unstructured, spontaneous, with many of the members reactive confirming Gilmore et al.'s (2001) definition of networking specifically in the SME sector. The lack of a structured approach by the members to relationship development whether within the group or with other stakeholders should reflects the need cited by Tremblay (2000) to continually invest in the process.

The research is presently being extended and a number of issues are being analysed in greater depth. This work is being conducted as part of a PhD, which is being pursued through the Department of Geography, Trinity College, Dublin. Other areas of research include an extension to other co-operative marketing groups both outside and within the garden sector to identify whether considering the different issues that are emerging. The issue of socialization and its affect on levels of involvement could also be explored particularly in relation to gender difference.

---

**Parnetourism: Partnerships, Co-operation and Networking in Tourism.**
**A destination focus**

*A project entitled Parnetourism, which is being funded under Interreg IIIA is presently being undertaken by the Tourism Research Centre, Dublin Institute of Technology and the Department of Geography, Trinity College, Carmarthen, Wales. The work focuses on product providers involved both directly and indirectly with the tourism industry in Counties Wexford and Carlow (Ireland), and Pembrokeshire and Carmarthen (Wales). The research, which involves three stages and includes questionnaire completion, workshops and training seminars, explores the idiosyncrasies of partnerships, co-operatives and networks in tourism destinations. Results from the quantitative phase were that the respondents considered that although marketing and networking were important advantages of group involvement, it was the wish to be part of the community that was seen as the greatest advantage. Meeting people and sharing ideas were also seen as advantages. Issues such as the lack of time, the lack of financial resources were noted as the main disadvantages as well as the fact that the same people undertake the work all of the time. The main reason why respondents tended to contact the group was to seek information with only one person mentioned the process of networking. However, the sharing of information is seen as a major contributor to networking. Contact tended to be on a monthly basis with the phone rivalling the popularity of the email as the method of communication.*

*Factors for successful networking included co-operation and communication, leadership and direction, with deterrents to success being a lack of involvement, lack of interest and lack of leadership. The reasons for involvement with a group was many, though having an asset and the seeking of information were the two most cited reasons why people became involved.*

*Work has also been undertaken in evaluating information which is being derived qualitatively from the product providers and support bodies, which explore in greater depth the issues of group structure and size, involvement, communication used, performance and training.*

# References

Berry, L. (1995). Relationship marketing of services – growing interest, emerging perspectives. *Journal of Academy of Marketing Sciences, 23*(4), 236–245.

Bord Failte. (1998). *Relationship marketing.* Dublin: Bord Failte.

Bord Failte. (2003). *Garden Facts 2001.* Dublin: Bord Failte.

Buhalis, D., & Cooper, C. (1998). Competition or co-operation: SMTE at the destination. In: E. Laws, B. Faulkner, & G. Moscardo (Eds), *Embracing and managing change in tourism.* London: Routledge.

Caffyn, A. (2000). Is there a tourism partnership lifecycle? In: B. Bramwell, & B. Lane (Eds), *Tourism collaboration and partnerships: Politics, practise and sustainability.* Clevedon: Channel View Publications.

Carson, D., Cromie, S., McGowan, P., & Hill, J. (1995). *Marketing and entrepreneurship in SME's – an innovative approach.* Englewood Cliffs, NJ: Prentice-Hall.

Carson, D., Gilmore, A., Perry, C., & Gronhanig, K. (2001). *Qualitative marketing research.* Beverely Hills, CA: Sage.

Connell, J. (2004). The purest of human pleasures: The characteristics and motivations of garden visitors. *Great Britain Tourism Management, 24,* 229–247.

Donaldson, B., & O'Toole, T. (2002). *Strategic market relationships: From strategy to implementation.* London: Wiley.

Drucke-Damonte, D. (2000). The effect of cross industry co-operation on performance in the airline industry in global alliances. In: J. Crotts, D. Buhalis, & R. March (Eds), *Tourism and hospitality management.* New York: Haworth Press Inc.

Garnham, B. (1996). Alliances and liaisons in tourism: Concepts and implications. *Tourism Economics, 2,* 61–77.

Gilmore, A., Carson, D., & Grant, K. (2001). SME marketing in practise. *Marketing Intelligence and Planning, 19*(1).

Gordon, M.E., McKeague, K., & Fox, M.A. (1998). Relationship marketing effectiveness: The role of involvement. *Psychology and Marketing,* (15/5) 443–459.

Gorman, C., & Reid, F. (2000). Developing Ireland as a successful garden tourism destination. In: J. Ruddy, & S. Flanagan (Eds), *Tourism destination marketing: Gaining the competitive edge* (pp. 437–443). Dublin Institute of Technology, Tourism Research Centre, Dublin, Ireland.

Grabher, G. (Ed.). (1993). Rediscovering the social in the economics of interfirm relationships. In: *The embedded firm on the socioeconomics of industrial networks* (pp. 1–31). London: Routledge.

Gray, B. (1985). Conditions facilitating interorganisational collaborations. *Human Relations, 38,* 911–936.

Gray, B. (1989). *Collaborating San Francisco.* CA: Joseph Bass.

Gronoos, C. (1997). Value driven relational marketing: From products to resources and competencies. *Journal of Marketing Management, 1,* 407–419.

Gummesson, E. (1999). *Total relationship marketing: Rethinking marketing management for the 4P's to the 30R's.* Oxford, UK: Butterworth Heinemann.

Gummesson, E. (2000). *Qualitative methods in management research* (2nd ed., p. 60). Thousand Oaks, CA: Sage.

Gummesson, E. (2002). Relationship marketing and the new economy: Its time for deprogramming. *Journal of Services Marketing, 16,* 585–589.

Hall, R.H. (1991). *Organizations: Structures, processes and outcomes* (5th ed., p. 227). Englewood Cliffs, NJ: Prentice-Hall.

Jamel, T.B., & Getz, D. (1995). Collaborative theory and community tourism planning. *Annals of Tourism Research, 22,* 186–204.

Judd, C., Smith, E., & Kidder, L. (1991). *Research methods in social relations* (6th ed). Fort Worth: Holt, Rinehart and Winston.

Kelly, C., & Kelly, J. (1994) in Stoel (2002). Retail co-operatives: Group size, identification, communication, frequency and relationship effectiveness. *International Journal of Retail and Distribution Management, 30*(1), 51–60.

Kotler, P. (1996). *Principles of marketing.* London: Prentice-Hall.

Kotler, P. (2003). *Marketing management (11th ed.,* p. 660). Englewood Cliffs, NJ: Prentice-Hall.

Lamb, K., & Bowe, P. (1995). *A history of gardening in Ireland pub.* Dublin: The Stationary Office, for the National Botanic Gardens Glasnevin.

Li, F., & Nicholls, J. (2000). Transactional or relationship marketing – determinants of strategic choice., *Journal of Marketing Management, 16,* 449–464.

Morgan, R., & Hunt, S. (1994). Relationship marketing in the era of network competition. *Marketing Management, 3,* 19–28.

Morrison, A.M. (1998). Small firm co-operative marketing in a peripheral tourism region. *International Journal of Contemporary Hospitality Management, 5,* 191–197.

Palmer, A., Barrett, S., & Ponsonby, S. (2000). Behavioural analysis of co-operative marketing organisations. *Journal of Marketing Management, 16,* 273–290.

Parvatiyar, A., & Sheth, J. (1994). Paradigm shift. In: J. Sheth, & A. Parvatiayar (Eds), *Marketing theory and approach – the emergence of relationship marketing: Theory, methods and applications* (Section 1, Session 2.1). Atlanta, GA: Centre for Relationship Marketing, Emory University.

Payne, A. (1997). *Advances in relationship marketing* (pp. 31–38). London: Cranfield Management Series.

Seale, C. (1999). *The quality of qualitative research.* Beverly Hills, CA: Sage.

Selin, G. (2000). Developing a typology of sustainable tourism partnerships. In: B. Bramwell, & B. Lane (Eds), *Tourism collaboration and partnerships.* Clevedon: Channel View Publications.

Sexena, G. (2005). Relationships networks and the learning regions: Case evidence from the Peak district National Park. *Tourism Management, 26,* 277–289.

Silverman, D. (2000). *Doing qualitative research: A practical handbook.* Beverly Hills, CA: Sage.

Stoel, L. (2002). Retail co-operatives: Group size, identification, communication, frequency and relationship effectiveness. *International Journal of Retail and Distribution Management, 30*(1), 149.

Telfer, D. (2002). Canadian tourism commission product clubs. In: E. Laws *(Ed.), Tourism marketing.* London: Continuum.

Tourism Ireland Limited. (2004). *Island of Ireland overseas visitors 2003.* Dublin: Tourism Ireland Limited.

Tremblay, P. (2000). An evolutionary interpretation of the role of collaborative partnerships in sustainable tourism. In: B. Bramwell, & B. Lane (Eds), *Tourism collaboration and partnerships.* Clevedon: Channel View Publications.

Wilson, D.T. (1994). Understanding the value of a relationship. *Asia–Australia Marketing Journal,* 2, 55–66.

Wolcott, H. (2001). *Writing up qualitative research.* Beverely Hills, CA: Sage.

World Tourism Organization. (2003). *Co-operation and partnership in tourism: A global perspective.* Madrid: WTO.

Yau, O., McFettridge, P., Chow, R., Lee, J., Sin, L., & Tse, A. (2000). Is relationship marketing for everyone. *European Journal of Marketing, 34*(9/10), 1111–1127.

Yin, R. (1994). *Case study research design and methods* (3rd ed.). Beverely Hills, CA: Sage.

Zueldin, M.A. (1998). Towards an ecological collaborative relationship management – a co-opitive perspective. *European Journal of Marketing, 32*(11/2), 1138–1164.

Chapter 11

# Information and Communication Technologies Supporting Destination Management: A Multimedia Application

Alfonso Morvillo, Maria Immacolata Simeon and Immacolata Vellecco

## Introduction

In the international tourism market — characterised by new origin and destination areas — the competitive environment has become increasingly uncertain, dynamic and turbulent due to market globalisation, higher technological innovation, increasing supply differentiation and demand complexity. In this scenario, local tourism development mostly depends on the attraction of the destination or supply system that is able to differentiate its products and strategically focus on its attraction factors so as to gain and enhance its competitive advantage.

Information and communication technologies (ICT) accelerate competition among destinations, a competition no longer based on material resources alone but also on their ability to generate intangible resources (knowledge and trust). ICT also contribute to differentiating destinations from other competitors so as to make them more visible and, consequently, much more visited by tourists. ICT provide substantial opportunities to build and enhance destination competitive advantages by creating virtual communication and relationship environments. These environments may have traditional "communication" purposes (i.e. products/services are perceived and appreciated by actual or potential users, e.g. promotion activities) or "transaction" purposes (i.e. on-line activities, such as hotel reservations, visits to museums), which generate additional benefits for users (Premazzi, 2001).

This paper is focused on ICT dissemination in the tourism industry and their strategic value as tools to support destination management. Based on an economic-managerial approach to the destination management concept (Section 2), this paper firstly analyses the determinants of rapid ICT dissemination in the tourism industry (Section 3) to understand how ICT and multimedia technologies can support destination strategic marketing and management (Section 4).

In the near future, multimedia networks — universal and interactive link tools — will have a high development potential, thanks to their effectiveness and flexibility. As an example of what was mentioned above, the project *Campania in Pillole* (Section 5) is presented, a multimedia application to promote tourism in Campania, set up by Institute for Service Industry Research – National Research Council (IRAT-CNR) with other partners. The project developed a *hardware and software prototype* that, through *Multimedia Messaging Services* (MMS), enables tourists to access information — sites of interest, suggested routes, opening hours of museums — on the historical-artistic heritage in Campania. This example of multimedia application is a tool to enhance a specific tourism destination; it favours an inflow of resources made available directly on-line or subordinate to the physical movement of tourists.

In the conclusion, the strategic role of technology is reiterated, viewed as a factor enabling aggregation among local stakeholders, products and services, and as a factor that may have an impact on the ways through which value is created for end users. However, this virtuous development mostly depends on the development (above all within the physical territory) of a culture and practice aimed at creating relationships, consortia and networks.

## Approaches to Destination Management: Analytical Perspectives

Although the literature includes many interpretations of the destination management concept, in this paper an economic-managerial supply-focused approach will be adopted. According to this approach the destination, being a local system of tourism supply, is not defined through geographical or administrative criteria but through a "number of activities and attraction factors which, located in a specific space, are able to provide an integrated supply, which enhances local resources and culture" (Rispoli & Tamma, 1995).

It is well known that there are two main streams of analysis related to the tourism destination concept, one focused on the demand side and the other on the supply side. For the authors adopting the demand-focused approach the destination becomes a unitary product, thanks to the tourist experience, while for the authors adopting the supply-focused approach this unitary nature is the result of joint actions implemented by the organisations located in a specific geographical area (Franch & Martini, 2002). Scholars focusing on the demand side view the destination as a whole set of products, services, natural and artificial attraction factors capable of attracting tourists to a specific site " …. . Destinations are competitive units within geographic areas, viewed as the products or sets of products crucial for tourists. The destination product includes a number of commercial tourism services, such as accommodation, catering, transport services, events etc., as well as product components which sometimes represent an integral part of a destination, e.g. its landscape or inhabitants" (Pechlaner, 1999). The common denominator is the experience made by tourists who, by selecting and combining the most suitable elements for their vacation, define the destination. Others, such as Tamma (2000) define destination as a system of supply linked to a specific area, identifying it as a whole set of products and producers taking on a specific structure, thanks to the joint management of resources and activities. The concept of tourism destination as a "system" implies not only many products and market segments, but also a multiplicity of interacting local actors playing different roles and contributing — through their actions, products and services — to creating the overall experience made by tourists within a specific area (Manente & Cerato, 2000).

In this case, going beyond a fragmentary view of resources, economic activities and management policies, the concept of *Destination* is then similar to the concept of Local System for Tourism Supply on which managerial and policy decisions have to be based (Tamma, 2000). The Local System for Tourism Supply has the following basic components (Antonioli Corigliano, 2002): a specific and limited geographical area, often with a distinctive landscape; a distinctive settlement pattern of its population; a distinctive historical, cultural, social identity; typical production patterns of the local community; an active role of the local institutions (supply of services and infrastructures, training courses, entrepreneurial development projects) to involve the various local stakeholders; and a population of interacting firms interested in creating a formal network based on hierarchical relationships.

The destination corresponds then to the whole set of products/services — *traditional and innovative, tangible services* (historical-naturalistic assets, firms, infrastructures) and *intangible services* (culture, traditions, competences, quality of life) — provided by a specific area (Pollarini, 2005). To increase the "value" of the area and its attractiveness — thus triggering a satisfaction-attractiveness-value virtuous circle (Ancarani, 1999) — the strategic analysis and marketing tools typical of the firms are applied to the area according to a market-oriented approach. Territorial marketing[1] analyses the stakeholders, clients/markets' needs, in order to build, maintain and reinforce profitable exchanges with local stakeholders (internal territorial marketing) and the outside world (external territorial marketing).

The management model is strictly linked to the conceptual definition of destination. Destinations and the relevant modern management model are developed through two substantially different approaches (Haimayer, 2003). In some cases spontaneous evolution phenomena start from the bottom, while more often the destination borders are defined from the top, and the destination formation process is managed by promoting and supporting local public administrations and tourism organisations. Actually, lacking a recognised leadership, institutions and policy makers promote the involvement of the various stakeholders in the development projects (Palmer & Bejou, 1995), combine local resources and competences, promote consensus (Bramwell & Sharman, 1999), social relationships and collective learning (Saxena, 2005) generated by turning implicit knowledge into explicit, codified and transferred knowledge.

At present different destinations and supply systems give rise to an increase in dynamic competition to enhance existing resources and attract new ones. In this scenario, ICT play a crucial role for the destination success, as they are electronic infrastructures capable of overcoming the supply fragmentation and developing an intelligent digital nervous system (Pollock, 2000).[2] ICT make less famous destinations as visible as those already well known on the tourism market (Buhalis, 2000). Additionally, ICT enable the complex grid

---

[1] Territorial marketing studies are quite recent. Beside Ancarani (1999) see also Varaldo and Caroli (1999), Bellini (2000), Valdani and Ancarani (2000) and Petrillo (2001).

[2] The metaphor developed by A. Pollock views the tourism industry of a destination as an organic and open system guided by a brain capable of receiving and elaborating stimuli from the external world and transferring central elaborations to peripheral areas.

of relationships among the various actors, users and suppliers of the destination to be integrated and co-ordinated, while reinforcing in the consumer's mind a systemic vision of the complex and heterogeneous basket of tangible and intangible products making up the destination. Actually tourists develop an idea of the destination much earlier than their actual visit; that is why operating in the *marketspace* generated by the digital revolution is crucial (Rayport & Sviokla, 1995).

## Evolution and Dissemination of Information and Communication Technologies within the Tourism System

ICT are a complex phenomenon, not only because of their various solutions and technological applications[3] but, above all, because of their pervasive spread across all fields of economics, albeit to a different extent.

The development of ICT and related economic phenomena have stimulated extensive research applied to different contexts. They have been analysed not only as a crucial sector from the economic point of view and because of their ability to produce effects on the productivity of the whole economy, but also as a tool to increase the efficiency and effectiveness of all main business activities and as a tool to create and exploit innovative business opportunities, which have generated deep changes in the traditional production, selling and consumption patterns (Cioppi, Savelli, & Di Marco, 2003).

The evolutionary path of the role of ICT as technologies enabling business transformation can be described (Figure 11.1) allowing for the scope of their potential benefits and the degree of transformation of the business they are applied to (Venkatraman, 1994).

The five stages — from the initial stage of local exploitation of the applications to the final stage of redefinition of the business scope, through the intermediate stages of internal integration, re-design of the business processes and network — have been steered by the connection capability of the technologies and by the favourable evolution of the cost-performance ratio of the technologies themselves. These stages are also the steps of a path towards an information society with more awareness of technological potential and an increasing creativeness in developing applications and identifying new fields of use.

Specific features of the tourism service market have created the conditions for it to become one of the first fields for ICT application, and a context capable of recording great advancement in terms of applications.

From the supply point of view, information is the fundamental link among the various firms, — usually small-sized firms — of the travel industry (airlines, tour operators, travel agencies, hotels, car rental firms, cruise lines). High information intensity was then the driving force (Poon, 1993) for rapid ICT development and dissemination; in few other economic activities is generating, acquiring, processing and disseminating information so crucial for

---

[3] The ICT industry can be broken down into two main areas: Information Technology (IT) and Telecommunication (TC). The former includes electronic information-based technologies and is sub-divided into two parts: hardware — software and services. The latter includes fixed and mobile networks, network systems and installations, telecommunication cables, satellites and telephony/data transfer services (Dossena, 2000).

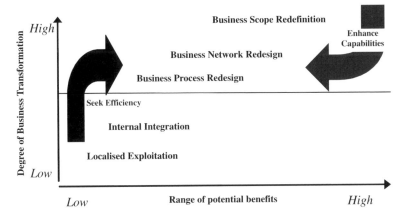

Figure 11.1: Five levels of IT-enabled business transformation.

daily activities. Moreover, because of the inter-firm complementarity, use of ICT in one sector stimulated the dissemination of the technologies in the other firms of the filière (Poon, 1993).

From the demand point of view, purchasing a tourism product largely depends on the description of and information on the product itself. There is growing need for information and directly developed customised tourism products; there is a need for an active, autonomous and flexible tourism dimension that can be achieved, thanks to the increasing use of information and telematic "connection" technologies.

In most economic sectors, computer science and telematics were used in the initial stages to achieve efficiency by cutting costs and streamlining repetitive and standardised procedures. The travel and tourism industry also experienced this phenomenon; however, in this case computer science and telematics were also immediately used as network technologies capable of ensuring (see Figure 11.1) a logistic and inter-functional interconnection within global organisations first (internal integration stage and business process re-design stage), and then an inter-organisation and inter-sector connection (network re-design stage and business scope re-definition stage).

Typically, ICT dissemination in the industry took place in three main periods (Buhalis, 1998), corresponding to the development of:

- Computer Reservation Systems (CRSs), in the early 1970s;
- Global Distribution Systems (GDSs), mid-1980s; and
- Internet, in the early 1990s.

With respect to electronic distribution through computer networks, which characterised the CRS's development, airlines were the technology leaders: thanks to the new systems equipped with central databases, airlines could control and distribute trip reservations at the global level, manage demand flexibly and integrate the whole range of front-office and back-office functions with a substantial cut in communication costs.

The gradual expansion of the geographical coverage and the need for horizontal integration (among airlines) and vertical integration (with other tourism services and products, such as hotels, car rentals, railways) led to the creation of global communication standards termed GDSs and, simultaneously, to the concentration of these systems in the hands of four global operators: Amadeus, Galileo, Sabre and Worldsplan.

These operators, whose majority shareholders are the airlines, could cover the earth's whole surface through a number of arrangements with local operators. GDSs are still networks of networks, which combine and integrate automatic booking systems of different tourism organisations and reach end users through travel agencies sometimes linked to the individual GDS by exclusive agreements. "GDS, like the early automatic booking systems, are characterised by a "closed" technological network, i.e. based on proprietary systems, the control of which is remunerated through a service price surcharge" (Martini, 2000).[4]

The firms involved in these processes are the main large multinational tourism organisations, such as hotel chains, airlines and car rentals, while SMEs are excluded due to the intrinsic properties of the sophisticated technologies, the high hardware, software and interconnection costs, and the need for skilled human resources. Therefore, these systems contributed to increasing the traditional duality, inherent in the tourism industry (Martini, 2000).

The Internet has profoundly changed relationships among the firms of the tourism system and between the system and consumers. It is a low-cost infrastructure that enables a large body of information, even multimedia information, to be conveyed, and goods and services to be promoted and distributed. Being an "open" infrastructure, the Internet makes a tool available to operators, which enables them to reach end consumers or be reached by them. From this perspective, small firms can compete on an equal footing with large organisations.

The properties of tourism products are ideal for e-commerce: they are complex products, which can be represented through the web, exploiting the potentials of the multimedia representation. Telematics also enables innovative use of information. By browsing, collecting and selecting information, tourists can "self-specify" their needs; thanks to ICT, they do not passively accept a pre-set tourism package, but play an active role in generating the tourism product, and make their choice based on the different attractions and opportunities suggested by the network.

The potential provided by the Internet to SMEs and consumers has originated widespread dis-intermediation and process/network re-engineering within the tourism industry.

At present the following organisation types can be found on the web:

- Tourism service producers, such as hotel chains and airlines;
- Traditional tourism intermediaries, such as GDS, tour operators, travel agencies, which have extended their business through an Internet website, even creating new brands; and
- Tourism intermediaries specifically created to operate on the web (e-intermediation), such as entrepreneurial undertakings linked to the New Economy, which operate through a website providing not only information but also the opportunity for on-line booking or transaction. This category includes both infomediaries (Internet Service Providers, generalist portals, vertical portals) with a high volume of traffic generated in

---

[4] As to the role and development of GDS, see also Buhalis (1998), Buhalis and Licata (2002), De Angelis (2004).

the website and substantial returns generated by the Internet advertising — and virtual travel agencies.

Many suppliers of tourism services developed e-commerce applications to make it possible for customers to have direct access to their booking systems. This drastically reduced the scope of activity of traditional intermediaries who underwent a strict selection process due to the decrease in intermediated flows and intermediation margins resulting from increasingly less dependent customers. Along with traditional travel agencies, also GDSs were affected by Internet competition and underwent a re-engineering process involving mergers and acquisitions or diversification towards virtual intermediation through on-line travel agencies.[5]

The co-existence of many operators and intermediation channels made competition more aggressive and generated new forms of supply arrangement by means of extensive co-operation among different producers and the creation of networks. The boundaries between the various types of intermediaries then became increasingly blurred (Rayman-Bacchus & Molina, 2001). Generally speaking, the possibility of taking advantage of the web depends on operator visibility and on the ability of the website to capture visitors (potential clients). In turn this depends on website accuracy and the availability of multiple hypertext links. Links are actually fast, cost-effective and enhance the website profile; they enable intermediaries who view the width of their network as a valuable asset to improve their competitiveness.

## Multimedia Technologies as Tools to Support Destination Management

Multimedia technologies — already considered as the new economic revolution promoted by co-operation and sharing of development objectives between information and communication technology sectors and political stakeholders (Lera, 1996) — entail the combination[6] of images, sounds, voice, videotexts and data, and provide many advantages in all stages of the communication process.[7] Consequently, if effectively used, they can drastically improve the quality of inter- and intra-organisation relationships.[8]

---

[5] Only Amadeus is still partially controlled by airlines; Worldsplan has decreased its worldwide presence in travel agencies and is part of Expedia.com; Galileo was taken over by Cendant, one of the largest and most diversified world-wide leaders in travel and tourism distribution. However it has widened its range of services to suppliers and customers. As to the latest dynamics of GDS also related to the development of new virtual intermediation players, see Mongelli (2005).

[6] The technical requirements to implement multi-media applications are quite complex. They depend on the breadth and speed of the transmission band, on the efficiency of the system architecture, which has to be able to store and manage high volumes of multimedia data promptly, on the protocols to transfer multimedia data and on the development of software to interface and process multimedia information (Gunasekaran & Love, 1999).

[7] In communication coding the process is faster and spontaneous; the message or language is more effective as it has at its disposal a higher range of signals to be processed; in the decoding stage, the message is better understood and feedback is more appropriate as the message is more likely to be received.

[8] For a review of the potential applications of multimedia technologies in many fields such as education, health, finance, retailing and entertainment, refer to Gunasekaran and Love (1999).

These technologies, thanks to their flexibility and effectiveness, are a fundamental tool to enhance the destination's distinctive competences and establish co-operative relationships aimed at creating and sharing knowledge and promoting a unitary image.

Using these technologies, virtual intermediaries are pursuing differentiation strategies increasingly based on the specific features of the network. From this perspective, the aggregation of the resources made available to consumers through the web increasingly takes on original forms involving operators of associated sectors, making leverage on specific resources, which cannot be imitated and transferred and becoming the focus of the network of products/services provided to tourists. This dynamic and constant search for originality becomes the driver for a constant re-inventing the destinations, identified through variable "myths" and redesigned through a constant re-definition of alliances and involvement of new operators (Stamboulis & Skayannis, 2003).

This is the direction followed by the tourism portals that promote specific geographical areas using the web as a tool to link local operators to the market and end users. At present three different categories of tourism portals on the web can be identified; they differ in the degree of involvement of the local stakeholders and the range of functions provided to consumers (De Angelis, 2004).

"Information" portals have a mainly promotional function, carried out through database networking and telematic access to information and tourism services provided in the destination. Usually management and data storage is carried out almost exclusively by a single actor charged by the local public administration.

"Link portals", in addition to the set of functions offered by information portals, make it possible to book and/or purchase the main tourism services provided in the destination, thanks to the link between the portal — whose objective is to attract potential tourists — and the website of the individual service providers through which the real transaction takes place. This category includes a large number of local operators, co-ordinated to standardise presentation of the supply.

"Integrated portals" or Destination Management System (DMS) are the last evolutionary stage of the e-business models for destination promotion and management. DMS are portals of countries, regions or destinations, where it is possible to find tourism information on the area, description of the main sites and attractions, along with tourism packages sold by local operators.[9] Information management, booking and/or purchasing are part of a system based on a common platform.[10]

Local organisations are highly involved in defining and up-dating contents and managing transactions and booking. "Through these tools local firms — performing their business within networks and providing tourism products addressed both to groups and individual tourists — can achieve good results in terms of volume of flows and profits. In this case, the success of the individual firm is strictly linked to the success of the whole network; it is based on the capabilities developed by each member to co-operate with its

---

[9] Examples of successful DMS are Tiscover in Austria or Gulliver in Ireland, whose distinctive strategic resources are represented by the underlying networks.

[10] From the technological point of view, DMS development was made possible, thanks to the integrated software and a Data Base system to use and re-distribute data through the Extensible Markup Language (XML) protocol.

partners, on mutual trust, on the ability to plan and develop local resources" (Della Corte & Sciarelli, 2003).

These information solutions provide many benefits for the demand and supply system:

- high quality, customer satisfaction and loyalty;
- new scope economies, network economies and switching costs;
- reduction of transaction costs;
- reduction of management costs; and
- higher efficiency and effectiveness in using information for strategic and marketing purposes;
- higher ability to plan objectives and monitor outcomes.

These tools also support the building or re-definition of a destination image, which is the result of a combination of rational/information factors and emotional factors. Emotional factors, that are usually the result of the tourist's experience, can be anticipated through a proper and effective combination of texts, images and sounds enabled by multimedia applications.[11]

In the future, new opportunities will be provided by the convergence of television, telephony and the personal computer which, by adding components capable of sharing technological and interconnection standards, make interoperability possible and combine the performances of the three sub-systems to design integrated services capable of maximising the generation of value for customers (Martini, 2000; Buhalis & Licata, 2002).

The technological convergence of the Internet, interactive digital TV and mobile phones will create further competition among service providers, intermediaries and destinations. Differentiation of the distribution channels as a function of the different devices — linked and interoperable, thanks to the development of proper technologies — makes it possible to have new market segments, identify new consumer targets and customise the products supplied.[12]

Tourism organisations will expand the provision of services through the Internet allowing for the expected increase of mobile terminals. However, the real challenge is the development of contents and information that can be distributed through different platforms (Buhalis & Licata, 2002). The different types of devices also differ according to their use, and the contents and formats of the communication they have to be adjusted to. Such communication exploits the possibility of combining the different types of signals (images, sounds, text, graphics), and must generate information and emotional effects suitable to the context. Simultaneously, a new competitive arena will develop — i.e. e-content suppliers — that will compete by defining their positioning according to the technological options chosen for distribution.

---

[11] An updated literature review on the relationship between the different components of the perceived image and the factors influencing its formation is available in Beerli and Martìn (2004). A wide review of destination image definitions can be found in Gallarza, Gil, and Calderon (2002), who also highlight the great variety of methods used to measure the construct, deriving from a multidimensional combination of attributes.

[12] To examine closely the diffusion and success factors of mobile marketing, see Scharl, Dickinger and Murphy (2005).

Moreover, the iterative nature of the new technological applications, enabling the user to be "located" by identifying his/her device, provides new, wider opportunities to develop marketing information systems. It will be possible to have a more exhaustive information database on actual and potential customers. Creating new and more exhaustive information sources can enable private firms to make more rational marketing decisions and act more effectively;[13] it can also guide public and private stakeholder networks in their destination strategic management (Ritchie & Ritchie, 2002).

On the other hand, it is also possible to implement more targeted marketing actions based on a relational approach[14] aimed at *customer retention* not only *customer acquisition.*

## The Project "Campania in Pillole"

Mobile Commerce is a technology that is developing as a result of the growing spread of mobile phones. It is an innovative channel to distribute products and services at the local level, as it enables operators to orient the supply (above all promotions) selecting potential consumers based on their presence in the site or their proximity to it.

Mobile Commerce makes it possible for consumers to purchase products and services "on the go", after identifying the supply available at the local level. It is thus, an opportunity for "last-minute" purchases and a tool to modify reservations as a result of changes at arrival or departure.

In this case, the mobile phone works as a wireless access node and enables the use of multimedia services consisting of short text messages, images and pictures. The main advantage is the "personal" nature of the communication reaching the individual person, not a place. This feature makes mobile phones competitive vis-à-vis traditional phones and the Internet (Ayres & Williams, 2004).

These systems have very high potentials, given the widespread use of mobile phone technologies. The number of mobile phones linked to the Internet has dramatically increased and it is expected to be higher than the number of PCs equipped with web browsers. Also MMS are expected to increase dramatically. MMS enable the development of innovative ways to use tourism services. MMS technology turns mobile phones into multimedia terminals, both in work and leisure time, and MMS messages enable prompt communication of images, audio files and texts regardless of the geographic location.

The project "Campania in Pillole" is an experimental application that has developed a *hardware and software prototype.* Using MMS technology this prototype enables tourists to have access to information on historical-artistic heritage, sites of interest, suggested routes and opening hours of the museums located in Campania.

---

[13] In order to identify the emerging marketing issues and practices in the hospitality and tourism industry, the recent contribution of Oh, Kim, and Shin (2004) offers a wide selected bibliography of 223 references.
[14] Relationship marketing is not a short-term solution to increase competitiveness in the marketplace; it is a long-term ambition to create loyalty — whether involving attitudes or behaviours — and increase the number of visitors in a specific destination (Fyall, Callod, & Edwards, 2003).

Campania has a well-known historical heritage and wonderful landscapes; tourism is one of its main economic activities and one of the main resources for local development.[15] In 2003 it was the southern Italian region accounting for the highest flows (arrivals and stays) of Italian and foreign tourists.[16]

The following partners, performing their activity in different fields, participated in the project:

- Advanced Consulting Equipe (ACE), a local advisory company;
- IRAT of the National Research Council; and
- Didagroup, leader company in design and realisation of broadband technological infrastructures and development of prototypes.

From the methodological point of view, the project was developed in two stages. To understand the interest in this type of service and the needs related to its modes of use, in the first stage an empirical survey was conducted through direct interviews with over 1000 Italian and foreign tourists. The findings confirmed that, although mobile phones are still used in traditional fashion, 70% of the respondents were highly interested in using an MMS service for tourism, if available.

In the second stage, a web-based prototype was developed (termed *www.campaniainpillole.it*) allowing for the needs identified by users. The prototype was designed allowing for two different types of use:

- *Pull*-based use, providing tourists with the possibility of asking for information about museums, tourist sites, events scheduled for the reference period, etc. Tourists who wish to visit Campania can have access to the website *www.campaniainpillole.it*, both before and during their tour. The website is developed to provide useful information on the suggested sites and tours. This free web service is combined with the possibility for tourists of getting detailed information on museums, tourist sites, and scheduled events for the reference period directly on their mobile phones. The answers to their questions (displayed in "frames" format) is sent to the tourists' MMS terminals on the days (and even times) selected to visit the specific sites.
- *Push*-based use, through which tourists can get detailed information during their visit (e.g. of a museum) by simple instructions sent to a (short) reference number. Thus tourists receive on their mobile phones multimedia contents related to the attractions of a specific site.

### Prototype Development

The project was finalised with the development of a prototype portal providing a body of information to users in order to make it possible for them to identify monuments, thematic tourism routes and other cultural attractions offered by the cities selected by the portal. The

---

[15] The strategic nature of the project, due to its potential impact on the local economy, was recognised by the Regional Government of Campania that co-funded it within the framework of measure 3.17 of the POR Campania 2000–2006.
[16] Billi, S., & Biasi, M. (2004).

portal has a number of innovations as to the technologies used to develop the model and the service provided.

**Portal architecture**   The portal was designed to be a local tourism information hub. As a function of this objective the technical attributes of the prototype were defined along with its carrying structure. The solution adopted implies both the creation of a large *database* — acting as a capacious tank for all rapidly changing contents — and the use of standard paging up elements through which also rough data can be packaged in the same graphic format as the rest of the website.

Browsing is modular to enable future extension of the contents without substantially changing the graphics and structure of the website; it is also more user-friendly, thanks to the arrangement of the data by thematic section. Additionally, this solution made it possible to maintain the maximum number of information levels below the home page within the traditionally adopted values, so as to prevent random browsing in the many topics covered.

Graphics was designed to make the website more user-friendly and effective in conveying information. Graphics, in general, is a critical point of design as on it depends how fast pages can be do*wnloaded*; too heavy pages — overloaded with images and animation — distract the visitor's attention from the portal information contents and slow access times to pages making information retrieval more difficult. Therefore, graphics was intentionally designed to have quite a spare style. In the headline (title graphics) — whose main function is to inform visitors of the web page they have landed at — a clipart and a number of images were introduced to enhance the visual impact and arouse the visitor's curiosity. A logo with the partner firms' brand name is also reproduced on each web document and page.

The search engine can be easily identified and found in each internal page of the website. Browsing buttons were introduced to help visitors browse the website and obtain and read the information included in the text links. Specific attention was paid to the homogeneity and consistency of the pages making up the body of the portal, so as to highlight the shift from the portal environment to the sites including the information found with the support of the search engine. The browsing level was made higher by including in each page a number of utility functions such as "back" or "back to Homepage". Users can then follow a backward process of the visited pages within the portal.

Portal levels are illustrated in Figure 11.2.

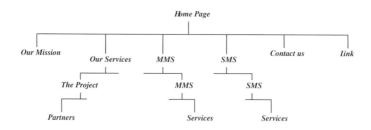

Figure  11.2:  Arrangement of the portal levels.

To develop the portal, a detailed analysis was made of the innovative technologies for interfacing mobile units and PC, such as wireless Bluetooth and technologies and protocols to send multimedia messages. The technology used to develop the portal is the ASP (*Active Server Pages*), a *server-side technology* (Figure 11.3) particularly suitable to the needs of this portal as it enables users to create documents, which can provide information and meet browser requests differently.

The technologies involved in the development and operation of *ASP* are:

- A server web supporting an active server;
- ODBC (*Open DataBase Connectivity*);
- Server database (*Access*); and
- Transmission control protocol/internet protocol (TCP/IP).

**Services provided**  The services provided by the website can be accessed inside a reserved area, which can be entered by the user after registration. The services provided are the following:

- Print area
- Newsletter
- Area B2B
- Sending of MMS
- Search engine
- Area B2C

The most innovative service provided by the portal is the possibility for browsers to receive on their mobile phones an MMS message, which enables them to take with them "information pills" related to a specific monument or work of art or to the opening hours of a museum. Therefore, tourists using the Internet to organise their tourism route, can look for monuments, museums, typical food products and get from the portal all pieces of information facilitating their visit. An internal search engine helps browsers obtain information as fast as possible.

Within the section labelled MMS it is possible to find four categories of monuments related to each city included in the website:

- Churches
- Monuments
- Museums
- Excavations

Figure 11.3: Technology *server-side.*

With respect to each category of attractions, additional information can be found: architectural information, historic information, general information and information on typical aspects of the site.

Information is arranged and structured in advance within multimedia messages. Each multimedia message available to be sent consists, in line with the MMS technology, of a text file and a jpg format image showing the specific architectural work the message refers to.

The website includes a database where all multimedia messages available for sending have been arranged. Based on the city selected, the category of architectural monument and the type of content, users can have a preview of the specific message they would like to receive. The multimedia message (included in the database as a file with MMS extension) is then previewed by users on their monitor and they can ask for it to be sent to their mobile phone.

Sending multimedia messages is currently provided according to the *pull* (or *on demand*) technology and requires users to pull them into their PC — after identifying the information needed — by downloading the contents found.

The pull-based technology was chosen as it better meets the logics underlying service provision; it is the client who, in a synchronous manner, stimulates the server to send data. A push-based technology — where the client who shows interest in a specific category of information receives information from the server in an asynchronous manner — can be used to widen the range of services provided. For example, users can ask to be informed of any theatre performance in the city, or of events such as fairs, festivals, concerts and other performances. In this case, the server will send the message not when the user asks for the information but when and if the event announced in the multimedia message specifically created will take place.

The "SMS-sending" service is an alternative to the "MMS-sending" service, designed to enable users to receive the same information contents that can be obtained through MMS, also as a simple text message without any image. Namely, the user registered in the website who wants to get information on the monuments located in a specific area, can ask the information to be sent to his mobile phone as an SMS, if this is not able to receive MMS. Also in this case information is arranged in the same sequence and levels adopted for MMS.

Additionally, thanks to the portal, registered users can file MMS, video messages or simply their own photos in a dedicated space (within the section "Free Album and/or FotoAlbum"). By doing so tourists (users) can save and maintain the culture and architectural information with photos attached, organising their tour without the support of tourist guides or other paper literature. Through this personal photo album users can view all multimedia or video messages filed, send them to their friends' mobile phone or e-mail and create new multimedia messages using the photos filed.

## Conclusion

This project was developed only for demonstration purposes. For this reason it only refers to four sample cities of the region of Campania: Amalfi, Benevento, Caserta and Pompei. The prototype is the starting point to develop and market a package of multimedia services that can be used through MMS, providing real time information to visitors of tourist sites.

There are many potential developments of the service (advertising, e-commerce, mobile entertainment). Also supply can be differently developed, for example, combining service and purchase of a pre-paid card, such as the Campania "artecard", through which it is possible to have a bundle of MMS, which can be deducted from the card credit.

The operators of the mobile Value Chain (mobile operators, internet service providers (ISP), web application service providers (WASP), technological organisations, etc.) showed a high interest in value-added services that currently account for only about 10% of the profits. However, the objective is to double this percentage and promote general packet radio services (GPRS) new generation terminals, with colour display and compatible MMS, i.e. capable of supporting more complete services ranging from public utility to the so-called "infotainment".

This example of multimedia application is a tool to promote and enhance the value of the tourism destination; it contributes to an inflow of resources directly triggered on line (e.g. hotel reservation, car rental, etc.) or subordinate to the physical movement of the tourist. These tools do not necessarily have to originate *within* the area enhanced by them but — if they are able to attract resources in the area — they can become a resource *of* the area.

ICT and above all multimedia technologies enhance the distinctive competences of the destination, while becoming a factor that creates and differentiates tourism supply systems. Actually they can be a fundamental resource for the destination, both with respect to its infrastructural components and soft components (applications and competences).

They also affect the pattern of the business models and the modes through which value is created for end users (Vernuccio, 2002). The Internet, for example, on the one hand enables the SMEs excluded from the networks dominated by large firms to obtain direct visibility with consumers, avoiding one or more intermediation stages. On the other, consumers can have direct access to the supply system, purchasing products and services and performing an active role in the building of the service package purchased.

Multimedia technologies, as link technologies, also facilitate the need for coordination among the players involved and enable the supply system to be redesigned by aggregating firms within virtual environments. They are thus a new way to govern systems of firms, which will be used by policy makers as a driver for local development.

The technology interacts with other resources, providing the destination with the possibility to present itself and establish relationships within a virtual environment. In the virtual space also new relationships are created (e.g. with potential users) and the opportunity to recombine knowledge resources increases. Technology then improves the common language, organisational efficiency and information flow, increasing the value and the competitive ability of the destination.

However, this virtuous development depends on the development, within the physical territory, of a culture and practice aimed at creating relationships, consortia and networks. In other words, the various organisations and policy makers have to enter into cultural and economic agreements as a result of integration and concerted actions.

For the mutual benefit of all its components, the telematic network can draw a map, which enables the tourism system to represent itself as a whole system, while providing network users and potential tourists with all the information on how to reach the virtual and physical destination so as to take advantage of the information and economic offers which can be found in both.

# References

Ancarani, F. (1999). Il marketing territoriale: un nuovo approccio per la valorizzazione delle aree economico-sociali. *Economia e Diritto del Terziario*, (1), 179–198.

Antonioli Corigliano, M. (2002). Turismo, nuove tecnologie e fattori competitivi. In: M. Antonioli Corigliano, & R. Baggio (Eds), *Internet & turismo*. Milan: Egea Publishing.

Ayres, R.U., & Williams, E. (2004). The digital economy: Where do we stand? *Technological Forecasting and Social Change*, *71*(4), 315–339.

Beerli, A., & Martìn, J.D. (2004). Factors influencing destination image. *Annals of Tourism Research*, *31*(3), 657–681.

Bellini, N. (2000). *Il Marketing Territoriale*. Milan: Franco Angeli.

Billi, S., & Biasi, M. (2004). La domanda turistica. *XIII Rapporto sul Turismo Italiano 2004–2005*, Mercuri, Firenze.

Bramwell, B., & Sharman, A. (1999). Collaboration in local tourism policymaking. *Annals of Tourism Research*, *26*(2), 392–415.

Buhalis, D. (1998). Strategic use of information technologies in the tourism industry. *Tourism Management*, *19*(5), 409–421.

Buhalis, D. (2000). Marketing the competitive destination of the future. *Tourism Management, 21*, 97–116.

Buhalis, D., & Licata, M.C. (2002). The future of eTourism intermediaries. *Tourism Management*, *23*(3), 207–220.

Cioppi, M., Savelli, E., & Di Marco, I. (2003). Gli effetti delle ICT (Information and communication technologies) sulla gestione delle Piccole e Medie Imprese. *Small Business/Piccola Impresa*, *3*, 11–50.

De Angelis, M. (2004). Il ruolo strategico delle ICT nei Sistemi Locali di Offerta Turistica. In: E. Bellini & F. Bencardino (Eds), *Conoscenza, ICT, Territorio: un approccio interdisciplinare*. Milan: Franco Angeli.

Della Corte, V., & Sciarelli, M. (2003). Evoluzione del marketing nella filiera turistica: il ruolo dell'information technology. *Congresso internazionale "Le tendenze del Marketing."* Università Ca'Foscari Venezia, Venezia, 28–29 November.

Dossena, G. (2000). Le imprese nel business ICT: brevi cenni. In: S. Frova, G. Dossena, & A. Ordanini (Eds), *Infostrutture e società dell'informazione*. Milan: Franco Angeli.

Franch, M., & Martini, U. (2002). Il ruolo delle tecnologie per l'informazione e la comunicazione nello sviluppo delle politiche di marketing delle destinazioni turistiche alpine. *Convegno "Le tendenze del marketing in Europa"*. Ecole Supérieure de Commerce de Paris, Paris, EAP, 25–26 January.

Fyall, A., Callod, C., & Edwards, B. (2003). Relationship marketing. The challenge for destinations. *Annals of Tourism Research*, *30*(3), 644–659.

Gallarza, M.G., Gil Saura, I., & Calderon Garcìa, H. (2002). Destination image. Towards a conceptual framework. *Annals of Tourism Research*, *29*(1), 56–78.

Gunasekaran, A., & Love, P.E.D. (1999). Current and future directions of multimedia technologies in business, *International Journal of Information Management*, *19*(2), 105–120.

Haimayer, P. (2003). Politica del turismo e destination management nell'Arge Alp. Un primo bilancio. In: H. Pechlaner, K. Weiermair, & C. Laesser (Eds), *Politica del turismo e destination management. Nuove sfide e strategie per le regioni dell'area alpina*. Milan: Touring University Press.

Lera, E. (1996). Towards multi-service personal communications: Perspectives for a sector structure evolution. *Telecommunications Policy*, *20*(7), 481–496.

Manente, M., & Cerato, M. (2000). Destination management per creare valore. In: H. Pechlaner, K. Weiermair, & C. Laesser (Eds), *Destination management. Fondamenti di marketing e gestione delle destinazioni turistiche*. Milan: Touring University Press.

Martini, U. (2000). Imprese turistiche e mercato virtuale di Internet. Opportunità e problemi rispetto al dualismo del settore. *Convegno "Economia virtuale e opportunità reali".* Università degli Studi di Padova, Vicenza, 2 June.

Mongelli, T.L. (2004). Nuove tecnologie per il turismo: Internet, Telematica ed Innovazione. *XIII Rapporto sul Turismo Italiano 2004–2005,* Mercuri, Firenze.

Oh, H., Kim, B.Y., & Shin, J.H. (2004). Hospitality and tourism marketing: Recent development research and future directions. *Hospitality Management, 23,* 425–447.

Palmer, A., & Bejou, D. (1995). Tourism destination marketing alliances. *Annals of Tourism research, 22*(3), 616–629.

Pechlaner, H. (1999). Alpine destination management and marketing in Italy. *Turistica,* Year VII (2/3), April–September.

Petrillo, C.S. (2001). Un approccio strategico relazionale per la valorizzazione turistica del territorio. In: C. Pugliese (Ed.), *Governo del territorio e sviluppo turistico. Innovazioni manageriali, aspetti giuridici ed economici,* Quaderni IRAT, no. 27.

Pollarini, A. (2005). *La comunicazione del prodotto/territorio, Le città della cultura, comunicazione e marketing territoriale.* Rome, 11 February.

Pollock, A. (2000). Sistemi intelligenti per gestire la destinazione. In: H. Pechlaner, K. Weiermair, & C. Laesser (Ed.), *Destination management. Fondamenti di marketing e gestione delle destinazioni turistiche.* Milan: Touring University Press.

Poon, A. (1993). *Tourism, technology and competitive strategies.* Wallingford: CAB International.

Premazzi, K. (2001). Cyber-marketing territoriale: l'attivazione di un sito web per la valorizzazione del territorio. *Micro & Macro Marketing, X,* 277–300.

Rayman-Bacchus, L., & Molina, A. (2001). Internet-based tourism services: Business issues and trends, *Futures, 33*(7), 589–605.

Rayport, J.F., & Sviokla, J.J. (1995). Exploiting the virtual value chain. *Harvard Business Review* (November–December), 75–85.

Rispoli, M., & Tamma, M. (1995). Risposte strategiche alla complessità: le forme di offerta dei prodotti alberghieri. Giappichelli: Turin.

Ritchie, R.J.B., & Ritchie, J.R.B. (2002). A framework for an industry supported destination marketing information system. *Tourism Management, 23*(5), 439–454.

Saxena, G. (2005). Relationship, networks and learning regions: Case evidence from the Peak District National Park. *Tourism Management, 26,* 277–289.

Scharl, A., Dickinger, A., & Murphy, J. (2005). Diffusion and success factors of mobile marketing. *Electronic Commerce Research and Applications,* (4), 159–173.

Stamboulis, Y., & Skayannis, P. (2003). Innovation strategies and technology for experience-based tourism. *Tourism Management, 24,* 35–43.

Tamma, M. (2000). Aspetti strategici del destination management. In: H. Pechlaner, K. Weiermair, & C. Laesser (Eds), *Destination management. Fondamenti di marketing e gestione delle destinazioni turistiche.* Milan: Touring University Press.

Valdani, E., & Ancarani, F. (Eds). (2000). *Strategie di Marketing per il Territorio.* Milan: Egea Publishing.

Varaldo, R., & Caroli, M.G. (1999). Il marketing del territorio: ipotesi di un percorso di ricerca. *Sinergie, 17,* 73–84.

Venkatraman, N. (1994). IT-enabled business transformation: From automation to business scope redefinition. *Sloan Management Review* (Winter), *35,* 73–87.

Vernuccio, M. (2002). Marketing territoriale e turistico. *Rete, Economia e diritto del Terziario,* (2), 601–628.

Chapter 12

# Regional Tourism Co-operation in Progress

Tuovi Soisalon-Soininen and Kaija Lindroth

## Introduction

During the last few decades, companies have developed a wide range of forms of co-operation — using different interorganizational structures and networks — in such areas as distribution, marketing, foreign market entry, and product development. For example increasing global competition and limited resources have forced companies to participate in co-operative groups in order to create new innovative products or facilitate entry to new market areas. Even the public sector has shown interest in supporting the development of co-operative networks between small and medium sized companies, e.g. through funding.

Networks are important in all sectors of economy but their significance is especially great in tourism, which is characterized by the interdependence of its different actors (governments, non-profit organizations, and commercial enterprises), by the generally small scale of its actors, and by the fragmentation of its markets (Pearce, 1992, p. 5). In the regional tourism context, the tourism destinations (a single district, town, or city, or a clearly defined rural, coastal, or mountain area) all have a complex and multidimensional "total tourism product" based on different kinds of natural, social, and cultural resources and services as well as hospitality and tourism services. These resources are owned by a variety of public, private, and non-profit actors (Davidson & Maitland, 1997, p. 4). However, tourists regard the tourist product as a whole, they are not interested in who built the object, or who provides the service. All these factors require actors in the tourism sector to co-operate in order to offer a total attractive product and through this improve the destination's image.

Business networks have been studied through many different approaches, e.g. Araujo and Easton (1996) have identified 10 different traditions. We contribute our study to the industrial network approach developed by European marketing scholars, mainly centered on the Industrial Marketing and Purchasing Group (IMP). The industrial network research concentrates on studying total networks of relationships: it sees industrial markets as exchange relationships between multiple organizations. According to Håkansson and

Tourism Local Systems and Networking
Copyright © 2006 by Elsevier Ltd.
All rights of reproduction in any form reserved
ISBN: 0-08-044938-7

Johanson (1988, p. 372), "... (industrial) networks emerge and develop as a consequence of interaction". The network research has basically a descriptive and explanatory purpose; it tries to understand systems of relationships from a positional perspective (from a focal firm's viewpoint) or from a network perspective (one holistic perspective of the whole system). The analytical focus is on individual, interconnected relationships forming network structures. The time perspective is dynamic and long-term (Mattsson, 1997, pp. 456–457).

However, the majority of research has focused on the general characteristics of organically evolved networks, and on their structure and development processes (Möller & Halinen, 1999). The new challenge in the network research is the managerial aspect.

The development of complex networks requires the company management to show new capabilities: since the companies are dependent on each other, acting in the same network, the managers should understand the effects of any action on all the companies in the network. The managers need a "network view" (Ford & McDowell, 1999). Möller and Halinen (1999) distinguish in their network management framework four levels that all need different but interrelated managerial capabilities:

(1) Industries as networks (how to gain the understanding of the network, the network view or the network visioning capability),
(2) Firms in network (how to manage focal nets and network positions),
(3) Relationship portfolios (how to manage company's relationship portfolio), and
(4) Exchange relationships (how to manage company's exchange relationships).

In this paper we will concentrate on studying firms in network. Accordingly, we will use the "network" term to refer to macro networks and the term "net" to refer to intentional nets of a restricted group of actors. For example Mattsson (1985) proposes the term net to be used for the relevant subset of the network when one focal organization is being studied. The term "network" concerns the situation when the market is studied from a macro perspective (see e.g. Salmi, 1995; Äyväri, 2002). However, the net can also be defined without a focal firm consisting of all the actors that are more closely connected to each other than to those outside the net (Mattsson, 1998).

In tourism, the establishment of a network, particularly one involving small and medium sized enterprises, often takes place at the recommendation of a public sector authority. It is therefore important for the individual actors as well as the policy makers to understand how single activities are related to the development of the network as a whole. This is important to the individual actor as well as to policy makers. The manager or coordinator of the developing network is often a public organization, i.e. tourist office or another public organization, which manages the EU funded resources. This may generate problems: first, the position of the tourist organization as a "neutral" actor does not give the possibility of choosing the partners, second, tourist organization's role as a coordinator might not be accepted by other actors, and third, the actors of the destination might not have common visions of the objectives of the network. Furthermore the continuation of the co-operation after the end of the funded period has shown to be difficult. Therefore it is important that the co-operating actors and the coordinator have an understanding of the development process of the network, in other words, a network view.

The aim of this study is to increase the understanding of the development process of networks in tourism. The development of networks includes the question how to manage the evolutionary process. The coordinator has to know what kind of motivations the partners have in order to be able to involve them into the process. The actors have different backgrounds, different views of their environment and their role in it, and different opinions of the purpose of the new network. Additionally, the coordinator has to know its own role in the development process, its possibilities to motivate the emergence of the new network, and has to be able to manage the process.

The objectives of this study are:

- to describe a regional tourism co-operation development process,
- to analyze the management of the network in its different phases,
- to study the roles of the actors in the existing network, and
- to identify the future needs.

The empirical part of the study is based on a regional tourism development case in the province of Eastern Uusimaa, Finland.

## Managerial Views of Network Development

Networks are stable but not static (Easton, 1992, p. 23). New relationships between companies are formed and old relationships disappear. The continuous interaction between companies offers the opportunity for innovation in an environment with which both are familiar. Håkansson and Lundgren (1995) identify two interrelated dimensions in the evolution of networks: firm behavior and network pattern. Firm behavior describes individual companies, their changes, and the development of relationships with other companies. Network pattern characterizes the way in which the changes in firm behavior create specific evolutionary processes in the network.

Both public policy and the activities of individual actors are important in the development process. Critical issues in supporting the development process are: how much money should be invested, to whom it should be distributed and when. As different problems are critical in different phases of development, the interaction strategies of the actors vary. Public policy should not only favor individual projects, but also aim at supporting networks as a whole (Lundgren, 1993, p. 167).

Networks consist of several actors with different interests and different views. The differences are results of various backgrounds and histories of the actors, of their positions, knowledge, and ambitions in the network. Furthermore, actors are linked to other specific actors through exchange relations and are influenced by them (Håkansson & Johanson, 1993, p. 44).

Managing networks and network evolution is a big managerial challenge. Understanding networks, their structure, processes, and evolution is essential to successful network management. The network view (see e.g. Ford & McDowell, 1999) is important in order to be able to analyze the evolution of the network and to find opportunities for strategic development.

At the net management level a company's behavior can be analyzed through the focal nets they belong to and through the positions and roles they have in these nets. The managerial challenge is to develop and manage nets and net positions (Möller & Halinen, 1999). Network position defines "how the individual fits into the network" Henders (1992,

p. 5). Position can be seen as a result of long-term, interconnected activities by both the focal actor and other actors in the network.

Gemünden and Ritter (1997, p. 297) introduce the concept of network competence as "the resources and the activities of a focal company to generate, develop, and manage networks in order to take advantage of single relationships and the network as a whole". Net management capability includes mobilizing and coordinating the other actors' resources, and activities (Möller & Halinen, 1999). According to Ritter (1999), the elements of a company's network competence can be divided into network management task execution and network management qualification where the former consists of relationship-specific and cross-relational tasks and the latter of specialist and social skills.

Mobilizing various different actors of a company and developing co-operative attitudes and mechanisms in that interaction with others seem to be critical in the goal performance in networks (Håkansson & Snehota, 1995, p. 6). When studying corporate collaboration in technical development, Håkansson & Eriksson (1993) found four key issues concerning the handling of cooperative development processes: prioritizing, synchronizing, timing, and mobilizing. In prioritizing, the problem is that of choosing partners, synchronizing concerns the way in which the company's and the counterparts' activities and resources are related to each other. Timing of activities in the networking process includes timing in different levels: timing within the single company, a relationship, and different relationships. Mobilizing other actors in favor of a certain technical solution is one of the key issues in order to succeed in the process.

Likewise, Biemans (1992) suggests that successful cooperation consists of selecting the right partner, identifying and motivating the right persons, formulating clear-cut agreements, and managing the outgoing relationship.

## The Case: Premium Visit Co-operation in Progress

### Research Method

The IMP research has largely focused on the temporal aspects and the development of relationships. Additionally, recent research has emphasized relationship development in connection with the development of the other relationships of the network actors. Because of this, relationships should be studied as a part of the total business network to which they are connected and in their interaction with the broader business environment (Halinen, 1996).

In the longitudinal approach, both retrospective and real-time data have their strengths and weaknesses. The combination of the two methodologies has proven to be a good strategy to reach the advantages of each approach (Halinen, 1996, p. 53; Leonard-Barton, 1995, p. 60).

Gummesson (1991, p. 30) states that qualitative interviews and observation provide the best opportunities for the study of processes. In the longitudinal research, it is important to find reliable and valid incidents (empirical observation) as indicators for an event (a theoretical construct). A good process model of innovation development strings the events together "in a particular temporal order and sequence to explain how and why innovations unfold over time" (Van de Ven & Pool, 1995, p. 163).

In this study real-time data was supplemented by retrospective analysis of the early stages of the co-operation process. The qualitative data was gathered through personal interviews, observation (occasionally participant observation) and written documents (project documents, co-operation contracts, records of meetings, and newsletters). The personal interviews were carried out during winter 2004. The 10 companies interviewed represented the different roles, volumes, sectors, and geographical locations of the 27 companies in the net.

### Background Information

The region of Eastern Uusimaa, comprises 10 municipalities with a population of nearly 100,000. Due to its long history, the region has a plethora of cultural and historical venues with old and valuable architecture. It can also boast associations with many of the best-known artists in the country — both past and present.

The centre of the province, Porvoo, has long traditions as one of the most popular domestic day-trip destinations thanks to its central role in Finnish history, its mediaeval town plan and wooden architecture from the 18th century. The region as such does not have great tourism traditions, but can be described as a stopover for tourists traveling from the capital to the Lake District or as a day-trip destination for tourists using Helsinki as their base.

The tourism strategy of the province for 2001–2006, defines the vision of the area as that of the treasury of cultural history of Finland. According to the strategy, the aim is to make sure that the province will increase its visitor numbers more than other areas in Finland and the tourism revenue in the province will grow faster than that of other provinces.

Lately the exceptional private tourism cooperation of the province has attracted a lot of national interest. The highest tourism authority in Finland, the Ministry of Trade and Industry, carried out a research in winter 2003–2004 on the regional cooperation models used in the country with the purpose of highlighting the best practices in regional tourism management. The report shows recognition for the work done in Eastern Uusimaa. This is very valuable, as the results have been achieved without any official regional tourism development body, unlike in most other provinces in the country.

In the following chapters we will describe the different phases of regional tourism co-operation in Eastern Uusimaa. First, we will look at the EU-funded project that initiated the development process. Second, pay attention to the unsubsidized Premium Visit net that continued the co-operation process. Finally, identify emerging future issues: the actor's needs and expectations, and other issues that might affect the future of the co-operation. Focus will be on the management of the net, its actors, timing, goals, and the results of the net.

### EU-funded Project 2000–2002

Traditionally, developing tourism in the province of Eastern Uusimaa was in the hands of municipal tourist information offices. This started to change as a regional development company, Posintra Ltd, owned by municipalities, educational institutions and private businesses in the area, was established in 1998. The business idea of Posintra was to boost the business activity of small- and medium-sized companies in the area as well as to facilitate regional co-operation. The projects run by Posintra were funded by the EU and focused mainly on tourism. One of the projects aimed at building up networks around focal firms in several sectors.

The large tourism project around a focal firm initiated in 1999 mainly focused on product development, marketing, and better awareness among the players of each other's products. A local tour operator, Porvoo Tours (owner plus two employees), established its position as the focal firm for the emerging net of businesses participating in the project. Porvoo Tours as practically the only regional distributor of group travel products had an interest in enhancing the tourism supply and finding new, professional suppliers. The external funding was necessary in order to start the co-operation as most tourism companies in the area were micro businesses and as the municipalities within the province always had invested minimally in tourism.

To most actors project work as such was something new and provided a totally new challenge. Posintra had a full-time employee devoted to tourism, an objective outsider who started to pull the strings and initiated lots of new activity. He organized the practical work: chose the participants with the help of the focal firm, managed the training sessions, provided help with the product development, and took care of the communication within the group.

The owner of the focal firm assisted in choosing the partners, participated in planning and implementing of the project activities. She was also the motivator and the soul of the group. She understood the need for co-operation among small businesses in order to enhance the region's tourism supply. For her own business, it was also vital to improve the existing offer through a well functioning net of tourism actors. This shows that both of the managers of the project had the network view required for successful co-operation of the net.

The project coordinator and the owner of the focal firm selected 25 companies for the project. These companies were either existing partners of the focal firm or new ones that they found promising. Unlike most of the regional development projects, this one had the possibility to influence the selection of the partners thus creating a good basis for future co-operation.

The timing of the project was perfect as the region was lacking in this type of co-operation although the need for that had already been recognized by various bodies in the region. There was also an increasing demand for better-developed tourism packages instead of the traditional day tripping. Additionally, new tourism businesses and potential business ideas had emerged in the area. The project provided the actors with the necessary resources for intensified co-operation.

The goal of the project was to increase the competitiveness of the companies through networking and intensified co-operation. The aims set for networking included product development, joint marketing through the focal firm, as well as increased exchange within the relationships. In terms of business operations the challenges were pricing, customer service, internal marketing as well as joint practices for contracts.

The results of the project were clearly seen in enhanced networking skills of the participants, intensified co-operation, new product packages, and increased sales. Also contract models between the focal firm and the partners were formulated and implemented. However, the planned communication system, the joint Internet portal that had been heavily invested in, failed. The actors were not ready for this type of communication system that gave all the actors access to each other's business information. Instead, electronic communication was based on regular email information, mainly taken care by the focal firm.

*Premium Visit 2003–*

With the EU-funded project coming toward the end, the participants started to make plans for continued co-operation. The focal firm suggested a model of a net where the members elect a board. This was supported largely by the members and the newly organized partner-ship continued operations. The net was named Premium Visit. The five board members rep-resented the different types of companies involved in the net. Together with the focal firm, the board decided on marketing activities, membership criteria, and other relevant issues. The focal firm was satisfied with the board and saw it as its unofficial company board.

Membership criteria approved by the net included the following: New members had to be recommended by an existing member. They also needed to comply with the quality requirements of the net. They had to be trustworthy companies and show successful results in business. In spring 2004, the net had 27 members, the majority of them already involved in the project, others new. The annually revised contracts with the focal firm could be made at two levels: full membership or subcontractor.

The goal of the net remained more and less unchanged with emphasis on increased mar-keting and sales activities. Also product development continued to play a central role in joint operations. The action plan in spring 2004 included, e.g. the planning of new winter products.

After more than 1 year of the Premium Visit net operations, the members showed great enthusiasm and optimism for the future co-operation. In terms of business results, the com-panies involved had shown an improvement. Awareness of the companies and their prod-ucts had improved, as had the mutual trust in partnership.

Based on the 10 interviews of the net members carried out in winter 2004, certain roles could be identified. The turnover of the companies was used to divide the companies into three groups. The first group (2 companies) had a turnover of over one million euros. In spite of their volume and resources, these two companies were less active in developing the net than furthering their own business interests, e.g. participating actively in the mar-keting activities. The second group (5 companies, including the focal firm) had a turnover of 100,000–1,000,000 euros. These companies seemed to be active developers of the net and could also show a substantial increase in their business, thanks to networking. Regardless of the smaller volume, they had a big impact on net development.

The third group (3 companies) had a turnover of 30,000–100,000 euros. Of these three companies, one was an active new partner, one a subcontractor, and one an ex-member. Their contribution to the net varied accordingly. The new partner proved to be an innovator and an active developer of the net. The subcontractor had a positive attitude, but had cho-sen to concentrate on his own business activities due to lack of resources. The ex-member had a negative attitude and showed a lack of a network view. His expectations of network-ing focused on the direct effect on his turnover and he failed to see the total impact of the co-operation.

*Future Issues*

Based on the 10 interviews a wide range of needs was identified. These needs were twofold: those concerning the relationship between the focal firm and the net members, and those dealing with a variety of networks and business development issues. The contracts between the focal firm and the members comprised marketing and sales activities. The problem lies in the fact that the marketing contracts are signed for 1 year only, thus making it difficult for the focal firm to draw any long-term plans. Additionally, the active members may also create their own strategic nets for business purposes, which endangers the position of the focal firm as distributor.

The more general issues included needs for product development as well as development of the overall image of the region. Furthermore, members were in need of consultation in taxation and legal matters. Another area that was brought up in interviews was that of personal development and the management of the versatile tasks of an entrepreneur.

The interview results suggest that the private net faces huge expectations from its members. This is probably due to the fact that there is no other actor in the region meeting these development needs. However, the Premium Visit net is primarily a distribution channel that cannot respond to all expectations arising from the membership.

## Conclusions

This paper aimed to describe a regional tourism co-operation development process by analyzing the management of the network in its different phases, studying the roles of the actors in the existing network, and identifying the future needs. The following conclusions could be drawn: first, the different elements of network competence, relationship-specific and cross-relational tasks as well as the specialist and the social skills were recognized in the persons of project coordinator and focal firm owner. They had the capability to mobilize and co-ordinate the other actors' resources and activities. This was essential in motivating the actors and identifying the joint goal.

Second, this successful co-operation was initially based around the focal firm and the fact that it was possible to choose the most potential partners for product development. Later on, the Premium Visit members guaranteed the quality of the net by defining the membership criteria for newcomers. Additionally, the marketing and sales agreements between the focal firm and the members were formulated clearly and implemented during the project.

Third, the net actors' roles were not dependent on their resources. The actors active in the net were also active in building their own co-operation with other companies. This could also be seen as a threat from the focal firms point of view as the distributor in the net. Fourth, over the past years there has been a clear shift in Eastern Uusimaa from a municipally led tourism management to private initiatives. This represents new thinking in regional tourism development as tourism development often used to rely heavily on external funding. Accordingly, this model has been recognized by both the Ministry of Trade and Commerce as well as tourism organizations in other regions in Finland.

However, the current situation has its shortcomings. The active members of the net are all small companies with limited resources. All their resources are geared toward their own business operations as well as the core function of the net, e.g. distribution and marketing. On top of this, they share a common view of regional tourism development needs with image building and product development as the most necessary actions. They are conscious of the fact that it takes more than their Premium Visit net to meet the regional development needs.

The favorable growth in visitor numbers and in the revenue from tourism spoke for the success of the increased co-operation. A plethora of new tourism entrepreneurs are active in the area and the product supply is substantially wider today than at the beginning of the networking activities.

# References

Araujo, L., & Easton, G. (1996). Networks in socioeconomic systems: A critical review. In: D. Iacobucci (Ed.), *Networks in marketing*. USA: Sage Publications.

Äyväri, A. (2002). *Verkottuneen pienyrityksen markkinointikyvykkyys*. Dissertation, Helsinki School of Economics and Business Administration, Helsinki.

Biemans, W. G. (1992). Product development within networks. In: H. Håkansson, & I. Snehota (Eds), *Developing relationships in business networks*. London: Routledge.

Davidson, R., & Maitland R. (1997). *Tourism destinations*. London: Hodder & Stoughton.

Easton, G. (1992). Industrial networks: A review. In: B. Axelsson, & G. Easton (Eds), *Industrial networks: A new view of reality*. London: Routledge.

Ford, D., & McDowell, R. (1999). Managing business relationships by analysing the effects and value of different actions. *Industrial Marketing Management, 28*, 429–442.

Gemünden, H.G., & Ritter, T. (1997). Managing technological networks: The concept of network competence. In: H.G. Gemünden, T. Ritter, & A. Walter (Eds), *Relationships and networks in international markets*. Oxford: Elsevier Science Ltd.

Gummesson, E. (1991). *Qualitative methods in management research*. London: Sage Publications.

Halinen, A. (1996). The temporal dimension in buyer–seller relationship models. In: P. Tuominen (Ed.), *Emerging perspectives in marketing* (Series A–10). Turku: Turku School of Economics and Business Administration.

Henders, B. (1992). *Positions in industrial networks: Marketing newsprint in the UK*. Unpublished PhD thesis. University of Uppsala.

Håkansson, H., & Eriksson, A.-K. (1993). Getting innovations out of supplier networks. *Journal of Business-to-Business Marketing, 1*(3), 3–34.

Håkansson, H., & Johanson, J. (1988). Formal and information co-operation strategies in industrial networks. In: F.J. Contractor, & P. Lorange (Eds), *Co-operative strategies in international business*. Lexington: Lexington Books.

Håkansson, H., & Johanson, J. (1993). The network as a governance structure, interfirm cooperation beyond markets and hierarchies. In: G. Grabher (Ed.), *The embedded firm*. Routledge: London.

Håkansson, H., & Lundgren, A. (1995). Industrial networks and technological innovation. In: K. Möller, & D. Wilson (Eds), *Business marketing: An interaction and network perspective*. USA: Kluwer Academic Publisher.

Håkansson, H., & Snehota, I. (1995). *Developing relationships in business networks*. London: Routledge.

Leonard-Barton, D. (1995). A dual methodology for case studies: Synergistic use of a longitudinal single site with replicated multiple sites. In: G.P. Huber, & A.H. Van de Ven (Eds), *Longitudinal field research methods*. London: Sage Publications.

Lundgren, A. (1993). Technological innovation and the emergence and evolution of industrial networks: The case of digital image technology in Sweden. In: S.T. Cavusgil & D.D. Sharma (Eds), *Advances in international marketing*. Greenwich, CT: JAI Press.

Mattsson, L.-G. (1985). An application of a network approach to marketing: defending and changing market positions. In: N. Dholakia, & J. Arndt (Eds), *Changing the course of marketing: Alternative paradigms for widening marketing theory*. Greenwich, CT: JAI Press.

Mattsson, L.-G. (1997). Relationship marketing and the market-as-networks approach — a comparative analysis of two evolving streams of research. *Journal of Marketing Management, 13*, 447–461.

Mattsson, L.-G. (1998). Dynamics of overlapping networks and strategic actions by the international firm. In: A.D. Jr. Chandler, P. Hagström, & Ö.Sölvell (Eds), *The dynamic firm: The role of technology, strategy, organization, and regions.* Great Britain: Oxford University Press.

Möller, K., & Halinen, A. (1999). Business relationships and networks: Managerial challenge of network era. *Industrial Marketing Management, 28*, 413–427.

Pearce, P. (1992). *Tourist organizations.* Essex: Longman House.

Ritter, T. (1999). The networking company, antecedents for coping with relationships and networks effectively. *Industrial Marketing Management, 28*, 467–479.

Salmi, A. (1995). Institutionally changing business networks: An analysis of a Finnish company's operations. In: *Exporting to the Soviet Union, Russia and the Baltic countries.* Dissertation, Helsinki School of Economics and Business Administration, Helsinki.

Van de Ven, A. H., & Pool, M. S. (1995). Methods for studying innovation development in the Minnesota Innovation Research Program. In: G. P. Huber, & A. H. Van de Ven (Eds), *Longitudinal field research methods.* London: Sage Publications.

Chapter 13

# Destination Competitiveness and the Role of Destination Management Organization (DMO): An Italian Experience

Antonio Minguzzi

## Introduction

### On the Performance of the Network

The term network defines a variety of subjects, with different but complementary interests involved in a long-term relationship in order to better utilize possible economic scales and specializations.

The Network Theory includes those theoretical elaborations which adopt the network organizations as categories for analysis (Marin & Mayntz, 1991; Ibarra & Andrews, 1993) affirming that interagency coordinating actions are set up by collective organization in order to manage the interdependencies that emerge not only from the exchange or competitive needs, for the same resources, but also from the necessity to solve commonly shared problems (Gulati, 1995).

According to the definition of Freeman (1984), "an organization is characterized by its relationships with various groups and individuals (including employees, customers, suppliers, government and members of the communities)" that "has either the power to affect the firm's performance and/or has a stake in the firm's performance".

In the classic management literature on interorganizational relationships and organization theory, Pfeffer and Salanick (1978) argue that organizations are not self-sufficient. The survival of the same depend on continued support from other actors within their environment. In particular, in describing the dependence of organizations on a range of other organizations, Pfeffer and Salanick (1978) argue that an organization's dependence on other actor is given by the degree to which the actor has a concentration of, and discretionary control over, resources that are important to the organization.

Tourism Local Systems and Networking
ISBN: 0-08-044938-7

Besides the individual strategies of single agents who aim to satisfy their own needs, the contributions made by the Network Theory also analyze those actions set up by inter-organizational systems in order to carry out the implementation of a collective strategy necessary for solving or managing problems (Astley & Fombrun, 1983). A single company's effective behavior is conditioned by the network in which it is situated and depends upon the Network's effectiveness in satisfying, through its coordinating actions, the company's recovery actions (Provan & Milward, 1995). In this light, the purpose becomes to research the usefulness in implementing a network policy. In other words, identifying clear and useful reference parameters necessary for a rigorous and long-lasting mapping of the underlying reasons of the creation of such an alliance (Palmer & Bejou, 1995). In this scenario, an organization that effectively manages its stakeholders must understand the following key concepts: (a) identification of the stakeholders and their respective perceived stakes, (b) the processes necessary to manage organization's relationships with its stakeholders and (c) management of a set of transactions or bargains among the organization and its stakeholders (Freeman, 1984).

In the recent tourism literature, many researchers argue the importance of the relationships between the different actors of the tourism destination. Gunn (1994) suggests that the implementation and success of a tourism development plan is often based on the support of the stakeholders in the community, which include the citizens, entrepreneurs and community leaders, guests.

### On Destination Management

Destination management consists of the integrated management of those processes necessary in establishing an exchange between a destination and its visiting tourists. Therefore, on one hand, it involves the management of services offered and tourist attraction factors, while, on the other hand, managing demand, dependent on tourist flow and customer satisfaction (Goelder & Ritchie, 2003).

Several tourism researchers have attempted to clarify the nature of the tourism destination. Hu and Ritchie (1993) conceptualized the tourism destination as a package of tourism facilities and services, which like any other consumer product is composed of a number of multi-dimensional attributes. For other scholars destinations are amalgams of tourism products, offering an integrated experience to consumers (Buhalis, 2000; Ritchie, Crouch & Hudson, 2001).

An analysis of the various definitions regarding the term destination often use region, district, area and locality as synonyms together with the adjective tourism to mean tourism destination (Keller, 2000). Based on the various models of tourism development outlined by Pearce (1989), it is proposed to define a destination as an amalgam of products and services available in one location, that can draw visitors from beyond its spatial confines.

Even if the most commonly recognized concept defines destination management by the product offered to tourists, interpretations vary when establishing whether the prospective should vary in the light of demand or supply. Some authors (Leiper, 1995; Ziltener, 1999; Martini, 2000; Pechlaner & Weiermair, 2000) support the demand aspect substantially and identify destination as a set of products, services, natural and artificial attractions able to draw tourists to a specific place. They affirm that geographical position does not coincide with destination, but is simply one of the factors that makes it up. Other researchers (Tamma, 2002; Brunetti, 2001) define destination as a supply system correlated with a specific area.

With this outlook, destination coincides with the notion of locality seen as a set of products, but the role of companies attitudes and their willingness to cooperate emerges as a critical factor (Fyall, Oakley, & Weiss, 2000; Medeiros de Araujo & Bramwell, 2002). A more systematic approach seems to regard the one which openly declares the various viewpoints (demand or supply) in its definition of destination and attempts to unite the limitations of the geographical area with product content (Manente & Cerato, 2000; Maltzer & Pechlaner, 2000).

Regardless of the definition chosen, the problem of management is posed as a coordinating issue among the individual agents. Each operator involved looks out for his own individual, direct and exclusive interests in developing tourism on a local level. However, he must realize that his actions influence other operators' actions due to interdependence networks. This evidence has led to the numerous studies which have analyzed the subject of destination performance in terms of "the locality as a whole" (Lundtorp & Wanhill, 2001; Kozak, 2002). While further studying specific categories in the demand system, for example small businesses (Tinsley & Lynch, 2001), or highlighting the critical role played by public organizations in area development (Kerr, Barron, & Wood, 2001).

Identifying the most suitable agents and means for destination growth does not sufficiently satisfy the necessity for further studies which would permit the identification of key and unequivocal variables in order to quantify destination performance and the success of programs set up to promote development (Kozak & Rimmington, 1999; Woodside & Sakai, 2001; Formica, 2002; Hudson, Ritchie, & Timur, 2004).

Often destinations are artificially divided by geographical and political barriers, which fail to take into consideration consumer preferences or tourism industry functions. An example of that is the Alps shared by France, Austria, Switzerland, Italy, often perceived and consumed as part of the same product by skiers (Buhalis, 2000).

While the previous discussion has outlined the general nature of a destination, here destination is considered to be a defined geographical region which is understood by its visitors as a unique entity, with a political and legislative framework for tourism marketing and planning (Buhalis, 2000).

## Research Framework

### About the Destination Management Organization in the Regional Tourism Development

The DMO plays a particularly critical and vital role in efforts to ensure that the expectations of stakeholders (both internal and external) are satisfied to the greatest extent possible (Ritchie & Crouch, 2003).

In Italy, tourism organizations are going through a period of change because sector policies have shifted from the central government to regional offices.

In this new context, the role of the DMOs is no longer simply limited to contributing to developing new tourism initiatives, but now includes the management of human and internal resources in various phases of evolution on a regional level in order to establish a relationship between the infrastructures present in the region and the existing market.

Therefore, it is imperative for DMOs to use legislative and management tools during planning and management of destinations in order to ensure that the benefits of tourism activity is shared fairly between all stakeholders and the sustainable practices safeguard the regeneration of resources utilized for the production of tourism (Buhalis, 2000).

DMOs tend to be part of the local, regional or national government and have political and legislative power as well as the financial means to manage resources rationally and to ensure that all stakeholders can benefit in the long term.

Considering the various models, we can note the following principle functions for the DMO at the regional level:

- to maximize the long-term strategy in cooperation with other local organizations;
- to represent the regional interests and the regional tourism industry on the national level;
- to maximize profitability of local enterprises and maximize multiplier effects;
- to develop an homogenous and coherent region image.
- to optimize tourism impacts by ensuring a sustainable balance between economic benefits and socio-cultural and environmental costs.

Today around the world the critical role played by the DMO is recognized like fundamentally for enhancing of the tourism on all different levels or type of destination: without the effective leadership and coordination of an efficacy DMO, a destination is ill-equipped to be either competitive or sustainable (Ritchie & Crouch, 2003).

**The case of an Italian experience in Abruzzo region**   *"Abruzzo Promozione Turismo" is a public sector agency for tourism promotion in the Abruzzo region.*[1]

The main key characteristics of this DMO can be divided into two groups:

- *destination marketing strategies*: the promotion of a territorial image, brand management and internet web site management;
- *development of local resources*: support for companies in the sector, the enhancement of local resources and the integration of the skills provided by participating companies.

In any case it is essential that a destination's DMO be functional from both the strategic and the operational perspective; the leadership and coordination roles that a DMO must perform are the essence of ongoing, long-term success (Ritchie & Crouch, 2003).

# Destination Marketing

Tourism theory has recognized the fundamental importance of marketing's quality of DMO. Because of this, the development of demand strategies is viewed as a major component of destination policy (Mihalič, 2000).

---

[1] Abruzzo is an administrative region situated in Central Italy. At present, "Abruzzo Promozione Turismo" is a public agency.

In the specific case of "Abruzzo Promozione Turismo", marketing plan can be divided into two main areas of intervention:

- *internal promotion*: advertising events to tourists already present in the region;
- *external promotion*: the plan used to attract potential tourists through product promotion and consolidation of the destination's image.

Concerning internal promotion, the DMO, on one hand, carries out promotional projects on a local level (advertising using all local media, billboards, sponsors, etc.), while on the other hand, it also directs promotional activity carried out by individual operators, thus, avoiding any incoherence between the perceived image and the diffused promotional message.

"Abruzzo Promozione Turismo" promotional activities executed outside the region aim to reassure a unitary strategy through direct intervention and modification of various operators actions. The choice between systems promotion and initiative depends on the object to be communicated.

Systems promotion enhances the overall offer supplied by the destination, in order to reach target segments. It operates through publicity campaigns, quality brand name promotion and image building providing an integrated product system. Initiative promotion promotes specific events taking place in the area (cultural/sports, and tour offers for predefined segments of the market, etc.)

Promotion operations can be aimed toward intermediary agents or the individual tourist based upon the clientele sought. Promotion used for intermediary operators refers to all actions which develop and consolidate relations with tour operators (fair/exposition attendance, tourism workshops, the preparation of ad hoc tourism information, the presentation of specific integrated offers). In order to further consolidate promotional operations aimed at intermediary operators (T.O., bus operators, travel agencies and non-profit institutions and associations) "Abruzzo Promozione Turismo" receives specific financing derived from Tourism Promotion Program (Legislative decree 54/97).

The purpose of this intervention is to increase the organization and planning for tour groups who arrive in Abruzzo by plane or bus, paying particular attention to those projects, which regard above all organized tours during the low season. Other initiatives refer to possible incentives for catalog publication and marketing operations sharing. The intention of the first action (catalog production) aims to provide an incentive for those catalogs (on paper and multi-medial), which promote tourism in Italy and abroad, which present hospitality offers in Abruzzo, rewarding increased page production and the presence of hospitality structures. With the advent of the Internet, much of the paper has been replaced by an effective DMO web site (www.abruzzoturismo.it).

The purpose of the second action (marketing) is to activate resources in order to increment tourism promotion through the project sharing presented by consortium and tour operator association, tour operators and travel agency networks.

Promotional activity aimed at tourists is carried out by a series of operations which aim to facilitate, on one hand, the relationship between local operators and clients, while on the other hand, focusing to diffuse and enforce the tourist's image of the region.

This operation can be divided into two main actions: promotion toward new markets and maintaining client loyalty from segments already familiar with the area.

Tourism promotion of the Abruzzo region toward new markets abroad takes place through exposition or fair participation, international relations management, the production of publicity in various languages, the sponsorship of unique events, for example worldwide motorbike show.

In relationship with client loyalty "Abruzzo Promozione Turismo" is developing some project for the future. Actually only a call-center is working to reply to the tourist questions about the region's resources/attractions.

## Local Resources Development

Tourism theory has recognized the fundamental importance of environmental quality for ensuring the future existence of most types of tourist destination. Marketing has for many years been the primary task that destination managers felt was their job. It is only in recent years that DMOs have acknowledged how significant their nonmarketing roles are in developing, enhancing, and maintaining destination competitiveness (Ritchie & Crouch, 2003).

The DMO's managers have to incorporate environmental objectives and practice into the current attitudes in order to stay competitive on the tourist market and many authors (Pizam, 1991; Middleton, 1997) claim that the quality of natural attractions are recognized to be a factor of tourism destination competitiveness.

The elements that make up a destination's (region's, district's, etc.) tourism offer can be grouped into three main areas: infrastructures, facilities and initiatives.

The Abruzzo model includes in these areas:

- Infrastructures
  - Communication lines
  - Internal viability
- Facilities
  - Accommodation
  - Welcoming and Tourism Information Office
- Initiatives
  - Sporting events
  - Free time Proposals

In regards to the infrastructures, Abruzzo DMO systematically conducts sensibility campaigns for local administrations concerning the problems related to tourist flow management. In this light, actions which aim to improve urban facilities take on an important role, in other words, the planning and execution of infrastructures related to reaching established client segments (realization of paths for walks, horse-riding and mountain bikes) and the construction of standard tourist road signs.

The initiative of development proposed by "Abruzzo Promozione Turismo" regarding structures principally refer to improving accommodation centers. Among the most important initiatives in this field, we point out the production of promotional material which contains detailed information regarding hotels and other forms of accommodation stimulating transparency and uniformity in prices applied to tourists. The creation of quality brands impose to those operators who ask for such denomination to obtain and reach determined quality standards. An example of quality brands is represented by the project "Bed and Breakfast" which consists in obtaining a specific trademark for this specific type of offer and provides mandatory regulations for all agents who intend to develop this form of tourism (a sort of auto-regulated code depending on the characteristics of quality and quantity).

The regional territory of "Abruzzo Promozione Turismo" has a series of peripheral visitor information centers. The purpose of these offices is to promote the development of local tourism and guarantee qualified information regarding local tourism offers, one of the first locations sought out by the visitor (Ritchie & Crouch, 2003).

These initiatives, in conclusion, include a set of services for the tourist which optimize and develop the nonmaterial resources present among the operators. Particular importance is given to sporting events and free time proposals, since they can influence the length of stay, survey market segments, innovate the product system.

On the whole, these various initiatives make the tourists' stay pleasurable, introducing them to the discovery of the destination and intensifying the relations between operators and tourists while also benefiting from customer loyalty. However, before this happens, it is necessary for DMO to favor the coordination between the various initiatives in order to carry a centralized promotion of all the activities offered.

## Research Results on Destination Performance Measures

"Abruzzo Promozione Turismo" concentrates its efforts predominantly on promotional activity, intervening neither in tourist product predisposition nor in coordinating activities of private operators, who have maintained a significant inclination toward individual management and decision-making. It also carries out a series of initiatives in order to encourage the development of tour operators' attitude in the region, as in the case of the publication of best practice issues. Therefore, the activities are represented by a relations network which is highly "oriented" from the territory toward the market. Figure 13.1 highlights the principle routes/circuits which are used by "Abruzzo Promozione Turismo" in order to improve destination performances.

In detail:

(a) the relations towards the tourism final market are more important than the relations toward offer system;
(b) the relations toward the market are on average (intermediary operators) in comparison to the offer;
(c) those initiatives aimed at reaching internal objectives (training programs) are lower than those finalized in proposing the system toward the external (promotion).

In studying this case, a few critical points regarding network functioning emerge:

- the formation of consensus regarding common product promotion policies;
- emphasizing the importance of a region's identity;
- promoting local resources (tourist, cultural and environmental);
- aid to developing small businesses involved in tourism.

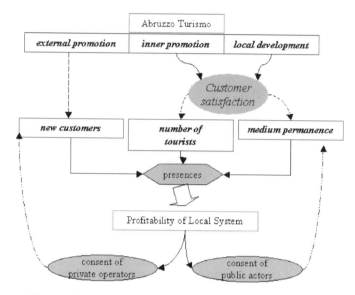

Figure 13.1: Network of Abruzzo Promozione Turismo.
*Source*: Our elaborations.

Some weak points emerge too:

- the existence of non-formal relations within the network;
- a lack of official documentation necessary in order to analyze the effectiveness of DMO activities.

Through direct intervention and by involving local agents, DMO plans and implements actions, which promote destination development. The availability and the enjoyment of services provided thanks to the agents involved and DMO supervision generate an increase in customer satisfaction. Customer satisfaction produces multiple effects on the number of tourists, highlighted by customer loyalty, which implies future visits and the average stay of each tourist in the region is influenced by the quality of proposals. These dynamics are further enhanced by external promotional campaigns, which describe destination as a unique and specific experience that aims to attract new clients. An increase in presence on the territory, through actions which increment both the number of clients and their stay represent the critical factor in the systems profits. Profits generate a consensus among the operators toward those actions taken by the central offices, increasing the legitimacy within public offices, assuring that, on average, increased financing.

Therefore, the initiatives set up by Abruzzo Tourism can be summarized in two principle actions: on one hand, preparing the lines of intervention for image development and consolidation of the region, while on the other hand, operating for the setting up of useful tools in order to improve the perception of the quality of regional offers as conceived by the tourist.

## Implications

The major implication that emerges from our study indicate that DMO activity is becoming more readily absorbed in company planning activities. Initially, programming is carried out by setting main objectives which are determined as product advantages and disadvantages and the company's positions (marketing policies). If the Marketing mix (product, promotion and publicity, distribution) is followed and is subjected to result control, an accurate and appropriate marketing strategy concept (plan) is developed. This plan demands that certain *natural cycles* are followed in company programming and favors the growing attitude of "constant improvement."

Product control becomes the natural and necessary outlet for programming promotional and marketing strategies given the manager's need to verify if the planned actions are taking place and if the objectives set have been achieved. Controlling allows the determination of which actions to implement in order to correct or improve results.

Controls are usually carried out through statistical analysis on tourist behavior and permanence (stay) in tourist areas. However, nowadays, these two indicators do not sufficiently measure the effectiveness of actions undertaken. Therefore, the next step requires the identification of strategic control of marketing activities that better suit the characteristics. In other words, continuous market analysis of both the external and internal situation, objectives, strategy, organizational problems, aiming to identify advantages and disadvantages and to rapidly propose changes in the overall marketing plan.

We have derived that the effectiveness of "Abruzzo Promozione Turismo" actions depends on the following factors:

- constant control over time;
- information quality;
- completeness of identified factors;
- type of analysis and modification actions.

In detail, considering the two impact directions by the activities of DMO (image perception and perception of service quality), as shown in Figure 13.2 (Tasks of Abruzzo Promozione Turismo), it is possible to identify various intervention categories in order to verify the incidence of actions taken (promotion and publicity) regarding customer attitudes. Including:

- the recollection and the image of the area;
- the ability to understand and assimilate messages provided by information systems and documentation produced;
- the difference between the real image and the advertised one;
- the degree of satisfaction;
- the effectiveness of the message;
- the effectiveness of individual promotional means.

Improvement in the offer system can instead be obtained above all through actions which enhance the quality of hospitality services offered and consequently the tourist's perception of quality (Medeiros de Araujo & Bramwell, 1999; Murphy, Pritchard, & Smith, 2000; Ritchie, Crouch, & Hudson, 2000; Yuksel & Yuksel, 2001). Training, the

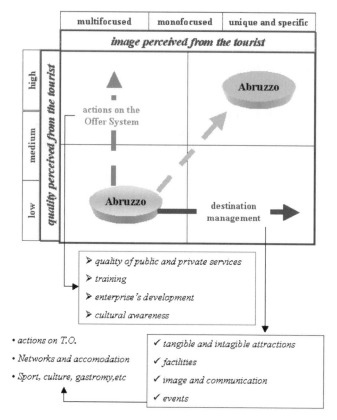

Figure 13.2: Tasks of Abruzzo Promozione Turismo.
*Source*: Our elaborations.

diffusion of best practices, the diffusion of technological and information innovations, the development of tourism attitudes by operators and residence attitude in welcoming tourists have been pinpointed (Pritchard, 2003).

From our studies, in conclusion, the following framework emerges, which highlights reference parameters necessary in analyzing DMO effectiveness.

The following conditions are necessary to obtain effective functioning of local systems:

(a) universally recognized clear guidelines;
(b) effective and efficient planning and organizational systems;
(c) flexible and accessible institutional and organizational organs;
(d) sufficient financial resources congruent with the initiatives to be carried out and stable over time.

Unfortunately, not all of these conditions are present within the internal and external scene in DMO's in Italy and perhaps this allows for the interpretation of differentiation in tourism development present in the country. In those areas with pre-set tourism initiatives favored conditions for DMO operations. However, DMO's do not always have adequate funding or adequate internal organization. In those areas, where tourism is a relatively new domain, variability in conditions is even greater thus pointing out that territorial promotional training is necessary for the various groups involved thus avoiding ineffective policies and actions of intervention.

At the end, we strongly agree with Ritchie and Crouch (2003) who argue that leadership and coordination are the key principles that the DMO must observe as it seeks to ensure high-quality, memorable visitor experiences.

# References

Astley, W., & Fombrun C.J. (1983). Collective strategy: Social ecology of organizational environments. *Academy of Management Review, 8*(4), pp. 576–587.

Brunetti, F. (2001). Il Destination management: aspetti problematici, significato e percorsi alla ricerca di una qualità ad effetto prolungato. In: M. Franch (Ed.), *Destination management. Governare il turismo tra locale e globale.* Torino: Giappichelli Editore.

Buhalis, D. (2000). Marketing the competitive destination in the future. *Tourism Management, 21,* 97–116.

Formica, S. (2002). Measuring destination attractiveness: A proposed framework. *Journal of American Academy of Business, 1*(2), 350–355.

Freeman, R.E. (1984). *Strategic management: A stakeholder approach.* Boston: Pitman.

Fyall, A., Oakley, B., & Weiss, A. (2000). Theoretical perspectives applied to inter-organisational collaboration on Britain's inland waterways. In: J.C. Crotts, D. Buhalis, & R. March (Eds), *Global alliances in tourism and hospitality management* (pp. 89–112). New York: The Haworth Press, Inc.

Goelder, C.R., & Ritchie, J.R.B. (2003). *Tourism: Principles, practices, philosophies.* New York: Wiley.

Gulati, R. (1995). Social structure and alliance formation patterns: A longitudinal analysis. *Administrative Science Quarterly, 40,* 619–952.

Gunn, C.A. (1994). *Tourism Planning* (3rd ed.). New York: Taylor and Francis.

Hu, Y., & Ritchie, J.R.B. (1993). Measuring destination attractiveness: A contextual approach. *Journal of Travel Research, 32,* 25–34.

Hudson, S., Ritchie, J.R.B., & Timur, S. (2004). Measuring destination competitiveness: An empirical study of Canadian ski resorts. *Tourism and Hospitality Planning, 1,* 79–94.

Ibarra, H., & Andrews, S. (1993). Power, social influence and sense making: Effects of network centrality and proximity on employee perceptions. *Administrative Science Quarterly, 38,* 77–303.

Keller, P. (2000). Destination marketing: Strategic area as inquiry. In: M. Manente, & M. Cerato (Eds), *From destination to destination marketing and management.* Venezia: Edizione Libreria Editrice Cafoscarini.

Kerr, B., Barron, G.N., & Wood, R.C. (2001). Politics, policy and regional tourism administration: A case examination of Scottish area tourist board funding. *Tourism Management, 22,* 649–657.

Kozak, M., & Rimmington, M. (1999). Measuring tourist destination competitiveness: Conceptual considerations and empirical findings. *Hospitality Management, 18,* 273–283.

Kozak, M. (2002). Destination benchmarking. *Annals of Tourism Research, 29,* 497–519.

Leiper, N. (1995). *Tourism Management.* Melbourne: RMIT Press.

Lundtorp, S., & Wanhill, S. (2001). The resort lifecycle theory. *Annals of Tourism Research, 28,* 947–964.

Manente, M., & Cerato, M. (2000). *From Destination to Destination Management and Marketing.* Atti della V CISET International Conference, Venezia.

Marin, B., & Mayntz, R. (1991). *Policy Networks. Empirical Evidence and Theoretical Considerations*. Frankfurt/Main: Campus.

Martini, U. (2000). Le politiche di marketing delle meta-organizzazioni. in Convention Le Tendenze del Marketing in Europa, University of Trento.

Matzler, K., & Pechlaner, H. (2000). Customer satisfaction management per le destinazioni turistiche. In: H. Pechlaner, & K. Weiermair (Eds), *Destination management*. Milano: Touring University Press.

Medeiros de Araujo, & Bramwell, B. (1999). Stakeholder assessment and collaborative tourism planning: The case of Brazil's Costa Dourada project. *Journal of Sustainable Tourism, 7*, 356–377.

Medeiros de Araujo, Bramwell, L, (2002). Partnership and regional tourism in Brazil. *Annals of Tourism Research, 29*, 1138–1164.

Middleton, V.T.C. (1997). Sustainable tourism: A marketing perspective. In: M.J. Stabler (Ed.), *Tourism sustainability. Principles to practice*. Wallingford: CAB International.

Mihalič, T. (2000). Environmental Management of a tourist destination: A factor of tourism competitiveness. *Tourism Management, 21*, 65–78.

Murphy, P., Pritchard, M.P., & Smith, B. (2000). The destination product and its impact on traveller perceptions. *Tourism Management, 21*, 43–52.

Palmer, A., & Bejou, D. (1995). Tourism destination marketing alliances. *Annals of Tourism Research, 22*(3), 616–629.

Pearce, D.G. (1989). *Tourist Development*. New York: Wiley.

Pechlaner, H., & Weiermaier, K. (2000). *Destination Management*. Milano: Touring University Press.

Pfeffer, J., & Salanick, G. (1978). *The External Control of Organizations: A resource dependence perspective*. New York: Harper and Row.

Pizam, A. (1991). The Management of Quality Destination. *Concept of a Sustainable Tourism Development, Harmonizing Economical, Social and Ecological Interests*. Proceedings of the association internationale d'experts scientifiques du tourisme, Vol. 33, *Quality tourism* — St. Gallen: Niedermann Druck.

Pritchard, M.P. (2003). The attitudinal and behavioural consequences of destination performance. *Tourism Analysis, 8*, 61–73.

Provan, K., & Milward, H. (1995). A preliminary theory of interorganizational network effectiveness: A comparative study of four community mental health systems. *Administrative Science Quarterly, 40*, 1–3.

Ritchie, B.J.R., Crouch, G.I., & Hudson, S. (2000). Assessing the role of consumers in the measurement of destination competitiveness and sustainability. *Tourism Analysis, 5*, 69–76.

Ritchie, J.R.B., & Crouch, G.I. (2003). *The competitive destination. A sustainable tourism perspective*. Wallingford: CABI International.

Ritchie, J.R.B., Crouch, G.I., & Hudson, S. (2001). Developing operational measures for the components of a destination competitiveness/sustainability model: Consumer versus managerial perspectives. In: J.A. Mazanec, G.I. Crouch, J.R.B. Ritchie, & A.G. Woodside (Eds), *Consumer Psychology of Tourism, Hospitality and Leisure*, pp. 1–17, Oxon, UK: CABI Publishing.

Tamma, M. (2002). Destination management: Gestire prodotti e sistemi locali d'offerta. In: M. Franch (Ed.), *Destination Management*. Torino: Giappichelli.

Tinsley, R., & Lynch, P.A. (2001). Small tourism business networks and destination development. *International Journal of Hospitality Management, 20* (4), 367–378.

Woodside, A. G., & Sakai, M. Y. (2001). Meta-evaluations of performance audits of government tourism–marketing programs. *Journal of Travel Research, 39*, May, 369–379.

Yuksel, A., & Yuksel, F. (2001). Comparative performance analysis: Tourists' perceptions of Turkey relative to other tourist destinations. *Journal of Vacation Marketing, 7*, 333–355.

Ziltener, W. (1999). La creazione di destinazioni in Svizzera. In: R. Mussner, H. Pechlaner, & A. Schoenhuber (Eds), *Management della destinazione*. Zurigo: Verlag Ruegger.

Chapter 14

# The Geographies of Tourism: Organizing the Space between Localisms and Global Networks[1]

Girolamo Cusimano and Maurizio Giannone

## Introduction

The thematic symbols and the ideograms interspersing the map of Sicily refer to the places visited by many travelers: Taormina, Agrigento and the Valley of the Temples, Palermo, Mount Etna.

Yet the tourist space of the island must comply with the rules of the administrative organization, which has divided the Sicilian territory into nine Provinces, each regulating its own sector for the most part.

Furthermore 20 public bodies, called *Aziende autonome di soggiorno e turismo* [tourist promotion offices], operate in Sicily; their raison d'être is to promote the tourist flow in their particular area of competence and interest.

Until recently, the tour operators' catalogues marketing the island's tourist supply featured almost exclusively the traditional 'Tour of Sicily', that is a one-week trip calling at all the most renowned tourist destinations. On the other hand, Sicily is recognized in its entirety on the tourist market; as a matter of fact, according to a study carried out by the *Italian Touring Club* in 1998, Sicily and Tuscany are the only Italian regions known as such, while for the rest of Italy the reputation of an individual location overrides that of the region to which it belongs (Touring Club Italiano [TCI], 1999).

Today, however, the pages of the tourist brochures dedicated to Sicily are covered with new destinations; they illustrate places not often included in the usual tours, places which find it difficult to successfully position themselves on the markets, but which represent some real 'niche excellencies' of the tourist supply.

---

[1] A part of the present essay is taken from the paper Cusimano G., Giannone M., 2004, "Tourism geographies and local development", in Swarbrooke J., Petrillo C.S. (eds.), *Proceedings of the 12th Atlas International Conference, "Networking & Partnerships in Destination Development & Management*, Irat-Cnr, Albano, Napoli.

---

By logging into the database PUNTOPIT of the Sicilian Regional Government website, dedicated to territorial and community planning,[2] it is possible to find a map of the geographical localization of the PIT, *Progetti Integrati Territoriali* [Integrated Territorial Projects]. These are the implementing tools of the local development policies of the European Union (EU) within the Objective 1 Regions, and thanks to them a whole organized set of public and private interventions are put into practice in a specific territory by making use of the integration of the planning among the different actions.

The PIT are devised starting from a core-idea of development, that is an idea proposing an innovative use or an increase of local resources.

In that regard it has been highlighted that the majority of the PIT put forward in Sicily are about tourist-cultural subjects; around 38% of the proposed interventions, as said before the largest amount of them, are of a tourist-cultural kind. Moreover the distinctive feature of most of the core-ideas of the Sicilian PIT (concerning about 80% of the regional territory) is a strong propensity to make a productive tourist-cultural use of the involved territories (Giannone, 2003).

The framework regulation on tourism issued in 2001 has introduced the concept of a local tourist system in the scenery of the regional and national tourist planning. These entities are also resulting from local partnerships, which aim at developing integrated and cooperative forms of usage of the territory. The scenario of the local tourist development is enriched with other tools of the sector-planning: the Wine Roads, the programme contracts, the Natural Parks, the Municipality Unions, the Leaders Projects, the Territorial Pacts, the Literary Parks and so on. These groups develop and carry out projects, benefit from public investments and propose themselves as tourist destinations.

The activism inspiring the local communities in Sicily (and elsewhere) motivates us to conceive a new geography of tourism, rather new *geographies*, where the territories claim their right to make decisions about their own development patterns with a bottom-up approach. By doing so they have subverted the categories traditionally used to name and measure tourism spaces.

## The Territories of Local Development

All the most recent legislation issued in Sicily and in the rest of the country to support the enterprises and the territories' development is based on the assumption that the local level is the ideal geographical dimension in which to achieve results in economic growth.

As a matter of fact, during the last years a transformation process of the development paradigms has been started at a local level and has made it possible for large areas of the country to successfully spread *Made in Italy* in the international markets.

A new way of understanding and building economic progress is at the origin of the changes we are facing; actually during the last few years there has been an increase in the attention given to the spatial dimension of the economy, and above all to those phenomenon

---

[2] www.euroinfosicilia.it

of the geographical concentration of the activities which have made possible the increase in competition between enterprises and individual territories.

By becoming aware of the possibility to overcome the traditional constraints on development, the local communities and the businesses of the 'suburban' economy have started to claim an active role for themselves in the construction of their futures.

As a consequence, different subjects (different for organizational structure, for *mission*, for area of activity) have together built some development projects for their own territories which have launched those different local entities into a global dimension.

However, the process of economic emancipation of the territories implies the existence of dynamics following cultural patterns. The success of the productive microsystems as in the case of the districts or of the system-areas is linked to the affirmation of a strong collective sense of identification with the territory.

Within the local systems, where the value of interpersonal communication is stronger, the stakeholders strengthen their relations (even when they are functional to the pursuit of economic objectives) by sharing the values and the representation patterns inherent to the history and the dynamics of a social space.

Therefore a dimension of identity exists, making it plausible to establish a network among the different actors operating within a certain space. Those actors recognize themselves as part of a territorial identity, of a community bound together, for example, by the memories of a common past, or by the same code of values. But at the same time they acknowledge in the others the same sense of belonging: to an integrated community, to a collective experience or to a common culture.

The space marked by the network of relations forms the territory; a space, which has been 'politically' translated and represented through maps, administrative boundaries and, even, guidebooks. Since even the practice of tourism creates territories and produces maps, as any tourist map can prove.

The principles of the local development, actually, upset the order in which we usually represent (also to ourselves) the space around us, for the dynamic relation existing between global and local level causes the territories to develop and to organize following a non-definitive pattern.

As a consequence, the communities become aware of the need to diversify their territorial supply from that of the competing areas, so that the local networks are forced to continuously give new form to their own area of intervention if they want to connect themselves to the trans-national networks. That has happened, for example, with the tools of the so-called 'negotiated planning' (as the territorial pacts), the European Community planning (with the integrated territorial projects) or the sector planning (in the tourist sector, the local tourist systems). All those tools identify and mark the borders of the new territories without taking into account the pre-existing administrative borders (Giannone, 2002).

*Censis*, one of the most influential socio-economic research institutes in Italy, has presented a paper during the Local Economies Forum held in Rome in 2001, and not surprisingly, it has given voice to the need to outline a 'new map of local development' in order to acknowledge the 'changes taking place in the territory and the soft torsion made by the local policies to favour the new drifts of the international competition' (Censis, 2001). The paper referred to the emerging of a new geo-economy characterized by the diffuse presence of territories considered irresistible for local development. So next to the areas 'posing a new challenge', the map of Italy was dotted with 'productive macro-districts', with urban areas functioning as 'globalization gateways', as 'glocal' areas and as 'ideal aggregations of micro-city councils'.

But only three years after that, the President of Censis, in an interview, stated his theory that the districts did not exist any longer and that their productive activities, once operating within limited geographical areas, were then spreading over a wider space.[3] And his changing mind proved the dynamic nature of the concept of territory.

## Identity and Local Cultures

Inevitably the constant organizational evolution of the territories challenges the idea of identity itself. If we consider the importance that the new territorial entities have taken on within the framework of the local development policies,[4] we can observe that, as a matter of fact, they are giving origin to new identities. They do not necessarily rest on some shared memories but rather on the growth and development processes that the different subjects build among them. All the stakeholders fundamentally recognize not only their common *past*, but also, their common *future*. The possibility to work out the projects for the future is the result of this sense of unity, which is a distinctive element of the *local territorial systems*, 'interconnection nodes between global networks and territories, provided with an independent development ability' (Dematteis, 1997). And most of the territorial bodies operating today in the local development sector can be assimilated to them.

The actors of the system join together (not necessarily following an institutional pattern) around development projects. But the network of relations is effective also towards the external world. The system works as a node 'linking' super-local networks (regional, national, European community or global ones).

The relation between global and local entities, usually felt as a threat, represents the paradigm of a culture more and more delocalized, resulting from mixtures and syncretism, and carrier of new diversity levels (Cusimano, 2002). On the other hand the local culture, as said by M. Featherstone (1996), is a *relational concept*, a symbolic structure whose borders are marked on the space occupied by others. So the dichotomy the local entities experience today is not a contradiction, but it mirrors a changing world: on the one hand they are subject to forces pushing them to comply with the standards set by the globalization processes; on the other they tend to reassert the value of the local identity characteristics binding the entities themselves to the territories and to the culture they belong to.

This phenomenon is particularly evident in the tourist sector and above all in the trends of demand: in the holiday world distances have become shorter, fast-food shops have increased in number, quality standards have caused authenticity to fade and tourists get excited looking at Venice reproduced in Las Vegas. But at the same time the experience of travelling feels complete only if it allows the person to understand the most *genuine* and hidden essence of the tradition and of the local history.

---

[3] G. Turani interviewing G. De Rita in *la Repubblica. Affari e Finanza* , March 22nd 2004.
[4] In Sicily in 2003 more than 100 new bodies (territorial pacts, integrated territorial projects, programme contracts) were active in the local development field and many of them had influence in the tourist sector (Mercury, 2003).

Also the system of the supply is split between the ambition to pursue 'trendy' consumption models and the awareness of the significance (not only cultural but also commercial) of the local environment specificities. By stressing the local specificities the new territories can actually acquire a competitive advantage in so far that they succeed in creating the prerequisites for the usage of their own tourist resources.

## New Destinations: A Comparison between Two Experiences

New destinations and products are appearing on the market outlining, as we have just underlined, new tourism geographies: such as the Sicilian district called 'Terre Sicane' (Sicanian Lands), an area within the province of Agrigento which until recently had been left out of the ordinary tourism routes that involve the island. In the meanwhile, fully fledged tourist resorts are trying to diversify their supply by extending their geographical areas: *Cefalù*, mostly a seaside resort destination is, in fact, being promoted by tour operators together with the nearby *Madonie* mountain district. These two areas are the case studies' object, a research that has been carried out by the authors to investigate if the new territorial systems of supply based on the traditional instruments of local development actually meet the market of the tourism demand, and whether the actors within the local tourist system associate themselves with the new organizational entities.

The geographical areas studied by this research illustrate two different realities from many points of view, especially in relation to the structures of the tourist supply. The two sample areas have been selected with the purpose of investigating the actual position the two territories occupy, as many operators consider them potential tourist destinations even if they show remarkable differences. Indeed the first of the two territories, the *Madonie* one, has already been on the market for a long time thanks to the tour operator's catalogues which exploit and stress out the beauty of its environmental resources (there is a natural park in that area) and the cultural and artistic relevance of many of the ancient villages widely spread in the territory. Nevertheless the district has not been successful yet in conquering its share of the tourist market — or at least not to the extent the operators and the local communities expected — even though many instruments for planning and for tourism exploitation are already functioning in the area. As for the second case, the 'Terre Sicane', the tourist sector has just started being organized, its characteristics being a large concentration of local partnerships mainly aimed at the cultural and tourist promotion of the area through the implementation of specially tailored projects. As a matter of fact, many of those projects are linked to the figure of *Giuseppe Tomasi di Lampedusa*, the renown author of 'The Leopard', who spent part of his adolescence in those places, while some others aim at the rediscovery from a tourist standpoint of the rural Sicilian landscape so effectively described in the pages of that novel and of other genre literary works.

The different positioning of the two areas on the market, the different nature of their tourist products and the different level of organization of their supply systems make the two territories dissimilar to each other. In spite of that they have in common a dynamic way of planning which suggests the remarkable sensitivity of the local operators to the tourist development themes and to the strategic cooperation.

Such a phenomenon is familiar to most part of the Sicilian territory, where more than a hundred local partnership entities originating from the 'negotiated planning', and about 30 'PIT' — tools for the implementation of the EU policies — are currently operating, being almost all based on the leading ideas of tourism development.

The abundant presence of the typical instruments of local development strategies in the Island territory, each of them linked to some form of territorial organization (with its borders, its networks, and its *milieu*), it underlines the sudden change occurred over the past years in the geo-cultural outlining of the Island tourist space, whose current elements of interest are not only the traditional seaside areas or the historical and artistic sites but also a widespread cultural supply which is probably less attractive but for some aspects closer to the most typical productions of the local tradition.

The area of the *Madonie*, the first one investigated by the research, coincides with the west end of the only mountain chain of the Island, which faces the coast northward where the main economic enterprises of the area are based that are mainly linked to intensive agriculture and seasonal tourism. It is possible to detect the striking contrasts existing between the coast and the inland not only in terms of landscape and geo-morphological characteristics, but also in terms of culture, the latter given partly to the presence of more or less intense flows of tourists.

The *Madonie* territory certainly presents some generic characteristics which help making it particularly suitable for a possible tourism development: as a matter of fact, in spite of its developmental stage as a tourist destination, its incoming supply appears to be well recognizable as for how the target has been segmented (elegant *hotellerie*, agri-tourism and rural tourism facilities). But, the incoming sector is not fully developed yet, so that it can absorb and accommodate only a limited number of tourists (as accounted for by the most recent statistic surveys in the field). The tourist product put on the market is primarily linked to nature and environment but, lately, also to culture.

The *Madonie* district maintains a very close relationship with the seaside towns because of their geographical vicinity to the coastal resorts, which hold a powerful attraction on tourism, and *Cefalù* gives an example of the kind of tourist micro-system model to draw inspiration from.

Thus *Cefalù*, a renowned Norman little town located at the foothill of the *Madonie* mountains, besides holding a strong attraction on the international market of the sea holidays and on the cultural tourism demand because of its own characteristics, it ends up carrying out the function of 'call' for the flows of tourism, to good advantage also of the nearby mountain area (at least in the intentions of the stakeholders of the *Madonie* tourist district).

The other area, called *Terre Sicane*, covers a limited portion of territory situated southwest of Sicily; it also faces the sea and is enclosed between the southern side of the *Sicani Mountain* and the *Belice Valley*. In this case we are dealing with a territory/destination studied during the 'involvement' stage of its life cycle. The different stakeholders of the local system, in fact, have only recently become aware of the tourist potentials of that area, which, like many others in the Island, rely on the cultural aspects of its territorial supply to support its own tourist product. But within the productive system of the *Terre Sicane* tourism cannot be thought about as a prominent sector yet. Nevertheless over the last years the incoming system has undergone a remarkable development in this area, mainly oriented to the extra-hotel segments (agri-tourism facilities and bed and breakfast (B&Bs)).

The incoming figures are still extremely limited as there is a small number of beds; but it is important though to underline how the *Terre Sicane* territory has been present on the scene of the eno-gastronomic and 'wine tourism' routes for some time now, thanks to the important winemaking and foodstuff firms existing there, all very keen to make advantage of the economic opportunities originating from agriculture and tourism integration.

In the Terre Sicane territory the gap between local planning and tourist positioning of the destination is very clear. In fact it seems that there is no accordance between the great dynamism of the tourist-cultural exploitation policies (which have led to the actual creation of many territorial planning entities such as Territorial Pacts, Literary and Cultural Parks, and so on) and the substantial increase in the tourist market shares (difficult to reach anyway given the present incoming situation).

## Representing the Destination

The research, which is currently being completed, has been carried out taking into account the two ways of representing the destination which contribute to form its outside image: that of the outsiders (mostly tourists and tour-operators) and that of the insiders (local communities and operators, public bodies, etc.). The two perspectives match largely the interpretation models of the tourist space drawn up on the demand and supply systems, which are fundamental for outlining the destination's position and the marketing mechanisms of its supply.

The starting point for the research has been first of all to select the objectives, that is to check the correspondence between the destination/territory image perceived by the main stakeholders and the outlining of the tourist space originating from the new territorial planning instruments.

Then the sampling scheme has been drawn, and after that data have been collected using different methods of gathering (such as questionnaires, direct interviews, focus groups, etc.), extending the investigation to the tour operator's catalogues and to the material promoting the local tourist supply (promotion campaigns and brochures, etc.).

Particularly interesting is what resulted from the analysis of some of the questionnaires distributed to a sample of local operators in the two provinces. As for the *Madonie/Cefalù* area, for instance, a relevant part of the interviewees (75%) has underlined the higher competitiveness of the *Madonie* area as much as its supply is combined to that of *Cefalù*, while a lower percentage of the sample (69%) considers the *Madonie* tourist supply as competitive enough besides from its being connected to the promotional and trading system of the Norman little town.

The last input is the symptom of the 'weakness' of the tourist 'appeal' of the *Madonie* district, but it is contradicted by the position it occupies according to the perception of the local operators themselves who think that the territory expresses a well-defined 'mark': in fact more than 87% of the same interviewees think that the *Madonie* alone can be a tourist destination.

Keeping the same level of analysis the *Terre Sicane* operators' sample originates an interpretation model of the territory which shows even more contradictions than the previous one; in fact, on the one hand 69% of the interviewees describe the area as competitive or highly competitive from a tourist point of view (so that we can assume that a significant share of the local operators does not believe that this territory can be properly put on the market); on the other hand the whole group firmly believes that the *Terre Sicane* is a tourist destination, strengthening as a consequence of the idea of an area which shows a strong territorial identity and an intense socio-cultural common ground among the members of the local community.

The results of this part of the research, focused on the supply system only, seem to show that the local stakeholders can detect a territorial identity in the (self-made) models of representation of the new space entities in a more or less aware way. This process is probably fuelled by the economic development expectations associated with the explosion of the tourist phenomenon.

But at the same time the limitations of the product-territory marketing strategy – still weak in terms of territorial and tourist marketing policies – become evident.

## Some Possible Conclusions

It is not easy to express final evaluations at this stage of the research. Nevertheless it is already possible to utter some background general remarks resulting from a first level of analysis. In particular:

1) In Sicily, tourism is taking on the role of the leading force for outlining new geographies with a 'bottom-up' approach;
2) the tools of the so-called 'negotiated planning' and of the EU can give a contribution to plan new 'spaces for tourism', that is territories able to try and enter the troubled scene of the global tourism competition;
3) in the areas where a mature and clearly recognizable tourism supply already exists, the weaker and developing ones tend to join those with a well-recognizable 'mark' (as in the case of the *Madonie* and *Cefalù*);
4) sometimes the territories lacking an established tourist reputation seem to be self-referential: in fact they tend to overestimate the local identity factors (such as history, traditions, etc.) and to provide themselves with a 'territorial trade-mark' (as the experience of the *Terre Sicane* shows);
5) the new territories of tourism often tend to be described by local communities as unique, exclusive models, carrying some dominant identifying features which are considered appealing to tourists. But this way of representing them is not always done by the outsiders, so that the projected image is not always corresponding to the perceived one (with negative effects on the destination/territory positioning on the market).

Mitchell (2000), talking about de-territorialized identities, questions himself on what kind of 'geographies of belonging' are being built up nowadays. It appears evident that the traditional patterns of the world representation are not adequate to tell us about the ongoing transformations. Nevertheless, in the process of breaking up the tourist space triggered by the globalization phenomena, it is possible to observe a compensatory trend to stress the differences and the plurality. Taking this viewpoint, the territories can offer further growing opportunities for local, social and cultural groups.

# References

Censis. (2001). *Documento per il Forum delle economie locali*. Roma.

Cusimano, G. (2002). Sotto il segno della cultura. Mondo attuale e New Cultural Geography. In: C. Palagiano (Ed.) *Linee tematiche di ricerca geografica* (pp. 193–222). Bologna: Pàtron Editore.

Cusimano, G., & Giannone, M. (2004). Tourism geographies and local development. In: J. Swarbrooke, & C.S. Petrillo (Eds), *Proceedings of the 12th Atlas international conference. Networking & Partnerships in Destination Development & Management*. Irat-Cnr, Albano: Napoli.

Dematteis, G. (1997). Retibus regiones regere. *Geotema*, *9*, 37–43.

Featherstone, M. (1996). *Undoing culture*: *Globalization, postmodernism and identity*. London: SAGE Publications.

Giannone, M. (2002). Tourist local systems and territorial development. *Journal of Quality Assurance in Hospitality and Tourism*, *1–2*(3), 125–131.

Giannone, M. (2003). Sistemi Turistici Locali e PIT. In: *XII Rapporto sul Turismo in Italia* (pp. 696–703). Firenze: Mercury.

Mercury. (2003). *II Rapporto sul Turismo in Sicilia*. Firenze.

Mitchell, D. (2000). *Cultural geography. A critical introduction*. Oxford: Blackwell.

Touring Club Italiano (TCI). (1999). *La marca Italia*, Milano.

Chapter 15

# An International Project to Develop Networking for Promoting a Specific Destination: Emigration as a Tool to Enhance Tourism in Cilento Area

Paolo Di Martino and Clara S. Petrillo

## Introduction

The sustainability of a local development path is strictly linked to its local resources, territorial specificities and traditional skills; namely, not only to its natural resources, but also to its geographical position, morphological features, social resources (traditions and habits of the hosting community), artistic and archaeological heritage, typical agricultural products, social and eno-gastronomic traditions, handicraft, and even general atmosphere, hospitality.

In its turn when local development is based on the specific context, it is easier to comply with a second basic principle: i.e. the adoption of a bottom-up approach involving all local, political and institutional stakeholders. Territorial development has to be driven by the local community, which is familiar with the territory and interested in preserving local resources so as to guarantee a long-term generation of income flows and maintain proper life quality standards. Creating synergic relationships between programmes or projects funded by different sources necessarily requires community agreement; their success can act as a stimulus for other areas to promote the development of a sustainable tourism. Moreover, the central government has to guarantee that all interventions are mutually consistent, part of an organic programme including priority objectives; it also has to foster local communities to have a proactive role in implementing development policies. By doing so, it is possible to adopt complementary top-down and bottom-up approaches.

Additionally, development policies, in order to be sustainable, have to be integrated; they do not have to protect individual interests but set out shared objectives, which — in the medium-long term — will have a positive impact on individuals as well. This requires a co-ordinated long-term planning based on a clear identification of the aims to be pursued

Tourism Local Systems and Networking
Copyright © 2006 by Elsevier Ltd.
ISBN: 0-08-044938-7

and of the tools to be used to involve the various stakeholders (through partnerships), and implement specific actions.

The Italian regulatory system provides for different tools to promote concerted actions and partnerships — such as territorial pacts or territorial integrated projects — facilitating the involvement of local stakeholders (institutions and social, economic and cultural operators) in outlining the development path of their area.

Specifically, with respect to protected areas, following the initial delay in setting out an organic regulatory framework, the need for a Park Authority was recognised, which could act as a "development agency", a promoting body and an aggregation centre for local stakeholders. Through territorial interventions focused on specific issues, many actions related to the various elements of the social-economic system are implemented; actually they are pilot projects sub-divided into different stages (increase awareness of the local community, establishment of the local partnership, design, management, implementation and operation of the project).

The Project *"Emigration as a tool to enhance tourism in Cilento area"* — developed and managed by the Institute for Service Industry Research of the National Research Council (IRAT-CNR) and funded by the Ministry for Foreign Affairs — is included in this framework. It is a pilot-project for an integrated territorial development focused on the local "tourism" system of the area including the National Park of Cilento and Vallo di Diano (PNCVD). The general objective was to enhance tourism by developing the synergies resulting from an integrated management of its competitive factors: local resources and Cilento communities living abroad.

The territory included in the project comprises the National Park of Cilento and Vallo di Diano, stretching for a large area of the region of Campania (southern Italy), characterised by valuable natural and cultural resources, well-known at international level. However, hinterland areas and coastal areas are quite different: along the coastal line economy is mainly based on international tourism (thanks to the famous archaeological sites of Paestum and Velia and the beaches located in the area). On the other hand, its particular geographical position, combined with an insufficient communication system, has generated a sort of isolation of a number of hinterland areas, only marginally involved in tourism flows; these areas are less dynamic and characterised by agricultural and forestry activities. However, while this isolation slowed down the economic development, it also made it possible to preserve its landscape and environment, which now represent the main resource to guarantee a rational and long-lasting development.

The Park resources are the platform from which a sustainable and self-propelling economic development process can be started: the integration on between the two areas can be achieved through a more rational use of the resources and a better time and space distribution of tourism flows, thus determining lower environmental costs and higher social-economic benefits for citizens.

It is then necessary: to stimulate the demand for tourism activities also in periods of the year other than summer time and in the hinterland areas as well; to drive it towards scarcely promoted and/or visited cultural and natural resources and towards typologies of alternative tourism (naturalistic, sport, recreational, tourism for elderly, etc); to link tourism activities in the coastal area to agricultural and forestry activities in the hinterland areas. This can be achieved only by increasing the number of environmental friendly accommodation facilities, promoting typical agro-food products and handicrafts, organising guided tours and educational courses on environmental issues along with sport activities fully respectful of the environment, establishing new museums; these are proper tools to promote the area and create job opportunities for young people.

The aim of the Project was then to identify common objectives, develop and implement actions focused on the environment and on the role played by emigrants, capable of mobilising local stakeholders through co-operation-based relationships.

The tool adopted by the Project was the creation of a virtuous circle through which an entrepreneurial network, including both Cilento public and private economic subjects and economic subjects migrated abroad, could be established. Developing synergies resulting from the integrated management of Cilento competitive factors (local resources and Cilento communities living abroad) would generate benefits not only to tourism operators, but also to all economic and social subjects indirectly involved: farmers, artisans, shopkeepers, suppliers of complementary services, restaurant owners, haulage companies, travel agencies and the hosting community as a whole. Benefits and synergies will not involve the specific area only, but they will have a positive impact on the many communities of Cilento people living abroad which have been actively involved.

The project, carried out in partnership with a number of public and private companies, aimed at creating a model of territorial integrated management founded on local specificities. A key factor for development is the autonomous ability of the local system to attract the international tourism market through a network of relationships between the system itself and the population of Cilento migrants living abroad. Another key factor is the development and dissemination of a positive image of the area "using" migrants as a communication tool.

## Cilento Area

The project is focused on an area which is quite varied from the morphological point of view and stretches for an area of nearly 200.000 hectares, in the Region of Campania (Figure 15.1).

Cilento area is part of an Italian National Park ranking second as to dimension and importance: the National Park of Cilento and Vallo of Diano.

In 1997, thanks to its characteristics the Park was included in the prestigious network of the Biosphere Reserve of Unesco Mab (Man and Biosphere) aimed at preserving and producing natural and cultural values through a culturally creative and operationally sustainable correct management.

The area is also getting the Uni En Iso 14001 certification with its EcoParco, a programme aimed at developing a sustainable system of environment management. Last, but not least, in 2000 the area was awarded the Green Globe, a global environment programme for tourism locations characterised by a concerted effort of the public and private sector organisations involved in the local tourism industry to improve environment quality.[1]

The fauna in the area is highly diversified including a wide variety of habitats. Coastal and mountain areas, raging rivers and brooks, cliffs and forests generate a wide range of

---

[1] The Green Globe works with consumers, companies and communities to create a sustainable industry through the implementation of Agenda 21. Green Globe's vision is to become the Travel and Tourism industry's premier global eco-label, the brand that represents the established hallmark of environmental best practice.

Figure 15.1:  The National Park of Cilento and Vallo di Diano.

fauna populations with species of high naturalistic value. The flora population likely consists of around 1800 different species of spontaneous autochthonous plants: 10% of them are very important from the phyto-geographic standpoint, as they are endemic and/or rare.[2]

In addition to its wonderful landscape, the area is also rich in history and culture: these are the sites of the well-known myths of the nymph Leucosia, of Palinuro and Aeneas; here we can find the remarkable remains of Elea's and Paestum's Greek colonies, the Carthusian monastery of Padula, the city of Paestum (Poseidonia) — founded in the late 17th century BC by Greek settlers from Sibari; the ancient Capaccio, Caput Aquis, mentioned by Plutarch, where Crasso defeated Spartaco's rebel army.

The area is also very heterogeneous: unaltered environments and highly modified areas with urban centres and densely populated valleys.

Nowadays it is an area which, while still having an active role in the contemporary society, preserves the traditional features which generated it (layout of territory, pathways, cultivation pattern, settlement systems). Like natural species in geographical environments, various peoples found in this area a point of contact and fusion, a crossing point, a site for enriching their genetic endowment.

In the area human settlements can be found whose genetic endowment — due to a forced isolation in the past centuries, slow growth of the population and absence of

---

[2] For further details as to the many species in the Park refer to the Park web site www.parks.it/parco.nazionale.cilento.

immigration — is more homogeneous than other populations. Because of these attributes they were selected by the National Research Council to participate in an international project named "Genetic Park of Cilento and Vallo of Diano".[3]

The Park, then, in line with Unesco Mab Programme directives, will have to perform a specific social economic function, taking into account the inter-relations between cultural heritage and natural assets. All the area has increased its value at world-wide level as result of a "priority agreement" entered into to guarantee the creation of links amongst similar and interconnected ecosystems within the "Network", and disseminate information to all countries involved. One of the most important objectives of the Biosphere Reserves is investing in the future through scientifically correct training programmes, and disseminating information on the relationship between human beings and environment from a long-term and inter-generation perspective.

The Park of Cilento and Vallo di Diano — generated by a joint work carried out by Nature and Human Beings — fits in the category of evolutionary landscapes (Mixed Assets), being the result of historical social, economic, artistic and spiritual events and achieving its current "form" in association with and in response to its natural environment.

Cilento is a meeting point for sea and mountains, for Mediterranean and African cultures. The territory unites peoples and civilisations and preserves signs of this union in its distinctive features: Nature, Cultural Archaeological, Architectural Heritage, a Territorial Arrangement full of Middle Ages elements, the lively world of Traditions. Located at the very core of the Mediterranean area, it can be viewed as the Mediterranean Park par excellence, as it embodies the most profound spirit of the Mediterranean Sea, its bio-diversity, environment, and history which is the synthesis of the meeting amongst different peoples and civilisations.

Morphological configuration, historical–cultural traditions, fauna, flora, fascination of landscapes and environments made this land a tourism attraction site and oriented its development. Most economic activities are directly linked to tourism to meet tourists needs and support the many accommodation facilities located in the area.

Also in Cilento — like in other national regions and in particular in the ones facing the Mediterranean Sea — there is a gap between hinterland and coastal areas, being the latter better equipped to receive tourism flows. This implies a space and time (seasonal) concentration requiring specific measures to favour a more balanced distribution of tourism flows.

As the Park is mainly a hilly and mountainous area, its economy is mainly based on agriculture (mostly olive growing and processing). Woodland resources are similarly crucial and stimulate the building sector and duramen handicraft. Of course naturalistic resources are crucial for tourism which, above all in the past years, is developing also thanks to the establishment of farm tourism facilities. These facilities are an excellent solution for an area which, along with its historical and artistic heritage, has a strong farm cultural tradition. Cilento has a wonderful coastline with a deep blue sea, sandy or gravel beaches, jagged coastlines, luxuriant and nearly primordial headlands and small bays. Along with well-known seaside resorts, there are a number of villages where fishing is still a primary income source.

---

[3] This project, through a methodology based on the analysis of the Human Genome (genome-wide search) aims at identifying the genes responsible for multi-factorial genetic diseases, the common gnomic regions "identical" from the descent standpoint.

The main characteristics of the Park's tourism system are the following:

- The main share of incoming tourism consists of outdoor tourism: actually, despite the fact that hotel and extra-hotel arrivals are more or less equivalent (302,000 and 294,000 respectively), the number of nights in complementary accommodation facilities — i.e. camping sites, registered houses and farm-tourism facilities — is four times higher than the number of nights in hotels (43,00,000 against 14,00,000). In fact the average stay in the so-called "outdoor facilities" is much higher: 14 days instead of 4, thus resulting in a proportional increase in the number of nights.
- A strong increase in tourism flows in the past 10 years: from 352,000 arrivals and nearly 4 million arrivals in 1990 to 600,000 arrivals and 5 million 600,000 nights in 2001, with an increase of 69% and 43%, respectively. However, the increase is quite unstable: there is a high discontinuity in the annual variation rate of hotel tourists (a 6% decline in 1991 against a 32% increase in 1998). A similar discontinuity is recorded in complementary accommodation facilities: the variation range fluctuates from −16 to +36% as to arrivals, and from −8 to +34% as to number of nights.
- A prevailing national tourism (82%) in hotels and this implies a shorter average stay as foreign tourists usually stay in the hotels for longer periods. Also in camping sites Italian customers prevail, although they have a lower weight and are relatively declining (in the 20 years investigated, from 66% to 59%), compared to hotel tourism. The number of domestic tourists is also increased due to the longer duration of their stay compared to international tourism; consequently nights in extra-hotel facilities prevail.
- A high number of hotels (173), number of beds (10,883) and above all alternative accommodation facilities — camping sites, tourism farms and houses (from 111 facilities and 24,000 beds in 1980, to 324 facilities and 45,000 beds in 2001). A comparison with the regional data highlights that 58% of the camping sites and 36% of the accommodation facilities (hotels) of the whole Campania region are located in Cilento. As to hotels, the supply in the area of Cilento accounts for 15% as to number of hotels and 17% as to number of beds of the whole supply in the Campania region.
- An overall improvement in the hotel supply: the sub-division by stars has improved and there has been a shift to higher-class facilities but, above all, a substantial decline in 1 star hotels.
- A progressive improvement in the use of facilities: the rate of increase of tourists has always exceeded the supply increase, thus generating a better use of the facilities and a doubling in the average number of nights per bed. However, the comparison between the gross utilisation indexes recorded by the facilities highlights a better use of the capacity in hotels rather than in complementary facilities. In fact, in the past 20 years hotels experienced an increase in the index of annual gross utilisation[4] — developed by comparing the number of nights with potential bed days, calculated by multiplying the number of beds by the days of the year — from 18% to 35%; while complementary facilities increased from 27% to 26%.

---

[4] The percentage index of net utilisation related to the days of actual supply to the public, net of the off-days would have been more effective. However, it was impossible to get information on the actual opening days of the facilities in the various months of the year.

## National Research Council Project "Emigration as a Tool to Enhance Tourism in the Cilento Area"

In 2002, the National Research Council, along with many public and private partners, participated in the call for proposals issued by the Directorate General for Italians abroad and Migrations Flows of the Ministry for Foreign Affairs. This call for proposal, made in partnership with the Ministry for Labour and Social Policies, related to System Action "D" named: 'Specific actions to promote stable links between the economy of Southern Italy and Italians living abroad" provided for in Measure II. 1 of the National Operational Program "Technical Support and System Actions" Ob.1 (PON ATAS) FSE IT 161 PO 001 adopted by the European Commission.

The aim was to promote actions to have Italians living abroad as partners in the internationalisation processes of the Italian regions included in Ob.1, and fund projects to be implemented at regional level. This general aim meets the need to improve the local development system of Southern regions through an approach including the following strategic objectives:

(a) Turning the phenomenon of Italian emigration into a local development factor;
(b) Implementing processes to integrate the various policies aimed at developing Southern regions (in particular the Internationalisation Policy identified within the Community Framework to support Objective 1), such as training and employment policies, and initiatives addressed to Italians living abroad.

To reach the strategic objectives mentioned above, the Ministry developed (within the duration of the PON ATAS 2000–2006), a multi-phase programme:

- PHASE A — *Promotion of the project development capability of the area.* Aimed at fostering the capability of the bodies and institutions performing on the market place of submitting ideas and projects to create partnerships between public and private stakeholders from the local institutional, economic, cultural, social, educational and employment system and Italians living abroad.
- PHASE B — *Creation of models of intervention on specific issues based on partnerships for the implementation of Regional Development Policies.*
- PHASE C — *Pilot projects.* To enhance the effectiveness of the intervention models identified, the Ministry for Foreign Affairs will promote the implementation of cross-regional pilot projects focused on specific issues through public procedures. The outcomes of the projects implemented will make it possible to outline the general guidelines for planning national and community resources.

The NRC project — *"Emigration as a tool to enhance tourism in the Cilento area"* — included in the first stage of the implementation strategy illustrated above, was aimed at promoting a linkage between the regional area and Italians living abroad — viewed as individuals with professional skills and special links with the markets, holding information which are usually not available and unique cultural values and ties.

Specifically, the priorities of the project were:

- creating new local partnership networks to establish a link with Italians living abroad;
- setting up new methodologies and contents capable of turning the existing links with the Italians abroad into stable factors for the area development.

The activities included in the Cilento project were developed in one-year time, from July 2003 to June 2004, in partnership with a number of public and private companies: the Regional Bilateral Body for Training in Campania, the company Broadcast Video Press, the company Riformed, the Association Magna Grecia and the Institute of Italy–America Studies (INIAS) from the New York University.

## Implementation of a Territorial Development Model

The aim of the project was to develop a model — which could be transferred and replicated — for the promotion and the environmental management of a tourism site through emigrants' support.

Within the local system of the National Park of Cilento and Vallo di Diano this model resulted in the creation of an entrepreneurial network including Cilento economic stakeholders, public and private operators involved in the tourism sector, broadly meant, and emigrated Cilento people living abroad.

The synergies created amongst the various stakeholders, the commitment of the public institutions involved and the involvement of private entrepreneurs (not only tourism operators strictly meant but also all economic and social stakeholders indirectly involved such as artisans, shopkeepers, suppliers of complementary services, restaurant owners, haulage companies, travel agencies and the hosting community itself) created a critical mass of resources and inter-relationships.

The development model applied to the local system "National Park of Cilento" was based on the following stages:

- Analytical research work on Cilento people living abroad and their associations with which it would be possible to establish structured relationships by creating databases based on specific criteria (number of people, professional skills, geographical distribution);
- Creation of an *Info-point* (Virtual Incubator) at the National Park of Cilento and Vallo di Diano, of an Export Info Point at the Italy–America Chamber of Commerce of New York and a telematic portal for an integrated promotion, crucial to link the various actors and networks, implement an integrated promotion of the area and increase awareness of environmental issues;
- Development of a database of the tourism firms carrying out their activity in the United States, whose owners originally came from Cilento; interconnection of these firms through the Virtual Incubator and the Export Info Point;
- Establishment of an Observatory of the tourism firms based in Cilento and of other Cilento firms producing typical products; networking with the Virtual Incubator and the Export Info Point;
- Organisation of training courses aimed at increasing the local communities' awareness of environmental issues and, consequently, enhancement of the local tourism system and of the role played by emigration in the history of the area;
- Integrated promotion of the local system National Park of Cilento and Vallo di Diano through a single portal which rationalises tourism resources and their enjoyment;
- Development — through promotional activities of the "Cilento" product carried out abroad by the Export Info Point — of a higher sense of belonging and dissemination of the Italian cultural identity amongst the Italian communities living abroad.

### Research Stage

The project started with a detailed analysis of the territorial, social and economic, of the area involved — meant as an integrated system including territory, nature, public and private stakeholders. The aim of this stage was to identify both the resources within the park area with a potential to be enhanced and their utilisation in order to promote the system on the foreign market.

In this stage data on the strictly economic–tourism resources of the area were collected, processed and systematically arranged in order to provide an exhaustive picture of the tourism supply within the Park.

With respect to the whole area and the various municipalities, the attempt was made to identify and analyse the tourism system: i.e. quantity and quality of the resources and of the professional and entrepreneurial skills used in the tourism sector.

A specific attention was also paid to the analysis of tourism accommodation facilities, broadly meant, to identify their typology, territorial distribution and development potential. To this purpose, data on the tourism system existing in the area and on the local productive system interested in internationalisation were collected.

As to the tourism system the data collected related to the different typologies of accommodation facilities and to intermediation and organisation facilities. This data were then linked to the ones on tourists arrivals so as to highlight the actual and potential production capacity of the area.

The first stage of the territorial analysis and survey gave rise to a research work on the field, a study of the contexts and data processing carried out both in the local area — National Park of Cilento and Vallo di Diano — and in the international areas involved — U.S.A. and, specifically, New York City. While in some cases the outcomes of the research work were very interesting and even innovative, in other cases they highlighted information already held by those who were familiar with the area, but never supported by a scientific research work. The outcomes of the research stage include:

**Database: "Cilento firms"**   The database on Cilento SMEs consists of 19,654 firms (data include: firm's name, address, capital stock, firm's scope and code, registration in the Register of Firms, date of opening and start-up). This database — which is a unique product not available anywhere else — is crucial to get a better understanding of the two key areas of the project; i.e. typical products and tourism.

The analysis of typical product producing firms which, as well known, are directly involved in the tourism system, was further detailed. 125 firms were accurately analysed giving rise to an exhaustive database including many data: firm's name, location, address, contacts, sector, typical products, additional information.

**Database, report and brochure: "Typical products as drivers for the development of Cilento economy"**   The aim of the study was to define the critical factors for promoting Cilento typical products. The focus was on the characteristics of the economy and of the typical products of the area — allowing for the data made available by official bodies — so as to investigate the context within which transactions amongst operators take place. Based on the research findings, we focused on each typical certified product outlining their economic potentials; a starting point to identify a suitable development policy aimed at enhancing their value.

The research work highlighted that Cilento typical agro-food products are a growth opportunity for the area, providing a development model to be adopted in order to fully exploit what is supplied by the sector. The area is also a leader in a sector where Italy is already a leader at world-wide level; the excellence quality levels of products such as the buffalo mozzarella, caciocavallo silano, Cilento white fig, extra-virgin olive oil, Paestum artichoke, quality certificated wines (Colli di Salerno, Il Cilento, Il Castel di San Lorenzo) are known at world-wide level.

The study also highlighted some crucial problems for the development of the sector, such as the firm's small size (many of them are micro firms), a limited entrepreneurial culture, constraints to financial exposure, which make the firms depending on merchandise brokers. Producers give their products to whole sellers without any specific label and whole sellers appropriate the value added resulting from the distribution process.

As part of the project activities a brochure was also published, specifically devoted to Cilento typical products. The brochure — which was widely disseminated — is subdivided into two sections: an initial section introducing the typical products and a second section sub-divided into micro-categories of products. With respect to each category, typical products are illustrated including information such as: raw material, processing technology, ripening characteristics, area and production time and other additional information. A specific attention was paid to the graphics of the brochure given its advertising purpose.

**Database and report: "Tourism supply system in Cilento"**    The work gave rise to a database consisting of 269 hotels, 212 extra-hotel facilities, 172 tourism farms, 39 travel agencies and tour operators. The database, although not covering the whole universe of the firms, is the most exhaustive document on Cilento tourism supply. The data collected made it possible to identify a number of specificities of the system itself, already known but never "proved" by an empirical evidence. For example, the *naturalistic* matrix of the Cilento tourism system is strongly highlighted: it is a system of accommodation facilities mainly characterised by "outdoor facilities" such as camping site, tourism farms, etc. On the other hand, the analysis highlighted a number of critical points, such as the lack of services to clients which would instead generate an increase in the quality level of the accommodation facility system.

**IRAT report "Tourism and environment in the PNCVD"**    A research work to highlight the link between the local tourism system and the environmental resources was also carried out.

The bibliographic review on the relationship between tourism and environment, the methodological analysis and the study and mapping of the environmental resources of the area were also made. The analysis was made by means of an empirical survey through the administration of a semi-structured questionnaire to 13 Opinion Leaders selected amongst major public and private institutions, such as regional and provincial governments, municipalities, trade associations.

An additional empirical research work was also carried out involving owners of accommodations facilities in order to investigate their awareness of environmental issues and their relationship with the Park Authority.

**INIAS database on Cilento people living abroad**   The survey conducted in the U.S.A is the first detailed analysis of a community of emigrants from southern Italy systematically and fully conducted in Italy.

Conducting this analysis was quite a complex task due to the high variability of the data collection systems and the high number of municipalities involved (over 80). A major effort was then made to complete and correct the Anagrafe/Registry of Italian Citizens (AIRE) database and standardize the data through Access software. Upon completion of the project, the database included data related to 31,081 Cilento emigrants, all members of AIRE.

**Research work "Tourism in Cilento — returning to the land of origin"**   An analysis sample was developed consisting of 521 return tourists (emigrants back to their land of origin for tourism reasons); it was founded on the database of Cilento people living abroad according to the snow ball technique. Emigrants were interviewed in two rounds: a face-to-face interview and a phone interview. The outcomes of the interviews were quite interesting and depicted the portrait of Cilento emigrants flying back to their origin town for tourism and affection reasons.

*Stage of Awareness Enhancement*

The application stage includes a number of initiatives:

- Establishment and operation of two *Info Points* — one at the Park at Agropoli and the other one at the Italy–America Chamber of Commerce in New York — which collected and arranged all information (calls for proposals issued by the various institutions, initiatives and projects promoted by the Park Authority and other bodies, regulations on environment, regulations on labour, incentives to SMEs) and disseminated them on the web site and to the operators applying to the information points. The Info Point at the Chamber of Commerce of New York provided information on the National Park of Cilento and Vallo di Diano to economic operators and other bodies, drawing them from the "telematic portal" or establishing a dialogue with the other Info Point based in Agropoli. The operation of the two information points was advertised also through two colour "technical schedules" written in Italian and English, including information on the info points and the portal content. Many American tourism operators were involved thanks to the co-operation agreements established with the Enit Office of New York and the Italy–America Chamber of Commerce of New York (the first Italian economic body in the U.S.A. founded in 1887).
- The *dedicated portal*, named www.progettocilento.it, highly interactive (i.e. which can be directly up-dated by the 80 municipalities included in the Park area), made a high number of up-dated and significant information available both to potential tourists and "return tourists". The "telematic portal", characterised by an excellent graphic and technological level, includes a high number of valuable information on the National Park area: initiatives implemented by the individual municipalities, festivals and events, guided tours, flora and fauna, calls for proposals, tax relief specifically addressed to the firms, tourism accommodation facilities, travel agencies, local typical products. These information, constantly up-dated for the whole period of the project, can be easily

accessed to by all those who are interested in getting additional information on the area: tourism, cultural, economic operators, potential tourists. Many users of the portal stressed its excellent quality. Through it the data related to each municipality located in the Park were made available (address, phone, fax, e-mail, etc.) along with historical, artistic, religious information and more general information on the natural resources of the Park, information on its main tourism routes and related accommodation facilities, local tourism operators and firms producing typical eno-gastronomic products (with a description of each product), service supply firms, etc. A number of tourism routes — the "portal" includes 8 of them — were also illustrated through traditional colour printed material, with texts in Italian and English and colour pictures. This printed material was also made because a number of American tour operators required the "telematic" tourism information included in the portal to be supplemented with "printed" information. Also thanks to the contribution by the Italy–America Chamber of Commerce of New York, around 20 American importers of eno-gastronomic products were identified and included in the portal. Therefore, also for the local agricultural sector development opportunities will increase as a result of the local consumption growth generated by the future increase in the number of tourists and in the exports to the U.S.A. A growth facilitated by the "telematic" relationship established between Cilento producers and foreign importers/consumers.

- At the end of the operation period of the information point and portal, a survey was conducted to gather data useful to check the "state of export of *typical Cilento products*". A number of economic players representing the universe of the firms investigated were identified.

- Thanks to the involvement of the Park, of some entrepreneurs and of the communities abroad, two tourism *routes* were developed based on the historical memory of the migrated Cilento people: "Palinuro and the Infreschi Coastline along the pre-historical paths" and "From Paestum to Padula". These routes, in addition to being illustrated in two tourism brochures and in a poster, were largely disseminated during national and international events and can be accessed on the web site. At Vallo della Lucania a *training course* and an internship on eco-management issues were organised. The 4 week training course was attended by 25 representatives of the tourism firms based in Cilento. Lectures were held by professors and researchers from the University of Salerno. Thanks to the training course the skills of the human resources employed in tourism firms were enhanced, combining competencies on organisational/management issues and competencies on technical–scientific issues, in order to have an immediate impact on the firms.

- The action aimed at *increasing local community awareness* included a number of innovative and crucial initiatives specifically addressed to the students living in the park area. The objective was to convince them that protecting the landscape, flora, fauna and the historical, artistic and religious heritage of the Park municipalities is not only a civic duty but a pre-requirement for the economic development of the area; without them tourists would not be stimulated to visit the Park, to get a better knowledge of it and enjoy it. The action started with a telematic didactic project recorded on the Internet at the web site programmidea@programmidea.it, disseminated in all schools located in the Park. The schools of the Park's municipalities were e-mailed a notice inviting them to participate in the project through the Internet. They were also asked to write a paper on the issues included in the project and participate in a competition. The competition was on: "Design and creation of an advertising poster to illustrate the wonders of the Park to Italians living abroad"; over 400 children participated in the competition and were officially rewarded.

### Dissemination Stage

The model implemented was disseminated — to be transferred to other areas — through a scientific conference and a book publication. The tourism routes developed were presented to the major international tour operators through brochures and press conferences and at tourism exhibitions. The connection with the emigrants abroad generated the idea of creating a Museum of Cilento migration, and building a Monument to the Emigrant.

Many dissemination actions were implemented at international level:

- Development, production and dissemination of a brochure and poster of the whole project, widely disseminated on several occasions.
- Events and congresses — press conferences, participation in tourism fairs such as the BMT (Mediterranean Fair of Tourism) of Naples, the BIT (Italian Fair of Tourism) of Milan, the Exhibition of art, restoration and conservation of cultural and environmental assets of Ferrara, the Exhibition of Rural Areas of Vallo di Diano.
- Presentation of the Project at Buenos Aires in the day dedicated to "Tourism and culture", within the 7th Edition of the "Italian Week of Magna Grecia". Argentine tourism operators were highly interested in the project. Also the Italian Ambassador in Argentina and many representatives of the Italian national institutions participated in the event.

## Outcomes

The project was finalised in June 2003 and achieved all its objectives, in particular the creation of a close link between the territory and the network of emigrants living abroad. There is also a higher propensity to view Cilento area as a testimonial of all the provincial district of Salerno due to the drawing effect that the promotion of Cilento area and products might have on Salerno economy.

The qualitative analysis highlighted the strong attractiveness of the eno-gastronomic traditions of the area. Cultural and archaeological resources, trekking and sea life are a major potential for a quality tourism. The role of tour operators is crucial but also word of mouth is paramount. The Cilento community living abroad might be the most useful tool to convey the message that Cilento is an area to be explored and loved, as it can be directly linked to ancient myths and to people's hospitality.

The survey also highlighted that the Project was quite successful in the whole area; this proves the effectiveness of the dissemination work and the acceptance of the Project by the local community.

In addition to the remarkable outcomes achieved — synthetically summarised in this paper — some points have to be highlighted.

Firstly, the several actions implemented to get an active involvement of Cilento operators and institutions in the project activities — such as meetings, seminars and participation in fairs — made it possible to identify and establish contacts with various operators and/or local bodies particularly interested in the initiative. They stressed the difficulty of involving other subjects thus confirming the starting assumptions of the project, namely the low level of willingness to co-operate and the "inertial" behaviour typical of southern-Italy entrepreneurs. Due to these difficulties, in order to re-launch the initiative we focused on specific actions — training courses and Information Point — in order to involve the highest number of local operators and stimulate their interest in the project.

With respect to the project co-ordination, the interaction amongst the project partners was very effective and this enabled to carry out a more effective co-ordination action and reach outcomes which exceeded our expectations. In a Project where the main objective is creating integrated territorial networks, the approach based on co-operation amongst partners was useful to create a positive atmosphere conducive to the involvement of the various operators.

Upon conclusion of the project, the portal developed is operational and extremely effective; it collected and made available thousands of information on the National Park and is an integrated, innovative tool characterised by a high potential. In fact it can be accessed by all those (foreigners and Italians) who want to know more about the area where the National Park of Cilento and Vallo di Diano is located and about its major attractions.

It is also worth mentioning the profitable relationship — which might lead to major economic developments — established between a substantial number of U.S. tour-operators and the tour-operators based in the National Park of Cilento, a relationship established thanks to the "telematic portal". The same can be said for the relationships between Cilento eno-grastronomic producers and U.S. importers.

## Conclusion

Allowing for the findings of the research work, some remarks can be made with respect to tourism development in southern Italy.

Firstly, it is confirmed that the initiative implemented by CNR and its partners is really a "pilot project", i.e. a useful example of an integrated promotion of a specific territorial area on the international market. Viewing emigrants from Cilento and their descendants living abroad, specifically in the U.S.A., as *testimonials* of their land of origin, as a fully free and effective tool for promotion thanks to the word of mouth, as a crucial potential factor for the economic development of the area, is an innovative, valid and effective intuition. Vice-versa, disregarding the meaning and the product of decades of migration and sacrifices made by thousands of migrants would be like cancelling over 140 years of history and wasting one of the most significant collective experience of southern Italy. It is worth reiterating that for an economic growth of a specific area, it is crucial to develop its system of values and its interpersonal and institutional relationships.

These actions may have a positive impact in enhancing local tourism and "de-seasonalise" foreign tourism flows. It is well known that tourist flows are mainly concentrated in the period between May and September, with a resulting under-utilisation of the accommodation facilities and unavoidable negative effects both on prices and, above all, on employment.

Areas such as the National Park of Cilento and Vallo di Diano can be re-launched through incentives and promotional actions targeted to specific consumers, such as elderly, high income people who have a lot of free time and wish to spend a period of vacation in a peaceful environment, where they can have clean air, mild weather and spas, visit historical, artistic, archaeological and religious sites, taste healthy and excellent food.

Additionally, some areas — thanks to the widespread presence of emigrants and their descendants — are the ideal target market for these promotional actions: first of all United States, Canada and Australia, but also South American countries. In these countries summer vacations fall on the period between December and the end of February, a period when temperatures are very hot there; a milder weather such as the Italian one would then be more attractive. Furthermore there is a general bias against South American countries; it is usually thought that their populations have very low-incomes or incomes below the poverty threshold. Actually million people living in these countries have the necessary economic resources to spend a vacation abroad; thousands of them fly every year to New York, Miami and Disneyland, Paris, London, Madrid, Lisbon, but just few of them arrive in southern Italy. When they visit Italy they follow the traditional route: Rome - Florence - Venice. This is because they are not aware of the resources that can be found in southern Italy; they are not stimulated to recover their cultural roots which, for all those who identify themselves with the western civilisation values — and then not only for those who have an Italian origin — can be found in "Magna Grecia".

The Project "Emigration as a tool to enhance tourism in Cilento area" confirmed our assumption and achieved its objectives. It also started a process which should be continued to optimise and disseminate the outcomes achieved and create — through a modern and innovative promotion — the tourism destination "Cilento" and, more in general, the destination "Magna Grecia". This objective could be surely achieved given the historical, artistic, archaeological, religious and natural assets which can be found in Mediterranean areas.

# Author Index

# Subject Index